a book about calling and confusion

Also by Patrick Dodson

Stuff My Dad Never Told Me About Relationships

as well as:
various podcasts on iTunes and at www.patrickdodson.net

Psychotic Inertia

a book about calling and confusion

by Patrick Dodson

{pause for effect}

Published by Pause for Effect Limited
709 New North Road
Auckland, New Zealand 1022

Pause for Effect books are available through most book stores and are also available in a variety of electronic formats. To contact Pause for Effect directly write to info@pauseforeffect.co.nz

ISBN 978-0-9864626-1-0

Edited by Anne Munro McGregor, PhD
with thanks to Meredith and Videne for proofing

Cover art and book design by Patrick Dodson

Printed and bound in the US and the UK by Lightning Source.
Lightning Source UK Ltd. Chapter House, Pitfield, Kiln Farm, Milton Keynes, MK11 3LW.
Email: enquiries@lightningsource.co.uk
Voice: 0845 121 4567. Fax: 0845 121 4594

National Library of New Zealand data
(Te Puna Matauranga o Aotearoa):

Title:	Psychotic Inertia - a book about calling and confusion
Author:	Patrick Dodson
Publisher:	Pause for Effect Limited
Address:	709 New North Road, Auckland, NZ
Format:	Paperback
Publication Date:	April 2010
ISBN:	978-0-9864626-1-0

First Edition

for Videne,
who always told me I could be president

if I wanted to

I still do

CONTENTS

introduction • **page 3**
where we look at getting unstuck by living from the inside out

part one • confusion
part one • confusion . . . . page 8

chapter one • create or die • page 9
where we look at the idea of finding v. creating our future

two • fear • page 17
where we discover how our fear of failure, being alone and not getting paid makes us hear voices

three • laziness • page 30
where we see how our quality of life has turned us into sloths, and God into Santa

four • selfishness • page 44
where we catch our selves trading our identity for a few bobbles, or some handsome guy

five • our need to know • page 52
where our fatherlessness, choice anxiety and lack of encouragement make us want someone, anyone, to tell us what to do with our lives

six • mindfuck • page 61
where our passive approach to life causes us to lose our individuality and makes us vulnerable to being screwed up by religious weirdness

seven • psychotic • page 71
where we expose our crazy talk which comes from transposing our unmet needs onto God, making Him into something strange

eight • God's turn • page 89
where we look at calling and guidance from God's relational point of view

part two • calling . . . . page 96

chapter nine • vocatio • page 97
where we look at the historical and sacred nature of a calling to be ourselves

ten • the general call of God • page 104
where we see that God's heart and intentions are intentionally broad and open so we can fill in the gaps

eleven • the extra ordinary call of God • page 111
where we look at the exception (Moses) verses the rule (you)

twelve • called to be yourself • page 119
where we see that your unique self is God's answer to a world in need

thirteen • teleology • page 130
where we flush out the last bastion of our deceptive hearts in wanting God to predict our futures

part three • creating the future • • page 136

chapter fourteen • restoration • page 137
where we see that in order to get back on that bike, we need our boldness, our strength, and our intellects restored

fifteen • recovering your call • page 149
where we take authority over our lives by going through a rite of passage that validates our identity and creativity

sixteen • free will • page 159
where we learn to choose wisely and stop asking God for parking places

seventeen • collaboration • page 173
where we look at the need to find people like us to work with, challenge, and mentor our development

eighteen • putting it all together • page 178
where we plan your life, not really, but really, kind of

nineteen • your gift • page 190
where we see that the one thing in the universe God does not already have, is what you could create

appendix a • page 203
On the Choice of a Profession by R.L.S. - 1888

appendix b • page 210
a bunch of scriptures to stick on your fridge

Inertia...

...a property of the universe by which you continue in your existing state of rest or uniform movement, unless that state is changed by an external force...

Introduction

People get stuck. Stuck in classrooms that bore them to death, or in jobs they grow to hate. People get stuck in places they don't really want to live in and wake up one day wondering why... Once people get stuck, they usually stay stuck, and as busy as they may look, not much ever really happens. Sometimes they get stuck by hitting a wall of indecision, but most people just busily plow a furrow so deep that after a while they can't even see over the sides or, as Somerset Maugham chides: "They are like train-cars traveling forever on the selfsame rails. They go backwards and forwards, backwards and forwards, inevitably, till they can go no longer and then are sold as scrap-iron."[1] It's called inertia ("a property of matter by which it continues in its existing state of rest or uniform movement, unless that state is changed by an external force"[2]). Some people survive this trap (made of the typical job, school or relationship) by escaping to the occasional party or overseas trip to deaden the pain. But if you're a Christian, your drug of choice is probably to wait for God to miraculously pull you out of that rut and set you on "the plan He has for you". And the rut gets deeper...

I meet people like this everywhere I go, and I go a lot of places. People who come out of high school with no clue as to what they want to do next. People who come out of college feeling like it was a waste of time, and still don't know what they want to do. People who then choose jobs that line up with their education (the one that bored them) or anything that'll pay the bills. People who have worked for years in a job they now despise, and despise who they're becoming... Because ultimately, what they become is someone else. And that someone else usually goes off doing really stupid things (substance abuse, relational abuse, materialist abuse) to take their mind off who they once were.

But in these same places, I also find people who know exactly who they are and what they want to do, and are doing pretty well. Or others who are still working it out, but are taking huge risks to have a go, just to see what happens. So what's the difference between a

1 "The Lotus Eater" in *Collected Short Stories, Volume 4,* Penguin Classics, 1993, page 176.

2 New Oxford American Dictionary.

person who is stuck and a person who is moving in the direction they love? What determines who does well and who does nothing?

There've been a lot of studies over the years to measure the determining factors of a person's or organization's success. They usually look at the *external environment* of these successes and failures to see what can be learned. For instance, Malcolm Gladwell found that success in moving through the hockey ranks in Canada was largely based on the cutoff birth dates for joining up. And he discovered that Bill Gates' success in software development had a lot to do with his having extraordinary access to mainframes at the University of Washington while he was in the eighth grade...[3] External factors do have a lot to do with facilitating our forward movement, but they rarely determine it. In fact, I think we focus far too much on the externals when it comes to understanding our lives and choices. It's a convenient way to not be responsible. I call it *living from the outside in*. Living from the outside in happens if you have a small view of self and a weird view of God. The external forces in your life tend to dominate your choices. You may call those influences guidance from God, but they rarely ever are.

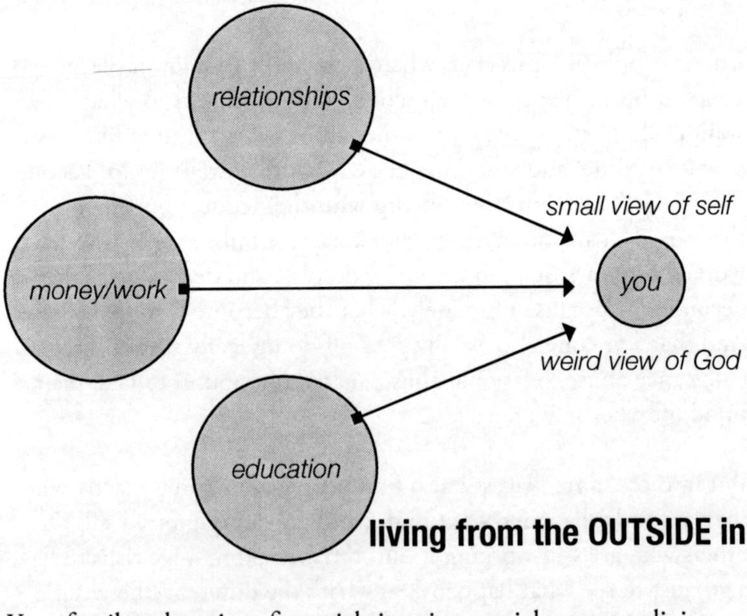

living from the OUTSIDE in

Your family, education, financial situation, social norms, religious expectations... are all external forces pulling you in different direc-

3 *Outliers*, Little, Brown and Company, 2008.

tions. We make choices based on these (like choosing a college major because of family pressure or because the job market is leaning a certain way) and end up on the same treadmill as everyone else. These forces dominate the person who has a small view of their identity (for instance, that they love children and want to help them), and from that singular piece, they end up making a knee-jerk decision (to be a teacher).

If, on the other hand, you have a clear view of yourself and your identity (including your passions, personality, intellect, skills, dreams...) and a solid view of how God walks out the future with you, then you determine what kind of education you need, who you want to work with, and where you want to live, etc. I call this *living from the inside out.*

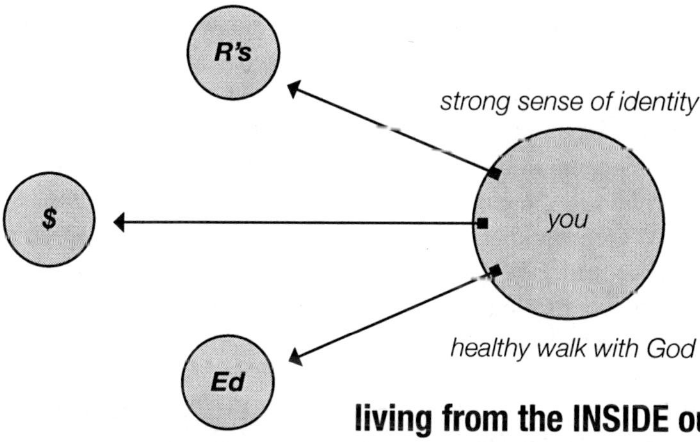

living from the INSIDE out

My experience has been that those who are moving forward in their lives with clarity about who they are and what God values, do so by managing the *internal factors* of their lives. They grapple with their motivations and issues of the heart (fear, laziness...), and develop their identity. They don't fluff around with questions about God's will or if they should do this or that. They make choices and learn from what happens. In effect, they create their future with God. By contrast, the ones who are stuck are often waiting for a word from heaven. Or from anyone who will give them permission to proceed. Waiting for something to save them. A relationship, a job offer, some mission opportunity... it comes in all forms, some even noble. But the environment is still controlling them because fear, laziness, and selfishness become internal anchors. And more often than not, even skywriting from God can't get them moving because guidance was never the issue in the first place.

I wrote this book for inert people. My hope is that they might understand their distinct and unique calling a lot more clearly. So they can know the difference between a command-and-control God and a loving Father and Coach. So they can get moving on the real questions of identity and creativity in a world that is dying for some answers to huge questions. But to do that, we have to first work on the internal factors. Our motives, issues of the heart, and our view of God. This is the only way to really deal with the fear that binds us, or the laziness that keeps us glued to the couch, or the selfishness that drives us to a shopper's way of life.

But my readers will have a problem. I mean, who wants to work on the issues of the heart, right? Who wants to go away for a few days and challenge our lazy or selfish approach to just about everything? We'd usually rather go for a three-step plan and a set of "guidance" scriptures to tape to the fridge. Assurances that "God's in control" and that it's going to be all right because the Bible says... So often we prefer blindly clinging to interpretations of certain scriptures that aren't even working in our lives because it's easier than working hard on the truth. We've been so willingly brainwashed that our bumper-sticker theology is now the only way we can survive in a complex world.

But this won't do. The only way to break the inertia, to do more than just survive, is to have some other force knock us into a new trajectory. And the best way to do that is to start with the heart. We must work the systemic issues that are holding us in place and keeping us from a better path. Because if we can, we'll see ourselves, God, and the scriptures in a whole new light. And even better, we'll be able to re-engage in the world around us with a lot more creativity and true love (and, hopefully, more money to do really amazing things :-).

So while the *subject* of this book is our calling, and dealing with the confusion that trips us up, the *process* is about the motivations and issues of our hearts – why we make certain choices and how we got stuck. What are those essential forces that move us (or not) or beg us to follow others? What's that thing inside us that obeys the "what if I fail" voice? Basically, we'll look at what *moves our will* in one direction or another.

If we're willing to address our fears, then I think this little read will be very freeing. If we're willing to acknowledge our laziness, this could be a great facilitator for action. If we can see where selfishness is getting in the way of our true soul and God-made self, then we'll learn how to be a creative blessing in our own neighborhood first and, maybe one day when we grow up, in the nations. If we can head down this road and work these issues, we'll be creating a foundation that could support the rest of our lives. Change always starts in the heart, so we gotta be willing to go there first. That okay with you?

Over the past 30 years I've been learning to walk with God. Not behind and not ahead, just with. Walking and talking, learning, choosing, learning some more... I'm sharing here what I've seen and heard because I really wish someone had done that with me when I was in my teens or twenties. Not as a prescription in the sense that this is how it must work for you, but as a process you can observe and personalize, which is totally possible if you start at the level of the heart. In this way, God can work out the details with you in a way that suits where you're at.

Psalm 51:6 says that God desires truth in the innermost man, and it's in that place that He shows us wisdom. This kind of truth is not academic; it means *being true* (honest, open) in our hearts so we can receive that amazing flow of wisdom, wisdom which guides us, not like carrots to horses, but rather advice to sons and daughters. My hope is that you would be open to getting this kind of wisdom and that the pages of this book can encourage you in the process.

Note on God: When speaking of God in this book I will largely refer to He. I know God is much more than any simple pronoun, but I don't know a better way to express this in writing; such are the limits of the English language.

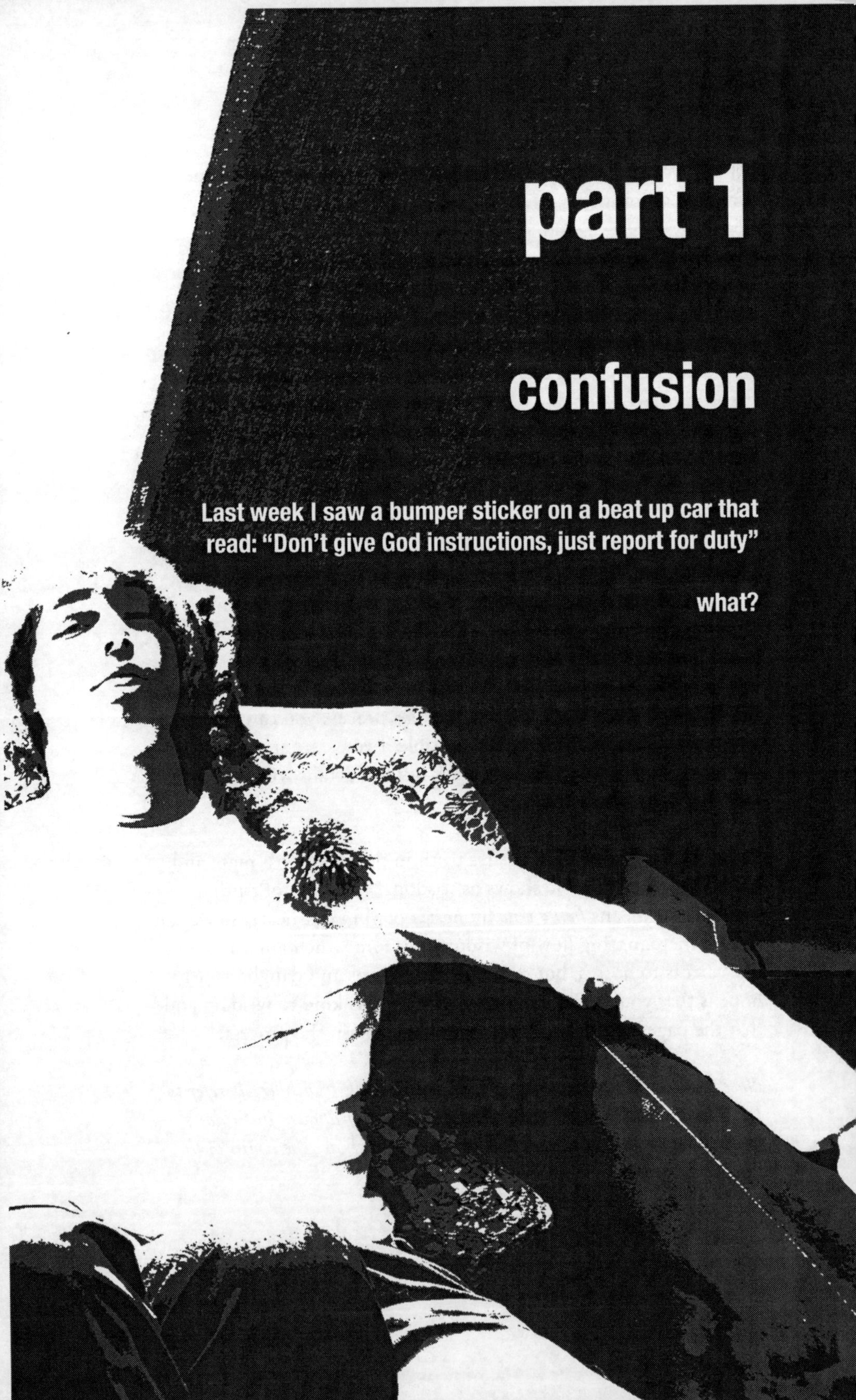

part 1

confusion

Last week I saw a bumper sticker on a beat up car that read: "Don't give God instructions, just report for duty"

what?

Chapter 1 • Create or die

We make decisions from our innermost being. The Bible calls this the spirit of our minds. These actions and choices come from our values, and our values come from our beliefs. Our beliefs come from what we think is true or real – in short, who God is. So, for instance, if we think God is a Commanding General, then we believe we are His soldiers, and our values will focus on obedience and order and plans and objectives... We will then make choices to wait on those orders, or blindly follow certain courses of action based on what we think is a command.

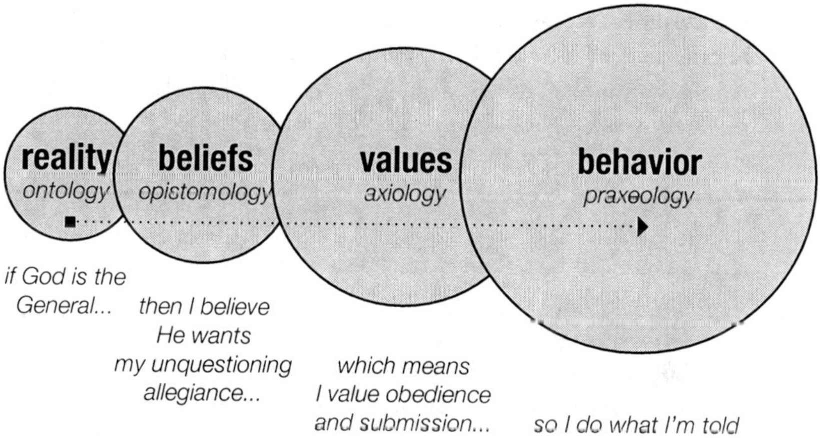

This plays out for just about any version of God we may have developed over the years. If the Sugar Daddy God is real, then we believe He's created the universe for US, and our values will reflect a consuming mentality. Our choices will then be about getting "as much as He has for us". If the Footsteps In The Sand God is real, then we believe He has everything under control and is carrying us whenever it gets tough, and our values will reflect a laissez-faire mentality. Our choices will be passive or perpetually delayed because "God's in control".

We all know that God is not restricted to one simple type and has many facets to His nature and character. He does command at times, carry us at other times, and always acts in the best interest of His children. But as diverse as He is, we generally lock on to certain aspects of God, or at least perceived aspects, and get stuck on believing, valuing, and choosing from that monotone perspective. Even at our best, we tend to default to a way of seeing God, or minimizing God, based on our needs at the time. If we're afraid to choose, God becomes the Omniscient One who knows all and will choose for us. If we're too lazy to act, then God becomes the All In Good Time God who has it under control and will let us know when He's ready. If we're too needy to unconditionally love others, God becomes the He Loves Me So Much God who'll bring us that husband or wife regardless of our relational development.

Now, if this was simply a matter of getting fixated on one single aspect of God and getting nowhere with it, we'd all be smart enough to see the trap and just move on. Or God would tap us on the shoulder (usually through the cause and effect of failure) and remind us that He ain't Santa. But our real problem lies in how we tend to combine many views of God that are all kinda off, namely the He Loves Us And Has A Plan For Our Lives God.

You're like, "But He does, right?"

If you say so. In fact, if anyone says something over and over again, it's like it's in the Bible. Yeah, God does love us, but what does that mean? Making choices for us? Is that loving? God does have plans and thoughts for us. What does that mean? A detailed road map that we simply must discover and it's all sweet? Is planning our lives God's idea or something we want because choosing is hard? Again, it's not that this isn't true in certain contexts, it's that we start with a basic need (like anxiety about the future) and slam a few scriptures together to create God in the image of that need. Then, presto, He has a plan for my life. Like when we don't know which college to choose and so we combine things like, "Don't lean on your own understanding" (Proverbs 3:5) and "God knows what's best" (not actually in the Bible, but it sounds close enough, right?) to allow us to sit back and wait for the answer. The real need here is to make an intelligent decision based on your identity, future goals, and what each college really offers (it's called research). But if none of those things is clear, then you take that need and project it onto God, who then *becomes* the kind of God who tells you which college to go to.

We'll work these details as the book goes on, but I just want to say at this point that when we project our needs onto God and combine a few bits and pieces of what we know of Him (usually out of context or from things He never even said), we make God into the image of our need instead of seeing who He really is. And since He doesn't play that game, we get really confused about how He wants to walk with us and what our calling actually means.

The primary question comes down to this: Is God the person who has a detailed plan for our lives that we must *find,* or is God the person who made us in His image so that we would *create* the future? If you look at all the various aspects of God's nature and character (as much as we can anyway) and then look at all the aspects of our selves (heart, soul, mind, etc.), what can we assume about the primary way we're to make choices and plan our futures? Find it or create it? Here's a very short list:

Note: This will be limited according to what I know of God, but you can add to this and then reconsider the question: Find the future or create it?

God's nature (*as it relates to calling and decisions*)
- Wise
- Caring
- Adventurous
- Passionate
- Creative
- Faithful
- Warrior
- Mother/Father
- Risk-taker
- Judge
- Dreamer
- Provider
- Teacher

Aspects of our design and nature
- Free to choose
- Intelligent
- Passionate
- Unique

- Familial/Relational (sons/daughters)
- Inter-dependent

When I look at the various ways God expresses Himself, I think we need to be very careful about taking one scripture and growing a whole life based on it. Like the way we think Jeremiah 29:11 means God has mapped out every day of our lives: "For I know the plans I have for you."[4] When I look at the dynamic and radical person of God, I have to assume that my life will be equally dynamic and that a cookie-cutter approach to guidance just won't work. Because there will be A LOT of times when you sense God saying, "So, what do you want to do?" or, "You choose". When I look at the amazing gifts of free will, intellect, and uniqueness of identity, I can only conclude that we've been created to create the future, and not to hobble through a lame life looking for open and closed doors. Why give us free will, intellect, and identity just to strip it all away and expect us to wait around like a puppy to be told when we're going on a walk. Doesn't make sense to me.

But that's my take after these 30 years. What I'd like to do with the rest of this book is walk through various ways of looking at this question. Now I know that if you frame the question a certain way, it's easy to answer. For instance, if I ask, "Do you find or create your future?", most people would say they create it (even if they've been looking for it for years) because "creating it" sounds cooler or maybe just resonates with something deeper in their soul, something they want to believe is true. But at this point we're not looking for the "right" answer. Instead, I need you to look back over the last five years and review the decisions you've made and how you've made them. Who did you think God was at the time and how did that view reflect on your decision-making process (have a look at that world-view graphic again)? I'm going to try and convince you that you were designed to create your future instead of simply finding it, and then I'd like to give some advice on how to make that happen. First though, let's start with your view of God and your resulting beliefs, values, and choices.

---

4 We'll look at the proper context later, but this verse literally says "I know the *thoughts* I have for you", and the "you" part is not about an individual, but about the people of Israel and Babylon together. Context is everything when looking at these verses and making choices based on them.

Please take some time to answer the questions below so you have a general idea of where your starting point is:

Who is God? What have you boiled God down to when it comes to decisions, planning, calling?

What do you then believe? What are the beliefs that have come from this view of God?

What then are your values? Based on your beliefs, what values have you formed?

What choices are you making? What are you actually doing (school, work, relationships) and how does it reflect your perspective of God?

How's that working for you? What have been the results of your choices and is there a gap between what you hoped God would do or be, and what's actually happening?

Chapter meditation

Note: At the end of some chapters I'd like to offer a meditation or devotional piece to consider. The point is to get off the treadmill. A lot of our built-up God-views have taken a deep root (based more on our needs than on our study of who He really is) and could use some renewal. And renewal takes time. So if this is working for you, take some time to not only consider these things but make a series of choices that seals them into the spirit of your mind (Ephesians 4:22...).

"It's for freedom that Christ has set us free."
Galations 5:1a

God hates bondage. He never intended for any of us to be enslaved. Not even to Him. Everything God does and is comes from His relational nature, and bondage is anti-relational. The requirements and fetters of bondage force the enslaved to act and think according to their oppressor. It demeans and dehumanizes creation.

Odd, then, that many of our concepts of God and what He expects of us fit into the master/slave model. Like we can only do what we're told, or that we are nothing and He is everything. Again, partial truths taken to the extreme because of our misunderstanding of the Father and, I think, an institution (the local church) bent on the idea of control.

Our place is one of worship and amazement at the person and wonder of God, but our bowing is not subjugation. He doesn't want our self-imposed slavery. We are sons and daughters and are co-operating our lives and the whole earth with a Father who has magnified our worth through Jesus.

Placide Cappeau, a French wine merchant and poet, was commissioned in 1840 by his parish priest to write a Christmas poem. The result was "Minuit, chrétiens" which became "O Holy Night". The first verse in the original:

> *Minuit, chrétiens, c'est l'heure solennelle,*
> *Où l'Homme-Dieu descendit jusqu'à nous*
> *Pour effacer la tache originelle*
> *Et de Son Père arrêter le courroux.*
> *Le monde entier tressaille d'espérance*
> *En cette nuit qui lui donne un Sauveur.*

Later, in 1855, the American classical music critic and minister John Sullivan Dwight translated the first verse to be:

> *O holy night! The stars are brightly shining,*
> *It is the night of our dear Savior's birth.*
> *Long lay the world in sin and error pining,*
> *'Til He appear'd and the soul felt its worth.*

This last line has captivated me. That until God's appearing, we are bound, but when He truly shows up, in our world, in our daily lives, *the soul feels or knows its worth*. This sounds like God. The freeing of the soul, the relationship, and the opportunity to co-create in the world. In this case, falling on our knees (as the chorus suggests) is out of sheer joy and relief, not bondage.

Do you know the worth of your soul? Its potential? What does it mean to you, that your soul is more valuable than the whole world (Mark 8:37)? And how does that value play out in your daily life and choices?

"Stand firm, then, and do not let yourselves be burdened again by a yoke of slavery."
Galations 5:1b

Chapter 2 • Fear

We do not have a problem with understanding our calling, or hearing God's voice. Ours is an emotional problem, namely fear. When it comes to making simple choices or really big ones like planning your future, you often hit a wall. A basic fear emerges – that things may not work out as you hope. Some people just cruise on past this feeling, while most of us stop and weigh things up. The weighing is cool, if the weights are balanced. If you're simply measuring how your real potential (identity + skills) will work in a given situation, then that's good research. But if you don't know your potential, then the *outside in* factors are going to dominate the consideration and the scales tip against you. You'll think/feel that you don't have enough money or talent or whatever to succeed, and you'll give up right there. Maybe you'll take a more manageable option or pray for an open door because you don't have the confidence to just kick one open.

The fearful guy in Matthew 25 simply buried and sat on the opportunity he was given. When his investor asked why he didn't at least put the money in the bank and get a little interest, his response was that he was afraid. Raw, unreasonable fear is usually what keeps us frozen in place.

Most people don't break down their own decisions and honestly own up to why they act as they do. This stuff goes on at the level of the heart or psyche, which then sends very basic thoughts or emotions to the reasoning parts of our brain. Memories of past rejections often hover in the background of our choices. These memories are the stories we tell ourselves about the past. They're not actually our experiences, but rather a chosen summary or compilation of experiences and sometimes even imagination.[5] Our minds can thus spin the past into a certain reality that tends to predict what will happen the next time we have a go. For instance, if you had a bad experience in school, you may not want to go onto college or do a masters because your story about a rotten education predicts more of the same. Or if you've tried to get some people together and

---

5 Daniel Kahneman, a Nobel Prize-winning psychologist, has an amazing TED talk on the riddle of experiences versus memories at: www.ted.com/talks/daniel_kahneman_the_riddle_of_experience_vs_memory.html

start a business that failed (which most do), then your memory/ story will remind you not to go there any more. The net result is a fear that justifies statements like, "I don't think God wants me to do that" or, "I'm waiting for God to show me what's best". I know there are times when that genuinely will be the right response to tricky situations, but for now, let's look at the roots of many of our choices.

So what are you afraid of? - **Failure**

One of the benefits of modern media is that you have instant access to all kinds of information. You know who the best bands are and who's hiring in the game industry. You watch very talented people constantly and get both inspired and a little daunted at the same time. This breeds a spirit of comparison, and comparison leads to self image issues, and self image issues lead to the dark side.

I've met lots of people, creative people with huge potential, who have completely given up on that creativity simply because they think they won't make it in the world of music or film or whatever, so they bury their talent and sit on it. On looking closer, I usually find they've been comparing themselves to people who have been working on their craft for decades and have got to where they are through that sheer hard work and a lot of failure. Remember the saying: Success is 10% inspiration and 90% perspiration. How would you know if you're good enough unless you give it a few years (because years is what it takes to *get* anywhere with your potential). The problem is that *we compare ourselves with where others have got to, not with where they started out*. And since it's impossible to go immediately from where we are now to where they are at their best, we think we'll fail. The fear of failure is the fear of not being like someone else's success. Take away the comparison and all you have to be is yourself. It's pretty stinking hard to fail at that.

Comparison is only one of the many roots of the fear of failure. Others have to do with money, or embarrassment, or just a raw sense that you won't be able to do the thing you'd really like to do. If you break it down, you'll see all kinds of emotions and thoughts based on past experiences, negative words spoken over you, or just a vacuous lack of identity. Whatever the cause, a fear of failure will keep you stuck or going in circles. On the other hand, articulating these fears gives you something to work on.

So what are they? *Write down any comparisons, rejections or past experiences that make you afraid to have another go.*

____

____

____

____

____

____

____

Failure is built into the universe. God had to know that free will was gonna lead to all kinds of mistakes; that babies were going to grab the cat's ear and get scratched. I'm sure He saw that coming, right? And it's okay with God because built into failure is the ability to learn and improve. Scientists use failure as an essential part of the empirical method and, as Freeman Dyson notes, "the whole history of science is a history of failure".[6] Even pain teaches us not to touch that oven again, or how not to screw up the next relationship we get into. Failure is also deeply connected with our sense of humor, the ability to put things into perspective and laugh at what our souls know is just another aspect of life. So failing isn't wrong, it's just failing. The problem is that we stigmatize the experience and link it with the loss of value as a person, and it ain't so. In fact, the people who are doing well are doing so because of their ability to learn from trial and error. Maybe it should be called trial and learning.

So when you're looking at a choice and think you might fail, be okay with it because the truth is you probably will. Steve Jobs failed running Apple computer the first time and got kicked out. Now look at the company. In fact, Americans in general are okay with failure (not that we always learn from it though). But regardless of how your culture deals with failure, you have to remember that you're also a citizen of the kingdom of God where failure is always an option. Accept that failure will be part of your growth process and you'll probably minimize the mistakes anyway.

6 From a conversation on "Speaking of Faith" (speakingoffaith.publicradio.org/programs/einstein/). Dyson is a theoretical physicist and Professor Emeritus at the Institute for Advanced Study in Princeton.

Being alone

We're designed to live in family, in a tribe. We hunt and gather together. We have an inter-dependent connection that runs deep and "it's not good for man to be alone" (especially men; you seen Jerry McGuire?). Even personal things like the creative process or cooking meals must have a community context or it gets tired real fast. And even in an indie- and alternative-obsessed culture, being alone is a painful existence. Deep down most of us have a fear of ending up alone. And alone is so counter intuitive to who we are that we constantly make choices, even compromises (like your last boyfriend?), to ensure that we do not end up by ourselves.

This can lead to a kind of herd mentality. Going to college because everyone else is, or getting stuck in a small-town job because that's what your friends are doing. Or staying under the control of weird leadership because you don't want to break out on your own. The trade-off is that even though you're surrounded by people at school or work, you often still feel alone. This is because you are not being yourself and therefore have not discovered *your* tribe. You can only be *together* with people if you start out being your self.

Many people give up pursuing a dream or course of action because they don't want to do it alone. And this is fair enough; it sucks taking risks by yourself. But if you compromise on your plans and hook your wagon to someone else's, you're just delaying the issue. I've read tons of case studies about women in mid-life who are pretty bitter about the compromises they've made to be with someone they now feel disconnected to[7]. They woke up one day and remembered who they were and what they wanted to do. Many of them started a new life. Some started businesses, others took on completely different roles in the home. The often radical change back to their original selves pushed buttons that led to divorce – to being alone... The compromise wasn't worth it.

What might you be compromising so you're not alone? *Write down some choices you've made or relationships you're in so you don't have to move forward alone. Some may be positive, but at least have a look.*

---

7 Please have a read of this if you are a woman or know any (which includes your mom, for all you WoW fans out there). It's called *The Wisdom of Menopause* by Christiane Northrup, M.D.

The truth is that you are enough by yourself. You don't need to be married to be complete or have a team of people who "get you" before you can take risks. In fact, the more you understand about the value of your soul and potential, the more you'll have to offer others. A solid view of self doesn't lead to isolation unless you're insecure or so far out there as a pioneer that it takes a while for people to catch up. There'll be many times when you'll have to venture forth by yourself. There'll be new territory that only you can see and even though it would be great to have some company, it's unrealistic to expect it. But this is not going to be your whole life. Once you've made some bold moves, others will want to join you, or you'll find new friends and comrades in the new space you're creating. If not, drag some people into it, because even though you have to branch out on your own, it's not good to *stay* alone. And, sometimes, you may have to slow down a little and move at the pace of the team, which can be frustrating, but at least you're moving.

God made us as individuals *within* social groups like family and our professional communities. Be comfortable with being yourself and then add that goodness to the group. I know this is a little easier for me as a Californian to say; we're obsessed with being ourselves. But even in more reserved cultures, the people that are confident about who they are often bless the larger social group by validating uniqueness. The fear of being alone is a compromise trap, so be okay with taking risks and dragging people into your space in good time.

Where's the money?

My dad's favorite line was, "Get a job". Generations of wisdom boiled down into three simple words. The undertone of this thinking is that there's such a thing as financial security. We all need a sense of security, but the idea of it being financial is a little crazy.

Even if you had a good job, you can't depend on that being around forever. And spending your life trying to build up a financial basis usually means you've spent your life on the wrong priorities (like leaving your family behind and eventually your own soul in the wake).

Now I think that working hard and creating value is a smart way to live – and the only way to pay the bills. But my security comes from the fact that I belong in a family, I am loved and eternally covered. From this security, I can take creative and financial risks that will multiply blessing over the decades (and pay the bills). But in the meantime, there will be some very lean seasons. Your parents know this, as did their parents, so they send these messages out to you hoping you don't die starving in the streets. When they say, "You gotta go to college", they mean, "Don't die starving in the streets". When they say, "Stop messing around with that guitar, my friend owns this company you could work at", they mean, "Don't die starving..."

The general message is that if you have a job, then you're going to be okay. But if you look around, there are a lot of people with jobs who still go on shooting rampages, or leave their families, or drink too much. A job is not a panacea that makes the rest of life a safe bet. And even if life was about having "stable employment", how do you even get such a job? Isn't your ability to get paid based on your knowing who you are, taking risks, and creating value that people want to pay for? Don't you have to have something worth trading or selling? And doesn't creating that thing mean some failing along the way? Like Madeleine L'Engle who got rejected around 24 times before some brave publisher was smart enough to see the value of *A Wrinkle In Time*, now a classic. So which comes first – a job and the money, or your ability to take risks and create something unique?

These generational messages go deep, and they should, because they're mixed with real wisdom, like "if you don't work, you don't eat" (II Thessalonians 3:10). But if they're tainted with generational fear, you end up obeying the curse and start making short-term decisions, often becoming a hireling for the rest of your life.

Another financial fear-builder is the subtle and not so subtle messages that the advertising industry calls creative selling. By "creative" they mean manipulating your basic needs for intimacy (sex sells), inclusion, and self image by showing you what you're not, and what you should buy to be different. The constant droning of marketing messages lowers your resistance with each reiteration, until you feel your core need is to have more money so you can buy these vital elements back into your life. Now you may feel that this is not you, and that you're not a sucker for the advertising man, but if you're human (with ears and eyes) and you grew up in the West, you've been affected.

So what do you need? *Write down the pressures you've been under to earn, and how that's affected the other dreams you've had. What choices have you made based on building "financial security" instead of developing your life, family, dreams.*

____

____

____

____

____

____

____

God knows that we need provision of all kinds (moral, physical, psychological...) and yet asks us to consider the lilies of the field (Matthew 6:25). How hippy is that? In the midst of real needs to pay the rent and that lame school loan, He wants us to tummy up to some flowers and meditate a bit? Really?

Really. What God is getting at is the basis for provision. It's seeking the values and the ways of His kingdom that teaches us how to create, and therefore earn. That worry (the result of fear) will not add anything to the mix, except more stress, which means more bad decisions (and added health bills). He's not being flippant or pseudo-spiritual, as in, "'It's all gonna be okay because I'm gonna pay the rent and when you get home, the fridge will be full!" He's saying that if we deal with the worry and fear, we can focus on a restfulness that allows us to see where the real value is. By value I mean the ability to create unique things of worth to yourself and other people. Whether that's a new song, a new cure for a disease or a better way to create cooking fuels for developing-nation villagers. The rest and wisdom that come from seeking what God's kingdom is about give us a secure platform from which to start inventing the future. And that kind of labor is worth its hire.

So what else are you afraid of? What's slowing you down? It could be that no one in your family has really launched out past the gates of local industries. Or maybe you have a pastor in your life who's keeping you bound under a weird view of God (which would be more your fault than theirs; I mean, can anyone really keep you in place if you wanted to move on?). Some people are simply afraid of what they think people think about what they're thinking... Dig deep and see if there is something that's keeping you from taking risks.

The reason I am pushing this is because it's fear that makes us go a little crazy. As in, "I'm just waiting on the Lord to lead me", when really He's waiting on you to get moving so you have something to talk about together. Or, "I'm waiting for a sign because I put out this fleece...", when we forget that the fleece was a response to the *fear* Gideon had in obeying the call he got. By the way, God's not really into being fleeced. Not His thing. He has in the past responded out of grace and kindness, but don't put God to the test simply because you're afraid.

Worse still is that these fears make us start hearing voices, like the one that tells you to say, "God told me to marry you", because you're too afraid to be rejected or even to get to know someone for that matter. Or you start seeing circumstances around you as God's guidance simply because something happened. This is called fatalism, and you need to know that God is not in the business of giving out parking places because you don't want to walk too far, or local jobs because you don't want to move out of state... He rarely manipulates the circumstances around us, but the fear in our heart often makes us believe that's exactly what's happening, even against biblical and historical wisdom. He's not controlling everything, but for the fearful person, God NEEDS to be in control because we're too afraid of a world where He's not. In this way, again, we create God in the image of our own need to be safe. It's called idolatry. Ironic, huh?

You know, there are a lot of good reasons to be afraid. It's not a safe or inviting world, and even if you know who you are and want to bravely go where no man has gone before, nobody else really wants you there. Sometimes your fears are based on real obstacles that need to be carefully considered before proceeding. But in that case, you're not really dealing with fear, you're dealing with challenge. You're being considerate or cautious, and that's fine. Fear is the thing that keeps you from trying at all. It's the exaggeration of certain issues that block your larger perspective because all you can see are the negative aspects.

There are some people who are just as concerned about the future as we are, but they move forward anyway. They've discovered what Susan Jeffers has learned: "You can accept fear as simply a fact of life rather than a barrier to success."[8] They're often unsure and second-guess themselves, but they keep taking risks. They face fears with a stronger sense of self and the reality of God in and with them. They just keep moving. Sometimes it's because they knew what they wanted to be at 11 years old and never let go. In fact a lot of us have a sense about what we want to be around that age. We may not be able to articulate it, but it's there deep inside. My nephew just finished pushing himself through law school where half the students are cut in the first year, just to keep things manageable. Upon graduating, he took himself to Uganda where he's been working for an NGO helping displaced children from the neighboring Congo to have legal refugee status (reserved for adults only so far). He deals with fear every day and a lot of horrific issues that are way beyond his capacity. He's been maligned and physically mugged but keeps showing up at work because he's committed to following through on serving these kids. I asked him once how he made his choice to pursue law and go on to work in Uganda. To him, it was a simple act of the heart, of faith, and of personal preference. That's all he needed, and now he is walking with and serving God. The cool thing is that he's doing it from both the heart and mind. And he's using the broad range of his identity (lover of justice, teacher, facilitator, friend) to fulfill the heart and intentions of God for some of the children in central Africa. He's overcome the fear by acting on his passion and dealing with the results as they come. Some people move heaven and earth to make good things happen while others wait for heaven to do it all for them.

---

8 *Feel the Fear and Do It Anyway*, Ballantine Books, 1988, page 4. This and her other work on the subject do a great job of demystifying fear and the sense that there's something wrong with me and no one else.

You may have identified with some of the fears and their roots in these pages. If you think that's enough to deal with for now, then I suggest you start a process to renew the spirit of your mind. Perfect love casts out all fear (1 John 4:18) but there need to be practical steps to make that real. To the Ephesians and Romans, Paul explains a simple but super-effective way to renew the spirit of your mind and deal with the inertia fear often creates.

1. Stop the behavior (Ephesians 4:22). *If you've listed things you're afraid of and the choices you made because of those fears, then I suggest you stop doing those things or find a way to change direction. If those choices have been more substantial (like courses in a university, or a job you've taken as a compromise), then take your time and make thoughtful decisions to finish your commitments or move towards a better plan. Don't just react because of what you've read here. And you never want to run from something; you want to purposefully move towards something better. If you don't have the better thing now, honor the commitments you've made and work on a better plan along the way.*

2. Start the renewal (Ephesians 4:23). *Start making plans and choices that specifically go in the opposite spirit of your fears. For instance, if you've given up your art or dancing because someone told you you're not going to make any money at it, then start it up again. Making money is not the point; being yourself and being creative is. And give this time. Read Sir Ken Robinson's book* The Element *(especially the part about Matt Groening holding on to his dreams).*

3. Learn how to be yourself again (Romans 6:17). *In this verse, Paul states that we can only change by being truly committed to that change, learning, and application. A. Make a commitment to some larger goals (maybe after you've finished this book and have a bigger picture, and had some time to process with family and friends). B. Figure out what you need to learn (via formal or non-formal education) in order to reach those goals. C. Finally, establish a practice that brings this learning into reality. We will go over this more in the section on calling.*

4. Be consistent (Ephesians 4:25). *I've found that in order to change something in my life, I need to make right choices for months until the habit is broken and a new one is formed. For instance, if you are*

starting a new project, you need to make hundreds of small choices that replace negative basic life experiences with positive ones. Each day you practice the guitar or study business, you're dealing to the fears and negative words spoken over you. This renewal takes years. The guy in Ephesians 4:28 had to stop stealing, get a job, save money, and become generous. That obviously didn't happen overnight. So give yourself time to counter the years of damage, but be consistent and deal with the fears as they come up. This may mean making really small personal decisions in the beginning, but it will lead to larger ones in the coming months. What you're doing is bringing the fears to a conscious level so you can choose against them with actions that are in line with your identity and not with the person you've been told to be.

5. Be excellent at what is good (or wise in what is good, Romans 16:19). *As I said before, we compare ourselves with people who have practiced (and failed) for years. The best way I know to deal with the fear of failure is to become amazing in your own right at the thing you love. Not wealthy or successful, but amazing as far as you're concerned. This means developing craft. Skills honed over years of plugging away at your creative process. No comparisons, just hard work.*

Chapter meditation

"A bruised reed he will not break, and a smoldering wick he will not snuff out. In faithfulness he will bring forth justice."
Isaiah 42:3

God is very understanding of our fears and psychoses. He completely sees the roots of these hindrances and gently walks with us until we're ready for the remedy. It's such a gracious and patient approach that I can only readily accept it in response. Such faithful kindness, like a mom who stays up all night with her frightened child, stroking the nightmare from its vulnerable head. God will not cut us off or move on without us. He will not extinguish the possibilities suppressed in our souls.

At the same time, He's not willing to abide the voice of some Gríma Wormtongue whispering death to His Théoden. He sees how the enemies of our souls have whispered fear via advertising ("you need more"), lame school systems ("you're not smart enough"), or fearful families ("get a job or else"), and He will bring those voices to justice. The way He does that is by reminding us of our potential. Speaking against fear with truth, the truth about our place as prophets, kings, and priests. He knows our potential and gently massages that truth like a balm into our week knees so that we can stand again.

But there is a danger to staying in the hospital too long; people die of other infections. The guy in Matthew 25 who sat on his talent eventually got punished by his own fear, and in this way God is reminding us that paranoia will destroy us. Franklin Roosevelt understood this when he spoke to a terrified and broken nation in his 1932 inaugural speech: "The only thing we have to fear is fear itself – nameless, unreasoning, unjustified terror which paralyzes needed efforts to convert retreat into advance." At a time when people had every reason to expect the worst, he knew that if left there, those fears would sink them into further depths of despair, and that would kill them in the end. Instead, he offered a realistic hope that they would "endure [...], revive and [...] prosper". He could say this because he knew that plummeting land values, frozen trade, and withering industry, as harsh as they were, still only constituted a material problem, which could be redeemed "if we face it wisely and courageously". FDR knew the real issue was a moral one. On one side, the unbridled greed of financial institutions and, on the other, the will of the people to change and deal boldly with the issues at hand. Sound familiar?

It's in this light that Roosevelt reminded the people of their heritage, and that these issues were "perils which our forefathers conquered because they believed and were not afraid". He spoke to the soul, knowing that would eventually deal with the material problems. In a similar way, God continues to kindly remind us of our potential by speaking to our soul: "Be strong and courageous, do not be terrified..." (Joshua 1:9). He says this as though it's possible to not live in fear. As though He's willing to be with us wherever we go. Not carrying us on His back, but teaching us His ways so that we can be "prosperous and successful" (verse 8). I think that means walking in the fulfillment of our identity in a Shalom or holistic kind of way.

So, like the other two guys in Matthew 25, we have to take the resources we've been given and just head out, take some huge risks, and invest what we've been given. They were probably concerned, careful, and even cautious, but they were not afraid to fail or lose and, in that sense, as soon as they took their first step, they were already successful.

Chapter 3 • Laziness

"Every man is, or hopes to be, an Idler. Even those who seem to differ most from us are hastening to increase our fraternity; as peace is the end of war, so to be idle is the ultimate purpose of the busy."
Samuel Johnson, *The Idler*, 1758

We do not have a problem finding the will of God. Our problem is that we are too lazy to do the will we already know. Loving our neighbors, honoring our parents, destroying poverty... the scriptures and our hearts are full of things we already know God wants us to do. We think we're stuck on the details, like how to go about it, or what our part is, but really we're just too lazy to even start the process or kick open some closed doors. So instead of doing good, we do nothing. After a while, doing nothing gains a strange power over us, a force that drains our will for a few more minutes of sleep. It's like we've inhaled some virus of the soul from a culture obsessed with early retirement.

Laziness is an ancient issue. Chroniclers of the ages from Aristotle (and his portrayal of laziness and the wicked in *Nicomachean Ethics*[9]) to Matt Groening (and his portrayal of laziness and the new cool: Bart Simpson) have all bemoaned and celebrated this human condition. Some in history have mocked the stylish nature of laziness, as in Oscar Wilde's 1893 play, *A Woman of No Importance,* where Lord Illingworth declares: "To win back my youth [...] there is nothing I wouldn't do – except take exercise, get up early, or be a useful member of the community." Others have extolled the benefits of laziness, like Jerome K. Jerome, who dedicated an entire collection of essays to the subject: "I am looking forward to the time when we men shall have nothing to do but lie in bed till twelve, read two novels a day, have nice little five-o'clock teas all to ourselves, and tax our brains with nothing more trying than

---

9 Aristotle links laziness to wickedness (note to surfers and gamers: this is the bad kind of wicked). He writes of the idle, "cowardice and laziness, [they] shrink from doing what they think best for themselves". This kind of inactivity leads to a sense of worthlessness – "And having nothing lovable in them they have no feeling of love to themselves" – which then leads to acts of cowardice and then evil. *The Nicomachean Ethics,* Book IX, chapter 4, II66b 2-29. Henry G Bohn, London page 242

discussions upon the latest patterns in trousers."[10] It's an age-old story told right up to today. Start a dot com, sell the idea (not the work), and retire at 20. The only thing new about this story is the number of people in it. Back in the day, you had to have a wealthy benefactor to be a dandy, and precious few could afford to hang about talking about trouser patterns.

Today, thanks to social welfare (among other things), hundreds of millions of people can live their lives without doing a day's honest work. In the past 100 years, laziness has grown from the domain of a privileged few to the birthright of millions. From the largest middle class in the world (India) to the poorer tiers of the USA, a Playstation is only an arm's reach away (as in, "Mom, can you hand me the controller?"). Not that everyone mentioned in these nations *is* lazy, but the opportunity is there for more people than ever. So, whereas in the past you could not afford to be lazy, today it's a national pastime. This generation has more people with more expendable cash and free time than any other generation in history. And while that's been true for most generations in history (a slow steady increase in life expectancy and quality of life, etc.), there have never been this many people who can afford to do nothing or live off their parents. It creates a new network effect where 10 million people can now spend 15,000 man-hours[11] per day on World of Warcraft. Or another 25 million can be playing simultaneous online games in China. You could build three Strasbourg-style cathedrals a day with that kind of time. Once an upper-class opportunity, hanging out is now a daily event for millions around the world.

Now, I'm grateful for the decrease in poverty and the rise in quality of life around the world. I'm glad that three generations have worked so hard to make life better for their children. But an increase in quality of life can be both a blessing and a curse: "God, don't make me so poor that I steal from you, or so rich that I forget you" (Proverbs 30:8-9, my translation).

10 *Idle Thoughts of an Idle Fellow*, 1886.

11 A man-hour is the amount of work performed by an average worker in one hour. It is used to estimate the total amount of uninterrupted labor required to perform a task. For example, researching and writing a college paper might require 20 man-hours. Preparing a family banquet from scratch might require 10 man-hours. Source: Wikipedia.

Tricks of the mind

On one hand, this amazing quality of life in many nations could create huge opportunities for entrepreneurship or building on your dreams. But a sad fact is that it's much easier to do what you're told than to get out and make a way for yourself. Even if you hate working for the man, doing what you love requires a lot of effort and most people can't be bothered. In fact, a lot of Christians believe that if something is hard, it's not of God, or it's a "closed door". So hard now equals wrong. These same people will then go asking God for a better way, for His will, for clarity, an open door, or a sign... neglecting the obvious path in front of them because that way is full of weeds and rocks.

We often miss the obvious way and look for an easier path because of the complex psyche of laziness. A bloated view of self and the spirit of entitlement collide to create the idea that we deserve an easier life. This is developed over years of being either coddled or "welfared". Our minds are then fed by a pervasive culture touting ease as the lifestyle of choice, with people walking around in t-shirts that read: "Hard work has a future. Laziness pays off now." The battle cry of this generation is now "Mañana".

Fear of failure or hard work makes laziness an easier mental option, but there are deeper forces at work that make it really hard for the mind to kick the ass off the couch. For instance, the thought that money is all I need to be happy, or that it will solve all my problems. Once, when I was around 14, I was cutting our lawn with a push mower. It was a brutal kind of crabgrass and the blades were completely blunt. I went to ask my dad for help and he told me I needed a bit of elbow grease. My response: "Can we go and buy some?" It's the idea that difficult things will be dealt with by money, and money's provided by other people (parental welfare mentality). And we extrapolate this upward, developing a sense that "God will provide", which becomes another facet to this mind of laziness. The irony is that you must create value of some kind to get that money in the first place, and laziness doesn't create anything.

Note: While being lazy doesn't create anything, being at rest or idle in an intentional way (like a sabbath) can be an amazing source of creativity, perspective, and wisdom for your next project.

Back in the day

Growing up was good times. Or so we think now. We'll often look back on our past as a better time, without responsibilities or pressure, which is another trick of this lazy psyche – that what we need is to go backwards in time. Avoidance much? In his fascinating book, *Doing Nothing,* UC Riverside Prof. Tom Lutz talks about the mind of "slacker subcultures [...] mourning for a past way of life [...], a kind of primitive, natural, mythical past" where work isn't "a necessary evil that interferes with their real [...] life".[12] This nostalgic longing for a workless world ("The Life") is part of the surf culture Lutz explores (among many other subjects), spanning the work and writings of Stephen Hull, Tom Wolfe, and Jack London. But there are many other expressions of mourning or nostalgia, which play on the minds of people today, creating a sense of loss and even dread about the future.

Since the future has to be created, it's very hard to see. Looking back then becomes a natural way to deal with a complex world. Mourning easier times or dwelling on nostalgic longings tend to dominate our thoughts, because while we can't see the future, our selective memory of the past still comforts us. And this is where we get trapped. Even some of our choices to move forward get stuck in a time machine because we make decisions based on our bondage to the past. For instance, the perpetual student in some postgraduate art school (which Lutz calls "a classic venue for slackers") clinging to a romantic world they tried to create as kids, or a guy working construction because it's all he knows, and all he really wants to do is snowboard with his friends who keep moving away despite his pleas (as in, "Dude, college? But, the hill!"). The choices we make are often limited by our longing to recreate the past, and when this runs out of steam we're left with a sense of loss or dread, because we still can't see the future. And so we either do nothing, or worse, we do what we're told.

> I remember my poor grandmother once incidentally observing, in the course of an instruction upon the use of the Prayer-book, that it was highly improbable that I

---

12 *Doing Nothing: A History of Loafers, Loungers, Slackers, and Bums in America*, Farrar, Straus and Giroux, 2006, page 252. Lutz doesn't simply whine about lazy people; he looks at present-day subcultures from the perspective of history, including the confounding attributes of our idle forefathers, like Benjamin Franklin and Samuel Johnson, and how they changed the world.

> should ever do much that I ought not to do, but that she felt convinced beyond a doubt that I should leave undone pretty well everything that I ought to do.
>
> *Idle Thoughts of an Idle Fellow,* Jerome K. Jerome, *1886*

Doing nothing, or rather doing nothing important, is a mode of survival. The mind of the lazy finds a groove and fits into it. If moving forward is too risky or requires too much effort, then we'll just find a simpler path and stick to it. In this way we resign ourselves to a welfare mentality, where God is the government, and we wait for the cheques... The long-term results of this kind of co-dependence are really kinda scary, but we think it's all good because God's in control, right? The psyche of laziness twists our view of God and keeps us comfortably stuck.

Pressure on all sides

Aside from the mental tricks of "entitled" thinking, many people face outside pressures that make it seem impossible to be themselves or to follow their dreams, even if they had the energy. There's a kind of programming we absorb from our environment which can make certain choices seem inevitable, like the person who thinks, "I'm not rich enough to go to a good school", and so they don't even look into scholarships. Or the need to take care of a sick family member means you choose not to start that small business which may have actually helped the whole family in the long run. Or, at the other end of the spectrum, three generations of your family have gone to an Ivy League school, so come hell or high water, you will too. We can sometimes feel doomed by these circumstances and simply fit into them, even as a form of faithfulness to those guiding us.

There's been a lot of "Supermom literature" in the last two decades analyzing the almost obsessive focus some parents have on raising baby Einsteins. A century ago, children were seen and not heard[13], but today they are the mantlepiece trophy and all efforts are focused on their future. This kind of parenting can be as subtle as a well-organized schedule managing school, sports, music, and

13 Make that 110 years ago, or right before 1899, when Douglas MacArthur's mom, Pinky, moved with him to West Point so she could take an apartment nearby and watch him with a telescope to ensure he kept up his studies. Go Pinky!

the occasional play date. But for others it may mean paying tens of thousands to a college consultant so that your 17-year-old gets perfectly prepped for the college of your choice, or frantically making every day count for your budding young professor. Take little Steven for example:

> Steven Guzman is only 12, but he's booked solid. He wakes up at 6 every weekday morning, downs a five-minute breakfast, reports to school at 7:50, returns home at 3:15, hits the books from 5 to 9 (with a break for dinner) and goes to sleep at 10:30. Saturdays are little better: from 9 to 5 he attends a prep program in the hope of getting a scholarship to a private school. Then there are piano lessons and a couple of hours of practice a week. If he's lucky, he'll squeeze in his friends on Sunday. "Sometimes I think, like, since I'm a kid, I need to enjoy my life," he says. "But I don't have time for that."[14]

This kind of schedule may not have been your life, but there's definitely been a shift from telling your kids to go down to the empty lot and make a treehouse, to buying them "macrobiotic cupcakes and hypoallergenic socks" or hiring tutors "to correct a 5-year-old's 'pencil-holding deficiency'".[15] And while there has been a recent move back to a more natural approach, or "free-range parenting", the effects of over-programed, product-oriented childhoods have left a mark. As free-range parent Lenore Skenazy puts it: "10 is the new 2. We're infantilizing our kids into incompetence."[16] This pre-packaged childhood has created a kind of co-dependence on the environment around us (authorities, programs, provision), leaving us clueless as to how to create our own story or future. It's no wonder we grow up thinking God is going to keep the minivan humming.

In contrast to this is another kind of external pressure that can seem equally debilitating. Many people grow up in environments where they feel limited by money, family dysfunction or culture (like the need to care for parents the rest of their lives), or just the

---

14 Nadya Labi, "Burning Out at Nine?", *TIME Magazine*, Monday, November 23, 1998.

15 Nancy Gibbs, "The Growing Backlash Against Over Parenting", *TIME Magazine*, Friday, November 20, 2009.

16 Ibid.

need to simply survive. Others deal with more overt issues like teen pregnancy, drug use, racial prejudice or mental illness. These kinds of things can leave you feeling trapped.

On top of the feeling that you can't control your destiny, the Supermom lit can affect people struggling with hard issues by creating a kind of paranoia. For instance, *TIME Magazine* writers Po Bronson and Ashley Merryman cite: "A survey of young Latinos showed they had picked up this panic that colleges are too selective and too expensive. Many had not bothered to apply even to their local public college, assuming it was as expensive as the Ivy Leagues and their grades weren't good enough to be admitted. When they were told the facts, three-fourths of them said they would have applied to college, if they had known earlier."[17] In this case, a kind of fatalism kicks in ("Oh well, it wasn't meant to be"). And in the resignation to the circumstances, hard as they really are, you also resign your ability to break out.

So whether the pressure is about getting you into the "right" preschool so you can get into the "right" university, or just making sure you don't get shot today, that pressure to either perform or survive creates a kind of stress that makes you into something you're not. Living with this stress makes some people over-achievers, while others simply cope or check out. This is one of the trickier forms of laziness; conforming to the pressure around you, whether to make other people happy, fulfill the responsibilities placed on you, or just survive in a difficult world. Now I'm not saying that people under huge hardships or financial pressure or those taking care of their parents are lazy. They're obviously not. But the external pressures in our lives often kick in a survival mechanism where we shut down the ability to use our real identity and ingenuity, both of which could create a better life for everyone involved.

Dave Eggers lost both of his parents to cancer in one year, ending his university studies in journalism. To him, it also seemed like the end of his dreams and thus his life. He was forced to deal with a bunch of new realities that made life very different from what he had hoped for. At 21 he took on the primary care of his 8-year-old brother, moved from Chicago to Berkeley, and struggled to find a

17 Po Bronson and Ashley Merryman, "Baby Einstein vs. Barbie", *TIME Magazine*, Friday, September 22, 2006.

job. He did what you have to do and made it through day by day doing temp work, helping his young brother through school and trying to find meaningful relationships so as to not go crazy. At the core, Dave was a writer, and he did his best trying to start a new magazine, but who has the time?

To make a long but worthwhile story short, after nine years of struggle and learning he eventually moved to Brooklyn and wrote a novel titled *A Heartbreaking Work of Staggering Genius,* which became a best seller and a finalist for the Pulitzer Prize. He wrote more books, started a quarterly literary journal, got married, began an amazing homework tutorial center in San Francisco (826 Valencia), and was awarded the TED prize for networking 2000 people to help kids do their homework and become better writers. And just for fun, he writes screenplays like *Where the Wild Things Are.*

In effect, he overcame all kinds of hardship by being himself. It took almost 20 years from the point of his parents' death and the life he inherited to the place he is now. But when you hear him speak, with compassion and determination, you can see that he was never going to be a victim to these circumstances; he was always going to be a writer, teacher, father... He overcame the hardest kind of laziness, the kind where it's easier for the soul to shut down because that's what life's handed to you.

Not gonna work for the man

Finally, on top of our inheritance of ease, our spirit of entitlement, and the programmed expectations in our lives comes the last form of laziness I want to talk about. It's a valiant beast, bearded and cool. The kind of laziness that's so popular and yet so unassuming, nobody messes with it. It has a long family history of pirates and gypsies, of beatniks and hippies. It doesn't care what you think and so stays protected by the isolation of its own "genius". I call this kind of laziness Indieism.

The Indieist will not work for the man, and so he doesn't work at all. He shares the view of Charles Wright Mills, who referred to the middle class as "standardized losers, […] conformists who sell not only their time and energy but their personalities as well".[18] The

18 *White Collar: The American Middle Classes*, Oxford University Press, 1951, page xviii.

Indieist will not sell his personality; in fact he will not sell anything. He's above it all. And in that lofty position he imagines all the things he could do, but doesn't do any of them. Aside from showing up at parties and other people's events, the Indieist kinda cruises through life; all aspirations and art, but no creative power. You can lead this braided horse to water, but he's too cool to drink. He's all about the ideas and the opportunities, never about the action. He is "always inquisitive and seldom retentive".[19]

Many people suffer from this bohemian problem. They have all the opportunity in the world, or enough of it, but will not make the effort to engage those possibilities. Like Parliament's Sir Nose, they're too cool to sweat. They hide behind the present vibe of a culture obsessed with being independent, so much so that they don't know how to connect, collaborate, and start making something of value. They love travel, to keep moving, because putting roots down kills their flexibility. They're all eggs and no baskets. They love being in relationships, but not for too long. They're passionate about everything, but not enough about anything to do any thing. They're like Melville's Bartleby who does nothing because he simply "prefers not to". How cool is that?

I think this last form of laziness is the most insidious. It hides behind the current trend, the flow. It doesn't make much noise or complain, but simply looks good doing nothin. It's the thing inside of us that aspires but does not act. It's encouraged all the time, nurtured with "I loved that song you wrote" or "You made that dress? It's fantastic", but it never responds past the pleased blushing of a cheek. It's way too comfortable in its present state to really break out into what might look uncool – like really hard work. To the Indieist, God is awesome... but there's no real need or pressure to develop a working relationship.

Sloth

All of these various forms of laziness are a kind of sloth. And sloth has been called a deadly sin because, as Aquinas suggests, it's a "sluggishness of the mind which neglects to begin doing good".[20] It

19 Samuel Johnson, *The Idler*, Universal Chronicle, 1758.

20 *The Summa Theologica of St. Thomas Aquinas*, translated by the Fathers of the English Dominican Province, 1920.

can't even start to love, or try to bless others, and that's where the sting of death is. Os Guinness goes further by saying sloth "[…] is a sluggishness of spirit, feeling, and mind that eventually overcomes the body like an after-lunch languor. [...] it is a condition of explicitly spiritual dejection that has given up on the pursuit of God, the true, the good, and the beautiful."[21] In this way, sloth is the enemy of our calling, the sacred connection between our identity and the known will of God. This laziness suffocates any expression of our soul that might be beneficial to others.

Growing up, I was the laziest kid on the block. I would intentionally leave food on plates so my mom wouldn't ask me to do the dishes again. I showed up to high school at 11 each morning and cheated my way through the rest of the day. I was driving at 15 and at 50 have only recently taken up walking... I moved through a number of odd jobs just to put gas in the car, but had no real idea of who I was or what I could do with my life. Even after becoming a Christian, I just went with the flow of what other people thought was important. Eventually the momentum ran out of steam and I was forced to deal with my own laziness and lack of understanding about calling, decision-making, and how to create a future instead of always looking for it to be handed to me.

The essential thing is to know exactly how and why we're lazy so we can work on it and stop projecting our laziness onto expectations of what God should be in our absence. For me, it's always cutting corners. Looking for the straightest path between two points. And not in an efficient way, but rather to reduce any kind of effort on my part. It's looking at how hard something may be and not even starting. I can especially see this in my lack of creativity. I know that if I put in my 10,000 hours, I can master something, but man, 10,000 hours!? I know that I have talents, but hate the idea of all the discipline and effort it would take to develop them. I know that, at the end of the day, I can get by, so why try harder?

---

21 *The Call: Finding and Fulfilling the Central Purpose of Your Life,* Thomas Nelson, 2003, page 140. (Languor is the state or feeling, often pleasant, of tiredness or inertia.)

What comes to your mind in terms of why and how you're lazy?

____

____

____

____

____

____

____

The importance of crisis

Most of the important things I've learned have come through problems in my life. Hitting the wall on issues that forced me to review how I was living. If I was a lot more disciplined, I probably would've learned things before I smacked into them. But God in His goodness has given us a world of cause and effect, where we can learn through mistakes and failures. The Hebrew language has a word for this: *mashber*. Literally translated it means "crisis", and the same word is used for the traditional birth stool. The pressure of birth is a great model of what happens in crisis, going from a state of warm goodness in the womb to the pressure of popping out into a world where we must fight to breath. Now, God does not throw crises our way – we create them – but the potential to learn from the culmination of our and others' actions is huge. Crisis can be just the transition we need.

The Chinese characters for crises (危機) combines the character of *danger* and the character for *crucial point.* I came to one of these points after leading a small media institute in Germany for nine years. It was going in circles and I was going nowhere. I couldn't break out of debt cycles, or break into a new level of creativity in our work or community. This crisis made me review everything, which happens to be a good place to start. I booked a five-day trip on the Norwegian Coastal Steamer that traveled from Bergen to Tromsø. During that time with God I was able to see my patterns and a way forward. Had I not had the crisis, I would not have seriously looked at the issues and how to face them. I've found this to be true in dealing with all of the big choices in my life and in the life of our family.

This is going to be really important for the present generation because, as Tom Lutz points out: "Unlike the 1960's counterculturists, many of the slackers of the 1990s and beyond have not felt much power to change the world. The only thing that ever changes, many of them have suggested, is style."[22] This sense that we are powerless is not so much because the world is any more complex than it was in the '60s, but because there's so much "soma"[23] in the air. We're simply not fussed about the looming crises all around us. We're distracted by marketing messages and dopamined up by shopping. Always buying, rarely creating. Sometimes we need a little push to help us see what's about to go down and what we can do to face it. Sometimes we need a crisis and, trust me, it's on the way.

---

22 *Doing Nothing: A History of Loafers, Loungers, Slackers, and Bums in America*, Farrar, Straus and Giroux, 2006, page 299.

23 Soma was the Valium-like drug taken daily or sprayed into the air during riots in Aldous Huxley's *Brave New World.*

Chapter meditation

"This is a day of distress, of chastisement, and of disgrace. The babies have reached the *mashber* – birth stool, but the strength to give birth is lacking."
II Kings 19:3

There are three things I'd like you to consider in this meditation:

1. Your happiness?

In her book *Sloth*, Wendy Wasserstein mocks us with this wisdom: "With sloth, you will live a longer, happier, and more rewarding life by removing the nagging tug of passion, creativity, and individual desire [...]. Comfort is much more important than any achievement or social contract."[24] She's identified the inner message of our culture. But ironically, the lazy pursuit of happiness ends up as a pursuit of unobtainable lifestyles and jobs we can't stand. Proverbs 12:24 sums it up in this way: "The hand of the diligent will rule, but the slack hand will be put to forced labor." So what really makes us happy – the pursuit of happiness or the development of passion in connection with a social contract?

2. Your problems?

In a letter to a friend, Edmond Burke wrote in 1795 that "nothing is so fatal to religion as indifference". Indifference is a form of self-protection; it's how we manage our problems or the complexity of larger issues in the world around us. But it eventually diminishes our faith because we have nothing to practice on. We need to take action against the crises facing our communities and nations by using our faith and the knowledge of God in a way that creates solutions to financial crises, threats of terror and war, dealing with poverty wherever we find it... These challenges become a context for our calling, which then draws us into the fray. Looking at the bigger issues often helps us move past our smaller ones.

3. Your plans?

Sometimes the battle against laziness will not mean instant action, but rather careful consideration and long-term planning. Oscar Wilde once said in a dizzying essay: "To do nothing is the most difficult thing in the world, the most difficult and the most

24 *Sloth: The Seven Deadly Sins*, Oxford University Press, 2005. page 106

intellectual."[25] The quote is often used as a playful way to excuse inactivity, but his point was that doing anything was often easier (or lazier) than intellectually discussing the best way forward. If you want to make a significant dent in one of the world's larger problems, you may need to consider a long-term process of education, apprenticeship, and application. This could take decades, and therefore needs some serious planning, which is sometimes much harder than just diving in.

In any case, when the crisis comes, will you have the strength to learn from it and grow? How can you prepare now to deal with the big decisions coming your way (aside from finishing this book)? In what ways has laziness slowed you down in the past, and how will you deal with the next opportunity?

25 *The Critic As Artist*, Green Integer, 1997, page 99.

Chapter 4 • Selfishness

Along with fear and laziness, the third factor creating confusion is our selfish approach to making choices and planning the future. It's not an obvious selfishness or even the typical kind where we reject the ideas and the heart of God and just do what we want. Our selfishness is being okay with an average life, one that doesn't bless anyone or change our world for the better. It comes from living in a weird paradox somewhere between "What would Jesus do?" and "Follow the desires of your heart". We oscillate between a sense of guilt that we're not doing enough for God and just doing what we want. This is where selfishness kicks in; in the absence of real clarity from God and a clear knowledge of self (identity, intellect, talent) and its place in the mix, we revert to a kind of desperate searching and clinging to things *we think* will meet our needs for love, provision, value, and destiny. In this way, we're not even being our true selves, but instead, we compromise the ideas, values, and design of God by making dumb choices just trying to survive. Our self becomes self*ish,* and we abuse the core goodness God gave us by filling our souls with empty lifestyles.

I know that's an earful, so let me give an example.

Backstory: Maria loves taking pictures and would like to be a photojournalist one day. She's just finished high school and is not sure what to do next because photography is only one of her many interests, and making a life out of it is a huge stretch for her confidence. Her church organizes a summer outreach to Mexico and a few of her friends decide to go, so she joins them, loves the time there and is besotted by the children in a small orphanage just outside of the town they're in. *Maybe she could be a teacher?* Back at home Maria feels the pressure of the coming school year as her friends apply for college and her parents want to know what she plans to do. She loved the kids in Mexico and could see herself working with them, but this only adds to the list of interests without bringing any clarity as to what she *should* do. She also met a guy on the outreach and has decided to start going out with him. He's in his first year of university in her home town in California and has taken a huge interest in her. *Maybe she should stick around and marry this guy?* A friend has told Maria that there's a great photojournalism course back east and so she starts looking into it and is excited about the possibilities. *Maybe she should be a photojournalist?*

Problems: In her self, she's a story-teller and does this by creating images. God loves this about her but she doesn't know it because all she's heard is that "Jesus loves the little children, all the children of the world...". It's crazy how the simplistic tidbits of God we amass over the years of kinda listening at church form much of our theology. Maria therefore thinks all God's interested in is the missionary aspect of working with kids in Mexican orphanages, but since she's "not called to be a missionary", being a teacher would be a nice substitute. Then there's that guy. So forget going back east and taking that huge financial risk – it would be stupid since her family and potential husband are right here at home...

Selfishness: Since Maria does not know how much God values her true self, she has this weird sense that what God wants is for her to be someone else – a teacher, for instance. The simplistic connection between what she thinks of God ("all the children of the world") and what she's somewhat interested in (kids in orphanages) creates a gap in her soul, an emptiness (because the soul knows she's missing it) that Maria then tries to fill with this new guy, some kind of security, and a destiny that's doable. This is selfish, or an abuse of the self, because she's trying to get her legitimate needs met by extracting them from others in an inauthentic way. Instead of taking the risk (dealing with fear) to be that photojournalist, she's looking for a safer path. Instead of moving away from the ease of home to create a life outside of her present boundaries, she's creating a potential lazy rut for herself, which only becomes apparent years later when things don't pan out as she'd like. Selfishness happens when we're not being our true selves.

Along the way, Maria starts to justify her actions by saying, "This is what God has for me". Not because she knows it to be true, but because she's formed or conformed God to the image of her needs. Instead of letting Him be who He really is, the Father who would love to see her get out of this rut and make a life that is truly hers and therefore truly effective, she worships a different god.

God's will for Maria is not that she'll be a photojournalist or a teacher, but that she would be herself, His daughter, and as such, align the desires of her heart with the heart God has for her family, community, nation, and nations. This complex connection requires a deep relationship and understanding between Maria and God, but who has time for that? Selfishness looks for a simpler road, but you end up as someone else, serving some strange god. Most people just get a job, become materialistic survivors, and hang out at church waiting for something to happen. From there, it just gets ugly.

The paradox

Self is not evil. We can't love our neighbor unless we love (understand, value, cherish, develop) our selves. Jesus said the whole world was not as valuable as your self, your soul. It's true that we have to die to our self-focused obsession – being too self-absorbed, too dominant or too abusive creates all kinds of death around us. But we can't kill our souls. The soul can't die because it was designed to live forever. So on one hand, we have the self and the wonder of it being made in God's image, and on the other, the abuse of that self, which happens when we do not know, love, and co-operate with God's design.

Our confusion is that we think we need to throw the baby out with the bath water. If we have a great idea, we think it must die screaming on the altar of our lives because this is what God wants; for us to die to self. Anything that looks like *your idea* or something done in *your strength* must automatically be silenced because it's *just you.* We assume that we are nothing, God is everything, and therefore anything on my heart is naturally selfish.[26] Ironically, this is where the selfishness begins. We were never created to be empty clones or "the Lord's army". God is definitely not working in that paradigm, but since we don't know this, we try for a few weeks. We say things like, "What do you want me to do, God?", but find that we're not hearing anything. We think we can't hear because we lack faith or aren't radical enough. We think we just need to throw in the towel

---

26 I do think there are some things we should get rid of, like fear or laziness – put that crap on the altar. Or ambitions that are selfish and abusive. The simple truth is that you know the difference between being the natural you and when you're being a selfish pig, so just don't be. In fact, if you were really being your self, the way God designed you, you wouldn't be going around trying to suck the life out of the universe.

and go full time into missionary life... We're struggling to find Him, to do exactly what we're told, and He's not even on the same page.

Confused priorities

So is it "all about God?" Is that what God is looking for? Is that worship? Because if it is, there's no real question about your call. Just ask what He wants you to do, and go do it regardless of what you think about it. Regardless of whether you'll be effective, or helpful, or sustain a life and family doing that. In fact, if it's God, then you don't have to worry about any of these things because He knows what's best. Right? So we try. We pray, we listen, and we don't hear much. Or we get vague impressions that become riddles, like our faith is being tested. And while all this is going on, we're being pressed to make educational, relational, and financial choices. This stuff can make you psychotic. In the absence of a response, we try plan B. Be a nice person, be employed, and be a good church-goer. But since God's not in the business of cloning, we get really confused and this life becomes an unsustainable proposition. We start looking for other watering holes, like the mall, or the sports bar, or another relationship. Since the self can't walk out its true calling, it becomes greedy, and then sinks its evil-twin-brother claws into anything that will help it survive.

At this point we enter the malaise of the average Christian life, where the bulk of Christians are walking around dazed and doped up on a subculture that maintains this confused schizophrenia. One side of our subculture's personality talks about what Jesus would do, while the alter ego pretty much does what we want. We have a language that espouses God's will, Him being in control, and insists that it's ALWAYS about Him and never about us. But this is the language of our disease and not how God thinks. And since the language of our psychosis is not real (at least not what God was thinking), the practice comes out very different. Our families are as broken as the ones next door, our premarital relationships are as sexual and busted as everyone else's, and our jobs are empty ways to pay the bills, 'cause God is definitely not there either (we don't think He's interested because it's not "full-time ministry"). It's no wonder we race back to church each week looking for that next injection of spiritual Valium, because this split thinking is so very hard to live with.

So when it comes to choices, decisions, and planning our future, we talk about the will of God but pretty much have to make things up along the way. And in the absence of our soul flourishing in its element, getting a larger LED TV seems like a really good idea. It's a way of placating our need to be something more, getting stuff that dulls us back onto the couch, because engaging with the real world requires a soul alive, and ours is barely breathing.

Russ

When you don't choose or get to be yourself, there's a subtle agreement you make with the devil. Like the bad human in *The Matrix,* you'll sacrifice your dreams, but you still wanna live comfortably. You're not gonna be completely evil, but you're not going to change the world either, and in exchange for this compromise, you get to live the life typical.

In Norway from the 1st to the 17th of May, high-school graduates wear red overalls and a hat to symbolize they're taking part in Russ. It's a drawn-out graduation ritual that celebrates the end of high school and the beginning of the rest of their lives. For most people, it's basically 17 days of debauchery prior to final exams that are meant to "qualify" you for the next phase in life. Normally, I wouldn't use a word like debauchery; it sounds way too old school, like "infidel". But it works perfectly here because *excessive indulgence in sensual pleasures* is exactly what Russ is about. Along with tamer aspects like BBQs in the park or just lazing about the town center with your friends, there's the more overt form of letting your hair down, like in the party buses (*russebil*). These discos-in-a-bus can cost the parents who pay for them thousands of dollars, all to provide a way for their kids to roam around Oslo all hours of the night dancing, drinking, and getting reeeeal close to one another.

Now from the outside, this can seem insane. The amount of Ecstasy that gets popped or alcohol consumed would embarrass a sailor, and the pranks or dares seem just plain alien. (I saw a girl dragging a huge salmon on a rope all day in Oslo because someone dared her to). But to the locals, this has been a tradition honored by their parents and grandparents, and it's just part of a rite of passage one takes on becoming an adult. But I think this rite of passage has an undertone to it that is true of a lot of "spring break"-style passages into adulthood around the world. At the core is an agreement to becoming an adult, and a certain kind of adult. I think really it's a transition to join the industrial revolution.

The sense that I got during the few times of being around Russ celebrations, and other such events in the world, is that these kids know their lives are going to change. And not necessarily for the better. They know they're probably agreeing to some more years of school, which is not an exciting prospect based on the last few years they've had. They know that they'll probably get into debt to pay for that education and the general cost of living. And they know they'll have to get a job they probably won't love to pay off those loans and, by then, they'll be stuck. Which is why I think they go to the lengths they do, and why their families and cultures support this insane waste of money and boundless sensuality. Because these are the last days of summer, of freedom, of being yourself, because you are about to sell your soul and the rest of your life to THE MAN. The banal working-class existence that you see your parents living and surviving is about to be yours. Because despite decades of innovation and change in the world, especially in the last 100 years, most people are still going from a lame education to a factory of one kind or another, devoid of opportunity for them to be their real selves.

And so you party like it's 1999 because, for your soul, it's over. And once you sign up for that university major that you know isn't you, or that job where you'll earn just enough to pay for your weekends, you will have unleashed the core elements of selfishness that will drive you for the rest of your life. A core bitterness against having to do things you hate. A core regret that you didn't take the risks your soul was crying out for. A core fear that you better not stray too far from the pack or you're gonna be left alone. These deep fissures of the soul change you. The agreement with the devil (via popular culture and market exchanges) suffocates your true self and the claws come out. You've sold out and you know it, and dammit, somebody's gonna pay for it.

Exploits

Daniel 11:32 says that most people will be deceived with smooth words but the ones who know God will take action or, as one translation puts it, "do exploits". So where are the adventures? Sure, people will go on personal OEs to try out their individual wings, but it seems people don't aspire to make cathedrals any more like the eight generations of families that committed to the one in Strasbourg. Or write epic poetry about the fall of Lucifer like Milton's *Paradise Lost.* Or revolutionize whole industries as the Cistercian monks did with Northern European agriculture. We've become okay with average lives and low expectations. And while we reserve the right to screw up our own potential, at the end of the day, a life that's not blessing the world is a selfish life. Perhaps we accept the status quo because ultimately we really don't know the God of exploits the way Daniel did. He was describing a knowledge that comes from co-operative action, not head games and fairy tales about Jebus. Knowing God in reality is costly knowledge because in the knowing comes the responsibility to act. We are created to create, and to join Jesus in destroying the works of the enemy. Our souls are wired to do this, but our selfish agreement with popular culture is keeping us stuck and confused.

Chapter meditation

"Then he said to them all: 'If anyone would come after me, he must deny himself and take up his cross daily and follow me. For whoever wants to save his life will lose it, but whoever loses his life for me will save it.'"
Luke 9:23-24

We have to figure this one out. Does denying yourself mean suffocating the very soul God has given you, or could it mean something else? What does picking up your cross mean, in 2010? How do we lose our life and, by doing so, save it?

There have been a lot of times in my life when the status-quo answer to deep questions has left me numb and clueless. I've realized over time that I cannot get answers to questions about the deeper things of God from people. At our best, we can encourage each other in a better direction, but at the end of the day we must ask Him ourselves. I have learned more in this way than with any other form of discipleship, study or whatever.

So I encourage you to ask God to show you what denying yourself means from HIS perspective. Not mine, or your pastor's, or anyone else who may benefit from their particular interpretation over your life. We have to move away from our passive pursuit of truth and into an owning of our life and the questions that need answering. If we dig, ask, seek, or knock, we will get answers, and because we worked for them, we'll know what to do with them. The person who drops a few bills in the offering and sits back for the show will never enter into a dynamic walk with God because that scary place is reserved for those ready for the adventure. You cannot buy entry; you simply have to put some big-ass boots on and kick your way in.

Chapter 5 • Our need to know

Why do we think God has a plan for our lives? Thorough research maybe? Or an in-depth search through history and the scriptures? And if He does have a plan, is it something He's telling everyone else except for you? It seems strange to me that a lot of us have this idea that God has a detailed road map or will for us, but none of us knows what that is. Except for perhaps the person standing up front telling their amazing story of God's leading and the incredible results, like some fantastic provision, or how God led them to their second wife... I mean, good for them and all, but these exceptional tales leave most of us feeling we lack faith or need to go to some retreat, course or seminary to get on the same inside track.

I have worked with thousands of people over the last 30 years who really want to hear from God about their future. People wanting to know who God is and what they're to do with their lives. But I find over and over again, when we dig deep on the issues, that this need to know, even for people with really good hearts, is still largely based on a lot of fear, laziness, and the selfishness mentioned above. On top of all this though, I think that along with our *internal* issues, our need to be told is exacerbated by three *external* issues that we have to face sooner or later. They are our *fatherlessness*, our *choice anxiety*, and our *lack of encouragement*. Put all the issues together and you can see why we get very confused about God's will and our calling.

The ironic thing is that up until now our inertia is not even about what God wants or our ability to hear His voice. Our internal and external problems swamp us and block our ability to understand any of this *from His point of view*. We're not even on His wavelength yet. These six issues filter the Bible, history, and our view of God to the point where we're convinced He wants to control every aspect of our lives. Not coach and co-operate; control! Such a filter means it's very easy for our interpretation of scriptures to get real weird real fast. We can take one verse and create a universe of meaning from it. For instance, "Don't lean on your own understanding" (Proverbs 3:5) becomes "Don't use your mind at all". This is the language of co-dependence and He never intended us to go there.

External issues: Fatherless

The design of God was to foster a living view of Himself and the broad range of His familial nature through extended family. The wisdom of God is revealed through our elders, and the playfulness of God through our siblings... Two of the primary ways God reveals Himself is through our mothers and fathers. I think, in the main, our mothers do a fantastic job modeling the unconditional love and provision of God. And while our fathers have the capacity to establish value and destiny in our lives, the sad truth is that relatively few actually make this happen.

Some of you will know that in my life my father checked out early and I had no real clue as to who I was or what I could do, in part because of his absence. I'm not saying that dads are 100% responsible for this facet of our development. I just know that when they're absent as a result of either leaving or working too many hours, it has a massive effect on us and we miss some of the blessing God hoped they'd pass on. There are key elements they're meant to model, and when they don't, our souls don't know what "fearfully and wonderfully made" means. I found that even when I grew up and learned of the amazing love of God for me, and that I was made in His image, I still didn't grasp it in my soul or do anything significant with this head knowledge because something was broken in my heart.

God has given our fathers the authority to represent Himself. When they misuse or abuse that authority, it goes deep. When they don't pass on encouragement or help us cope with fear, we're left hanging, often unable to break out even when we've become adults. It's no wonder then that even in our 20s we approach God not as we would a coach who will help us jump into things with boldness, but as a fearful 9-year-old wanting someone to hold on to the back of the bike and not let go because we're afraid of falling. We transpose what we needed as kids onto God and hope that this time it'll be better. This leads to all kinds of confusion.

Our dads often did their best with what they had to work with. But we have to consider the damage of being fatherless. Once I acknowledged in my heart the full effect of this in my own life, I was more able to see how God wanted to re-parent me and what guidance looked like from His perspective. It was very freeing but still hard because now it meant I had to be a son, not a co-dependent child. There was a gap between childhood and adulthood I wasn't sure I could jump. I found that He was able to coach me through it, but largely by having me take more risks and responsibility. At the same time though, I could also move away from the idea that He wanted to control every aspect of my life, which by the way is not good parenting. Honestly, if we looked at the ways we think God wants to lead us and measured that against what we understand as good parenting, He'd look like a control-freak. Imagine as a 30-year-old son calling your dad and saying, "I did the last thing you told me; what do you want me to do next?" A good dad would ask why you're even asking the question (or why you don't have a life yet). But we've grown to believe it's okay to ask God these kinds of questions because "He know's what's best" and because we're afraid of screwing up. The truth is that He does know what's best, and telling you what to do is lousy parenting. What's best is that you learn to decide for yourself, with the identity you've been given and with an understanding of the priorities of God. That, in a nutshell, is the will of God.

External issues: Choice anxiety

You know how you look at your future and think, "Man, I would love to do so many things, I'm not sure which one to choose"? It's because you're able to do so many things. Psalm 139 says that we're fearfully and wonderfully made, meaning you're a complex mix of identity, intellect, personality, passions, physical abilities, and talents. You can't possibly think of yourself in terms of one career or vocation. You *can* do 20 or 30 things in your life, maybe not amazingly well, but you're definitely not one thing. Your parents or grandparents may have had to focus on one career because of their circumstances, and this may be partially true for you. But the way you're wired is to be able to synthesize many different aspects of your life into doing a new thing in the world, or a series of new things.

That's one side of the coin; your potential. The other side is the sheer number of options in a world of 230-something nations and 6+ billion people. As I said before, you have more access to travel, money, technology, and knowledge than any other generation in history, and that creates a near infinite number of possibilities for a partner, job description, and lifestyle. I've read somewhere that the average person in the West who graduates high school in the year 2000 will go through five different careers in their lives. Not jobs; careers. So the sheer number of options being presented to you is enough to freak anyone out and leave them slightly comatose, like a guy standing in a Home Depot aisle facing 30,000 products, dumbfounded into paralysis by the sheer choice before him.

Choice anxiety is the result of two forces slamming into each other; our huge internal range on one side and the sheer number of choices on the other. This can leave us daunted and unsure of what to do because we can see a whole universe in front of us. Even for the passionate among us who are clear about what they want to do with their lives, the growing options for using that passion are hitting critical and debilitating levels. Social theory professor and author Barry Schwartz sees his visit to The Gap one day as a perfect illustration of the dilemma: "I want a pair of jeans – 32-28", says Barry to the trendy saleswoman who replies: "Do you want them slim fit, easy fit, relaxed fit, baggy or extra baggy... stonewashed, acid washed, or distressed?... button fly or zipper... faded or regular?" By creating all these options, the store had helped some with diverse tastes, but whereas in the past buying a pair of jeans used to be a five-minute affair, it was now "a daylong project" and "a complex decision in which I was forced to invest time, energy, and no small amount of self-doubt, anxiety and dread".[27]

Some people may be better shoppers than others and actually appreciate 80 kinds of cereal on the store shelves. But Schwartz points out:

> As the number of choices keeps growing, negative aspects of having a multitude of options begin to appear. As the number of choices grows further, the negatives escalate until we become overloaded. At this point, choice no longer liberates, but debilitates. It might even be said to tyrannize.[28]

So on top of being relatively fatherless and dealing with the internal issues discussed earlier, choice anxiety is tyrannizing what little courage we have left to venture out and have a go.

---

27 *The Paradox of Choice: Why More is Less,* Harper Perennial, 2005, pages 1-2.

28 Ibid.

Part of the daunting feeling comes from the sense that you could do anything. The truth is, you can't do absolutely anything in the world. You do have boundaries, defined by the range of your identity and talents, and your range of opportunities is also limited to a degree. I think the real root of anxiety comes from not knowing your boundaries or your range. I mean, you still have tons of options based on the fantastic fact that you are made in God's image and do have unprecedented access to knowledge, etc. But this is a manageable problem when you truly know who you are. Anxiety is a direct result of a lack of identity, and while I hope to fully discuss this in my next book, I just want to emphasize here that the issue is not a lack of knowing what God wants; it's a lack of not knowing who we are. And to a degree, anxiety is also caused by not knowing how God wants to walk with us. But the cool thing is, we can work on that.

External issues: Not enough encouragement
Hebrews 3:13 says we're to encourage each other daily. It's not a suggestion, like if you have a special word from God... It's a command and one we generally suck at. Most of us can remember on one hand the number of significant words of encouragement we've received in our lives. At the same time, many of us can fill pages with the negative words spoken over us or with the internal crap we tell ourselves. So given the fact that we're facing a lot of internal fears and a daunting world of choice, this lack of encouragement is killing us.

The root of the word "encourage" is *cour.* It's from the Latin (and French) word for *heart*. We're meant to give heart or courage to one another because without that, we lack the bravery of soul to engage the world despite our issues or weaknesses. I mean, we do have a few strikes against us, but none of this would matter if we had the heart of a lion. I remember running a race in the 4th grade. I've always been lousy at school and never really tried that hard, thinking I was kinda dumb most of the time. But I can still remember that sunny afternoon at Monterey Hilltop Elementary. The teachers had organized a few races for recess, and I got roped in somehow. I'd been held back for almost a year before being allowed to go to school, and the extra time made me almost a head taller than most of the other kids, so in the race, my longer legs gave me a real advantage. The distance laid out was only about 60 meters but, when halfway through the race people started yelling my name, everything went slow motion. I saw them waving their arms with excitement, their faces beaming with my brilliance. I cruised to an easy win (poor smaller kids) surrounded by my peers. The strange thing is that life went on for everyone else as normal, but I changed that day. Based on a small measure of encouragement, I went on to focus on sports in school for the next eight years, finally becoming a Letterman[29] in my senior year when we went on to State Finals in basketball. A few kids thought I was something for a few minutes and it went straight to my heart.

The power of encouragement is huge, as we all know. But unfortunately, most of us don't know the substantial power of *regular* encouragement. We go looking for encouragement and rarely find it. Which creates a kind of cycle because we hardly ever encourage others as a result. We pass by each other daily, missing the opportunity to encourage because we're so needy ourselves.

So when you put all six of these issues together...
internal stuff:
- fear
- laziness
- selfishness

external stuff:
- fatherless
- choice anxiety
- lack of encouragement

...you can see how easy it is to create and project all kinds of expectations onto God, forcing Him to be what we need in our desperation, rather than who He really wants to be as a Father, Coach, and Friend. You may not feel all six problems at once, but most of us are effected by some combination that tweaks our view of God. And not only God, but what we read, what we hear at church, and then how we talk to each other. When we don't deal with this stuff, we have to construct a parallel world that makes our

29 A Letterman gets a large letter to place on their high-school jacket to signify that they've achieved in all four sports in the year: football, basketball, baseball, and track and field. I wasn't even that good but, man, a little encouragement goes a long way.

fear and laziness seem normal or, worse, like a total commitment to God, as in, "I'm waiting on the Lord"... And our fatherlessness and choice anxiety become faith that "God is in control". Ultimately, this leads to a kind of Christian psychosis, living in an unreal world where not even God is able to abide.

So we look to other people in authority to compensate. Take this kind of weirdness into a Christian institution (local church, mission agency) and you're vulnerable to lots of misleading teaching and abuse because in the absence of a clue, other people are happy to define the rest of your life for you in the belief that that's what God wants them to do... We'll look at this in depth in the next chapter, and it ain't pretty. But please bear with me; there is a method here.

Chapter meditation

"This is love for God: to obey his commands. And his commands are not burdensome, for everyone born of God overcomes the world. This is the victory that has overcome the world, even our faith."
1 John 5:3-4

There's something amazing about a simple faith. Trusting in the substantial ways of God allows us to overcome or resist submitting to / avoid coming under / withstand being dominated by the systems of darkness. The things I've described above are really the works of a fallen realm. But even in this space, the ways of God, applied through faith and made real by daily action, become a turning point that not only counteracts the strikes mentioned against us, but uses them to make us stronger and more able to love (the ultimate goal).

In his brilliant account of creation (*The Silmarillion*), J.R.R. Tolkien describes the forming of the world as a masterful song. A song with this beautiful power to create a living planet. A song that's so incredibly potent, even the enemy's song of dissonance cannot change the core makeup of the master's creation. And while the enemy's dissonance does affect and add some elements of destruction to the world, it cannot overcome the sheer wonder of a loving creator.

I've often meditated on how wonderful this fallen world still is. Even after millennia of human and spiritual influence and impact, it's a gorgeous place full of potential. And even in myself, with all the weight I feel pressing against my potential growth, there is this amazing spirit, ready to overcome all odds if I simply take on the relatively light yoke of the ways of God. I have a Father who will help *re-parent me.* I have boundaries that I can be safe and creative in, and all I have to do is ask for understanding of *who I am* (versus *what I should do*). I can encourage others and, in doing so, have encouragement *flow through me.* I can put the power and truth of God to work on internal stuff in daily practical applications (like through forgiveness and risk-taking). Because in this way, in Him, I am truly strong and will be raised as on the wings of eagles.

So go ahead and count the costs of how you've been affected internally and externally. But then put the ways of God to work on each revelation. So if you're lacking encouragement, encourage others. If you have too many choices, ask Him about your identity... In this way you'll have a practical outlet to deal with the issues and you'll naturally start to move out of this homemade psychotic subculture. The power of God is not there to remove us from the world; it helps us overcome it by changing it from the inside out.

Chapter 6 mind•fuck |as it sounds|

noun

1 a concept or argument which is fraught with contradictions, and is used as a control tool.

The Urban Dictionary, 2010

There's no delicate way to put this. When you walk into any Christian institution loaded with any combination of the six issues mentioned so far, somebody's going to screw with your head. And it's not because these people are evil or just want to control you; it's that when you offer your authority to anyone, odds are they'll take it. It's our passive approach to discipleship that makes us vulnerable to all kinds of crap, and this adds to our confusion.

But as we go through this chapter, please be careful not to place blame on the people around you. We have to deal with the internal and external stuff before we can even see these institutional problems at all. I don't know anyone who's gone into the church or missions to mess with people's heads. But I've also observed that if we continue to mindlessly give our authority to anyone long enough, Christian "leadership" will become confusing and often tyrannical. And I know that in bringing this up, I may alienate a lot of super-well-meaning people who think I'm attacking the church. So let me make it clear: We need to get together, and we need to find healthy ways to grow in God together. We need to be the body of Christ in the world, and that comes in all shapes and sizes.

We also need to stop our lazy approach to spirituality. We plunk ourselves down in front of whoever's got the "latest word", sipping our free latte wondering how inspirational this morning's sermon will be. We invest nothing and get little in return. And putting some money in that passing plate is not an investment; it's a knee-jerk response to an outdated system. But once you do put your money in the offering, you unleash all kinds of confusion on yourself, 'cause now you're paying someone to tell you how it is, and that was never the idea.

Here's how it works:

You may have grown up in church or came along later. In either case, you show up wanting to know God and to figure out your life.

And maybe you show up to check out the "prospects"... Anyway, you're sitting there with some combination of laziness and choice anxiety, or fear and being fatherless... From that position, you project your needs onto that poor guy in the front who's being paid to deliver the goods. Not that you're thinking this, but at the core, this is usually what's going on. Maybe you have a good idea while you're sitting there, sipping your now cold coffee. Like, you want to start a local cafe that can bring your musical, design, and hospitality skills together to bless the neighborhood. So after church, you walk up to the pastor and share the idea. Or maybe you don't, because you never share your ideas, and so you go back home or to work doing something you abhor. But then you read this book and you do approach the pastor because you now want to get the youth group involved or whatever and want to know what he thinks. So he asks you if you've prayed about this idea and if it's in the Lord's timing. And while he thinks it's a good idea, he wonders if it might be better for you to start "your ministry" by joining a program he's running to do evangelism in the neighborhood – something about inviting people to the church's new daycare center... So you say you'll pray about it and walk away, kinda deflated but feeling like you should plug into the programs in the church, because, well, it's the church... I'm not saying everyone asks their pastor for permission to do what they want, but I do think we often confuse our loyalty to God with loyalty to the institution.

Part of our confusion comes from the fact that we ask the wrong people for permission. We think our allegiance to God is the same as allegiance to the local church. That we must submit to a higher authority, which often means submitting our plans, our money and, to a degree, our lives. A lot of this kind of weirdness came out of the "Shepherding Movement" in the 1970s , where some in church leadership wanted to control who you were dating, how you were managing your money, and just about everything else, so they could "guide" you along your sheepish path. It's because of these kinds of abuses that "Christian leadership" is an oxymoron. It's why Jesus defines greatness as the ability to serve, not control. The church's role is to equip the saints for *THEIR MINISTRY*, not the pastor's program. But we don't get this and so we comply with things we know aren't good for us, and I think we do so because of the six issues already mentioned.

I have no problem with the pastor recruiting for his program. My problem is that we ask for permission instead of making the cafe happen anyway and dragging people along simply because it's a great idea. You don't need to ask the youth pastor if your friends can get involved. The church doesn't have a corner on the market of ideas and programs. It's there to support the ideas of the people, and not the other way around. But if you sit there passively looking for a ticket to heaven, then you'll have to go along for the institution's ride, and that cafe will never happen, or the church will run one and there goes the party.

Discipleship or tribalism

It's not good to be alone, and we do need to move forward as a group. It's actually the strength of the group that makes our movement dynamic and effective. But there's a difference between kicking a group into action and adhering to a herd mentality that often slows us down. People in a church or any Christian institution develop into a sort of tribe. And like most families, this tribe is a healthy part of our development. In fact, I've read some studies showing that people actually live longer because of their connection to a church. But there's a downside. When that church gets its money from the number of people attending, and some of those people want to go off and do something else, they are often dissuaded from doing so, because they're breaking rank. Sometimes the advice to stick around is well founded, but I've come across a lot of people who were discouraged in their forward movement simply because it would move them outside of the authority of the tribe.

I completely get this. Who wants people to leave the family or the tribe, especially if that tribe is doing good stuff, as a lot of them are. I don't particularly like attending large churches, but some of them are doing extraordinary things, like the fatherhood program at Imago Dei in Portland or the community development opportunities at Mars Hill in Grand Rapids. I would want all kinds of people to pitch in on projects such as these because this is truly being the Ekklesia.[30] All of us should be adding our strength to the efforts of

30 Both Jesus and Paul spoke of us as the Ekklesia because it was a well-understood term of their day. It represented a group of "go to" people who were the "called-out ones". Not called out of the city into the church of the suburbs, but called out to fix problems in the city that no one else would take on. You know, like the A Team...

the larger body of Christ whether we like fixing roofs or not. But what I'm mainly concerned about here is the tribe creating a form of spiritual weirdness that confuses people because we're not sure who's in charge. Are the leaders in charge because they're serving the community and we get to help, or because they're the "Lord's chosen" and we *must* follow? Honestly, after inheriting thousands of years of some really abusive Christian leadership ideas, I think the present expression of church has got a little tweaked in some areas.

For instance, while I don't know anyone who became a pastor for the money, I do know that once you introduce payment for spiritual services, you've just started a business. Now, if you were getting your income based on your "spiritual leadership", don't you think that would affect how you did evangelism, taught your audience, and spoke to their futures? You bet your mortgage it would. Even at our saintliest, we would skew the message towards our best interests. I've come across many professional pastors who are the nicest people in the world, but they're running a business and that messes with their message. Which is fine if we called it a business, you know, like going to the dentist. But since we spiritualize this transaction, church turns into a very strange beast and begins to change the way we perceive who God is and what He's saying.

The combination of a professional pastorate and our need for guidance creates two unhealthy aspects in the church; the spirit of control and, its evil twin brother, the spirit of being right (all the time). To maintain the status quo, and the paycheck, a lot of people confuse their financial position and their spiritual position. If church was just a matter of putting your money in the offering and getting a good sermon, then things would be clear and you'd be fine with the results. But you may also be inclined to shop around for other sermons, or musical performances... All good so far, except for that spiritual thing that adds a little twist to the issue. For instance, as you head out the door and shake the pastor's hand, thanking him for the eloquence of the morning's message, you mention the fact that you'll be heading across town next week to check out the competition, you know, to get your money's worth. At this point Pastor Bill holds onto your hand firmly and reminds you that "this is the place the Lord has you in". Wait, wasn't this simply a financial transaction, or is attending this particular church a spiritual demand from God? The problem is that it's now become both. You are "called" to this place. And you *have* to pay for it as well because "God commands you to tithe". It's a little awkward that the guy telling you to tithe, and to stay here "because that's what God wants...", is the guy whose paycheck comes out of that tithe. And it gets weirder from there. A friend recently told me that upon complaining to the Christian leadership (there's that oxymoron again) about what she considered an abusive situation, the leadership replied: "Since God has called you to this place, it's not our problem; you will have to take it up with Him."

I know people in situations like this all over the world but, again, it's not because being in control or being right is the natural and evil inclination of those who are trying to pastor the flock. The problem is that we're a flock. The problem is that instead of being kick-ass-ninja-warrior-neighborhood-loving people, we're rocking up to our stylish Starbucks-branded churches, chilling to the latest band practice (worship), and waiting to be served something entertaining, just like at the movies. Our complacency becomes a blank check and makes our "leaders" weird. I'm sure our pastors would be much better off if *we* provided the context. If we dealt with our six issues (or more) and showed up with a better question, they'd be able to use their gifts and help us move forward. And that question is not, "What does God want me to be or do?" You pose the wrong question to the wrong person and you will get the wrong answer. I also think our pastors would be better off if they had real jobs, but that's another book.

Here's the deal: Authority from God's point of view is *exusia,* or the power to serve. Anyone who wants to lead needs to be about servanthood. And we all understand that, we just don't practice it enough. But the main issue is that we don't understand submission in the proper light. If the sole purpose of people in "leadership" is to serve you, how do you submit to that? Most people would say that you do what you're told by those leading you. No. No. No. NO! How can they serve you if you just wanna obey? How will they even know what you need unless you tell them? How can their skills really help you go forward if they don't know the connection between those skills and your direction? If you think it's just about obedience, then you will freak them out, because after a while they'll start thinking they have the answers for your life and we're back where we started. We make them weird with our passive form of submission. So let me make this plain: If people in authority exist to serve you, then submission is *letting your needs be known so they can serve your direction*. It's that easy.

So imagine an environment where you're in a circle at the back of a local bakery and not in a poorly designed building with rows of clones facing the pulpit like that Apple "1984" ad. Imagine a dialogue where you're all talking about your identity and your plans and the right people are connecting with each other in order to serve. No hierarchy and no money involved. And imagine that the wisdom shared by the group (including those with teaching or pastoral abilities) encourages each person to get out and do some good work in the community as part of building up their businesses and creative talents... This is what fellowship could be or may be for you now.

Spiritual leadership? Are we still doing that Levite thing?

Sadly, most people don't make the effort to create organic fellowships like this, and they end up trapped in the controlling loop of professional spirituality. From this strange environment (called the average local church) come even stranger interpretations of what God said. For instance:

Make disciples of all nations becomes *do* ***evangelism*** *in the neighborhood*, and do it as part of our program or denomination…

Lean not on your own understanding becomes *don't use your mind at all*, and you don't have to because that's what the leadership is here for...

God has a plan for your life becomes *we have a plan for your life*, and your plans should be more like our plans because we know what God's will is...

Don't touch the Lord's anointed becomes *don't question or doubt our leadership*, even if you know we're having an affair...

Don't rob God, bring the full tithe into the storehouse comes to life again regardless of the fact that Jesus nullified the tithing system. All of a sudden it's back to a legal approach to money and God, and *don't question our authority* (see previous rule).

Note: I know that this may not be your experience (I mean, I hope it isn't), but you'd be surprised at the crap I've heard about and seen around the world in the name of "caring for the flock".

And on top of all these strange translations can come a general sense that if you were really spiritual, you'd work "full time" with the church. Because in the centrist language of the professional pastor, everyone else is a "lay person", like "there's the best, and then there's the rest". This dates back to the language of Eusebius, an early church father who spoke of two callings; one was the "perfect" or spiritual call, and the rest were simply "permitted".[31] Os Guinness says that this kind of language went on to develop "a kind of spiritual aristocracy".[32] I guess that makes me a part-time Christian, or – I don't even know what that means. So instead of a healthy family dynamic, we're now paying our "fathers", priests, and pastors to lead us and marginalize us at the same time. But again, this is more our fault than that of the guy up front who's been duped into thinking this is God's idea. The ekklesia was never meant to have hierarchies drawing all the resources of the community into some building on the corner, especially where a few people are paid to do the work of the whole group (teaching, visitation, outreach). Take away the money and all of us would have to contribute to meeting the spiritual and material needs of the whole neighborhood. But again, who wants to do that? It's so much easier to pay the priest.

Our general compliance and our need to be led eventually develop a sense that God is kinda like the leaders we've created. Controlling, a little greedy, and demanding of blind servitude. Am I being too harsh here? Maybe, but look at the language we use: "God's in control" or, "Put it on the altar" or, "I am nothing and You are everything" or whatever the latest worship dribble is. Look at what we think God wants of us and how He's supposedly leading us. Our present form of discipleship is not only going nowhere in our lives, it's making us co-dependent dweebs who aren't even focusing on the real issues. All to prop up a system that keeps us, as Keith Green used to say, "asleep in the light". Or, as Jesus called it, "the blind leading the blind".

31 Kirk and Heather Webb, "Calling, Postmodernism, and Chastened Liberals: A Conversation with Os Guinness" in *Mars Hill Review 8,* Summer 1997, page 71.

32 Ibid.

The Barna Group has estimated that the USA tithe comes to around $50 to $60 billion dollars per year. And that 18% of that is going towards buildings alone, which are worth an estimated $230 billion dollars.[33] Each year, we give roughly the equivalent of the UN's total development budget to improve our sound systems and sometimes even just our pastors' lifestyles (with a little left over for the community). Straight up, this is a misappropriation of funds, but one that's only possible when we give it away like we do. I don't blame the church. I blame our sheepish willingness to be led and fed in a way that keeps us waiting around for heaven because being of earthly use is too stinking hard. And maybe that's the real issue; our focus on the end times. The material world is all gonna burn any day now so why bother becoming an amazing neurosurgeon? Why bother doing anything of value if Jesus loves me and is saving me forever. Maybe we're glad to have that free coffee in the foyer, even if it is costing us $60 billion dollars. We got nothing better to do with the money.

All this helps to form a certain lens through which we translate common scriptures about guidance and calling. If we're sitting in church as "God's army", then God becomes the General commanding His troops. If we're all kneeling as co-dependent children, then God needs to be "in control" and we don't have to get up until He tells us to. If "God loves me so much", then He wants to give me the desires of my heart and even though I'm relationally retarded, He's still going to deliver "the one" to me any day now. I just have to keep praying through my list for exactly what I want...

It's no wonder that with these needs and filters, the language in the church has gotten so out of sync with the real heart and intentions of God. Which, by the way, when I'm done beating you with this stick, we will look at. It's just that if I start with the good news, you won't be able to hear it because this mindfuck has gone so deep, you couldn't be sure what's God and what's the result of the slow brainwashing you've actually been paying for. Which makes it really hard for God to break through, because even though skywriting (or tagging) is an option for Him, He prefers to speak to the heart.

---

33 Frank Viola and George Barna, *Pagan Christianity?: Exploring the Roots of Our Church Practices*, BarnaBooks, 2008, page 41. And, just for perspective and not to be mean, it should be noted that Christian Smith in his book *Pass the Plate* (page 52) points out that in 2005, Americans spent about $30 billion dollars on candy.

Chapter meditation

"For I know the plans I have for you," declares the Lord, "plans to prosper you and not to harm you, plans to give you hope and a future."
Jeremiah 29:11

If you're sitting in your air-conned church foyer dipping your free donuts and wondering what to do with your life, then this scripture looks pretty sweet. Like, it's all taken care of. God loves you and has a wonderful plan for your life... But if having read my vitriol commentary you've become weary and decide that if you don't look this up for yourself, to see the real context, then you're gonna be sold another bag of magic beans and end up sitting in this sterile foyer the rest of your coffee-drinking life, here's what you may find:

> This is what the LORD Almighty, the God of Israel, says to all those I carried into exile from Jerusalem to Babylon: "Build houses and settle down; plant gardens and eat what they produce. Marry and have sons and daughters; find wives for your sons and give your daughters in marriage, so that they too may have sons and daughters. Increase in number there; do not decrease. Also, seek the peace and prosperity of the city to which I have carried you into exile. Pray to the LORD for it, because if it prospers, you too will prosper." Yes, this is what the LORD Almighty, the God of Israel, says: "Do not let the prophets and diviners among you deceive you. Do not listen to the dreams you encourage them to have. They are prophesying lies to you in my name. I have not sent them," declares the LORD. This is what the LORD says: "When seventy years are completed for Babylon, I will come to you and fulfill my gracious promise to bring you back to this place. For I know the thoughts I have for you," declares the LORD, "thoughts to prosper you and not to harm you, thoughts to give you hope and a future. Then you will call upon me and come and pray to me, and I will listen to you. You will seek me and find me when you seek me with all your heart. I will be found by you," declares the LORD, "and will bring you back from captivity. I will gather you from all the nations and places where I have banished you," declares the LORD, "and will bring you back to the place from which I carried you into exile."
> Jeremiah 29:4-14

1. This is not a happy message about the love of God for you. It's about punishment in direct contrast to the other prophets saying it's all about "peace, peace, when there is no peace".
2. This is not a personal scripture. It's a word to *all the people* of Israel and Babylon. God is saying to the whole group to seek the welfare of the city because in its welfare is all of *our* welfare, because His plans are for *all of us to do well.* It's a corporate calling to bless everyone as a result of following the ways of God.
3. The Hebrew word translated here as "plans" actually means "thoughts", as in the King James version that reads, "I know the thoughts that I think toward you". This is very different from a detailed road map for your life.
4. The basis for all of this working out well is a proactive engagement in business development, family growth, and civic duty. Not a lame existence of hand-holding, but a dynamic initiative whereby we co-operate with God to do agriculture, relationships, and politics. That's where the party is.

So that's what I get out of it. How about you? Have a closer look at the scriptures you think are about God's daily leading, and try to look at them from His perspective. God promises to lead us all into wisdom if we stop being passive and go deeper, because deeper is where He lives.

Chapter 7 • Psychotic

Listen; after this chapter, I promise to be nice. Just bear with me for these last few pages and it's happy times from there. But for now, I gotta tell you that when it comes to calling and guidance, most of us, as a result of everything I've talked about so far, have become psychotic. And while this sounds tongue-in-cheek, I'm serious. Built on internal fears, laziness, and selfishness, and exacerbated by the external pressures of being fatherless, anxious about choices, and lacking in encouragement, we develop our own little world, an alternate reality that keeps us safe and sound – mostly. The combination of our heightened need and our weird religious environment is the perfect breeding ground for psychosis. I've alluded to this throughout the previous few chapters, but if you have the patience, I'd like to bring it all together and highlight the confusion we've built up about God, calling, making choices, and planning our future.

According to the National Health Service (UK): "Psychosis is a term that is used to describe a mental condition where somebody is unable to distinguish between reality and their imagination [...]. People with psychosis often experience delusions – where you believe things that are untrue."[34] It's not really considered a condition but rather a symptom of other issues. And while I may be stretching the clinical version as an analogy here, I do believe that the unique condition of Christians in the state I've been describing does lead to a mild form of psychosis, a state which has already been studied and documented. For instance, Natalie Tobert has studied the effects of spirituality and psychosis and found that in some cases, "psychosis was said to be an incomplete withdrawal from the spirit state, a failure to return to this reality".[35] Part of our religion-fueled confusion can make it difficult for us to separate the things we've "heard in the spirit" (or simply from the pastor) from what God is really doing or saying. In the context of psychosis and spirituality, Tobert was speaking mainly of how "mystics joined the inner and outer world",[36] mystics like the Quakers, Mohammed,

---

34 http://www.nhs.uk/Conditions/Psychosis/Pages/Introduction.aspx

35 *Psychosis and Spirituality: Exploring the New Frontier*, Isabel Clarke (editor), Wiley, 2001, page 45.

36 Ibid.

Moses... Most of us have not had these deep experiences, we've only looked on from the outside of their stories and tried to glean from their world. We haven't had a similar context of our own to understand what they were going through. This is one way we stretch out in a kind of armchair mysticism and it makes us a little crazy. We long for those experiences often as a way of escape. Or we want God to do the same for us because it's spiritual, and our lives are not... Closer to home for us, though, is what Gordon Claridge describes in the same book:

> People of anxious temperament have nervous systems that make them unusually sensitive to fear-provoking stimuli. This makes them more susceptible to phobias, panic attacks and so on... At a biological level, anxiety *disorder* therefore merely represents a transformation of processes that mediate healthy anxiety. So it is, the argument goes, with psychosis and psychoticism.[37]

Whether it's a simple fear of failure or full-blown choice anxiety, the "fear-provoking stimuli" will kick into gear certain responses. Sometimes it's the healthy response that spurs us into action. But what I've observed is that when a few of these six conditions we've spoken of combine, these natural processes stimulate a disconnect from the real world and drive us to the religious brink of our Christian subculture. And it's at this fringe that we gather and start talking crazy.

When we try to connect *need-based* spiritual experiences with biblical principles (I'm afraid, so God's in control), we often mistake the exception for the rule and it's this exception that disconnects us from reality, from God's intentions. There is a threshold between a healthy spirituality and a psychotic disconnected view and experience. Crossing that threshold often involves the exacerbation of core tendencies in our psychology or biology (mental/emotional issues like anxiety, or physical dispositions like a chemical imbalance). Since the perceived reality ("He will tell me what to do each step of the way") is not really true, you end up having to make choices along the way to keep moving. You make these choices and you learn from the outcome, but this is often in direct contrast with your spiritual views, so you form a kind of dualism. You live

37 Ibid., page 96.

in two worlds; one where you think God's in control, and the other where human beings control the world around you. This leads to a low-grade chronic psychosis that creates perceptions such as, "If it happened, it must have been God's doing or God's will because *I believe God is in control*". In essence, you become fatalistic.

Note: God has delegated the world to us for the most part. He can and does intervene, but our sense that He's controlling everything is delusional. He wants to interact and co-operate with us, which is where our prayer, faith, and action come in. We can ask for help or His strength to assist us with the task of taking domain, but to assume He's managing and manipulating everything is not a biblical, historical or present-day reality. And missing this point also means we miss how God actually wants to interact with us. He can heal, and protect, and counsel... but we need to get back on the right page to see any of this happen.

I know I'm making a tenuous connection here between clinical psychosis and the confusion we seem to live with. And I don't mean to belittle the serious research done or the condition of those suffering with more acute versions of this mental symptom. But I do want to highlight the real need to take this confusion seriously because, on one hand, a lot of people I work with walk in the daze of this low-grade dualism, and on the other, some people are walking into churches and shooting abortion doctors (who were attending that church) because they believe that's what God wanted.

Now you may never go that far, because you probably have a safe world-view built up in your mind, namely that God loves us, has a plan for our lives, and is in control of everything. And living in a small town in Iowa, this may even be working out just as you want it to. But it's not in Chiang Mai, where 12-year-old girls are being raped and tormented daily. And so when these two worlds (the one in your head and the broken one God has asked us to take care of) clash through the death of a loved one or the sheer shock of working in a refugee camp, people snap. So we gotta face our smug approach to living on planet earth before that world falls on us. We have to face the difference between an exception (like God stopping the sun once in recorded history) and the rule (where the climate responds to how *we* treat the planet).

The voices in our head

The craziness starts with the hero's journey. You know, the guy (and sometimes the girl) in front who's telling us this amazing story. Like when he wanted to go to a foreign country and convert the heathen but didn't have the money for the airfare. And how in prayer God told him to go to the airport with the team anyway... And so he does, and someone walks up to him with a ticket. Now usually, this is some sympathetic member of the team who fronted the money 'cause they're nice, or because they felt God wanted them to do so. And I'm okay with this being an angle, or somehow God's direct hand in this person's life. What I'm not okay with is the story ending there. I wanna know what happened the next day, and the day after that. Or the rest of this person's life. What else does God do? Or what else is He trying to teach us? How about working hard, creating value for others, saving money and having enough for buying a ticket the next time? Isn't that just as Godly as the one-off event?

We always hear the exceptional tales and then the guy sits down, or goes on to give a biblical basis for why this is what real faith looks like, leaving the rest of us feeling stink, or lacking in faith or the ability to hear God... Like when the guy at the church bake sale, looking fondly at his own Betty Crocker across the room selling her famous fattening shortbreads, tells you how a few years ago he was standing in worship and looked over at Betty with her hands raised high... and how right there God said to him: "She's going to be your wife." Whathe? Really? So after 5000 years of recorded history where God only brought three couples together, this guy is the fourth? Wow, I wanna be just like him. I want God to give me a wife. Oh wait. God rarely did that. In fact it was a MASSIVE EXCEPTION. The rule is that God would really rather teach us how to relate instead of *giving us relationships*. Because while it's completely possible that God did speak to this guy, the reality is that he liked her and made up the rest. And it's the making things up that's psychotic. Which is really unnecessary because aside from the momentary "visitations", he's probably a very nice guy. But if he keeps it up, and we all know people who have, he's gonna end up divorcing, like half the married couples in the Western church, and then he'll have to make up something else that God said, like how his new woman is the true soul mate. Honest, God said...

So what has God said to you lately? Is it something grounded in the breadth of biblical context that resonates with God's nature and character? Or is it crazy talk? Let's look at a number of typical psychotic episodes we've learned to accept. Let's look at the exceptions and the rules and see if we can't get a little closer to what God is actually saying or, more importantly, what God is actually like. And I say this because for the last 30 years as a Christian, I've observed how the voice of God or the "word of the Lord" has gone from being about how to know God and walk with Him to being about what *He wants you to do*. It's moved from a relational conversation to being all about guidance, just like in the army.

For the Bible tells me so...
"God's perfect will"

The idea: We think "knowing God's perfect will" for our lives is about clearly defined points we must reach in our future, which includes our job, who we're to marry, and where we'll live. Based on ideas like knowing "the perfect will of God" (Romans 12:2) and "I know the plans I have for you" (Jeremiah 29:11), we think that God has a detailed road map that we simply need to ask for and then follow.

Psychosis: Since we approach God and the scriptures with no real sense of identity, we have no real sense of direction either. Therefore, we create a world in our minds where God's perfect will is for us to make perfect choices, and we think these verses are about detailed directions for discovering "God's best" for us. So we ask God to reveal the perfect choice to us. But since this was never the application of the scripture, we don't hear God, we just hear ourselves and call it God. We tell other people that it's God's will for us to be a chef or a doctor or whatever, and we proceed. Ironically, our friends know we're a little crazy when we talk like this, but since nobody wants to call a spade a spade, we all keep the masquerade up.

The context: Romans 12 is talking about living a life for God in our diversity and uniqueness. It's about giving glory to God through everything we do and not conforming to the darkness around us. It's in living a godly life, being ourselves in God, that we reveal to the world God's perfect will. In other words, God's perfect will is revealed in health care or the running of a great restaurant when the *ways of God* are operating in those places through His people. Finding this perfect will is not, for example, finding the perfect restaurant; it's creating it with God's brilliant ways in culinary art and nutrition. Likewise, transforming hospitality or landscaping in your neighborhood reveals who God is through the work *of your hands*. So stop asking for His will as though it's a thing. Ask to know the heart and ways of God instead. Then go out and *make the thing yourself.* Like many of these scriptures, the Romans verses show us the *general will of God*, His heart and intentions, not a detailed map.

"Don't lean on your own understanding" (Proverbs 3:5)
The idea: God knows what's best and you don't. Based on this quote, we think that if we have an idea, it's a bad idea. We fear that using our mind, passion, talent or intellect will naturally add an element of evil, so trusting God with all of our hearts means using none of our mind. Our abandonment to God will allow Him to *direct* our paths.

Psychosis: The craziness comes from the idea that after giving you an intellect, identity, passion, free will, and an imagination, God would want to strip it all away and have you do nothing with it. And so despite common sense and a clear understanding of a good way to proceed with a plan, we toss it all in and "wait on the Lord". I know people who have shelved perfectly good ideas that would bless their families and communities and gone in strange directions just to make sure they weren't leaning on their own understanding. Or worse, some thought trusting God meant they weren't to use any of their ideas or gifts, so they passively waited for "a word" that never came. While the real answer (their identity and passion) was right in front of their nose, they couldn't see it because in their unreal world God had to direct their path.

The context: The sayings in Proverbs are about developing wisdom and growing a knowledge of God's ways. They're not about becoming a co-dependant. Verse 5 is talking about a complete commitment to God, to radical discipleship, and in this way dethroning the selfish or evil inclinations of our hearts. Like dethroning money as a key indicator for choosing a job, or choosing the welfare of your family over a disconnected party life in another city. So trusting God with all my heart means I want to know the ways of God so I can make good choices. Free will (the gift of God) means I must make these choices and be responsible for them. God's ways give me context and wisdom and therefore a framework for making the best choice. In this way, I am not *leaning* on a self-centered context but on a godly context. Our confusion lies in the way we match "don't lean on" with "don't make a choice at all, just listen and do what you're told". Where's the wisdom or learning in that? Verse 6 builds on this by saying, "in all your ways, know Him, and He will make your paths straight".[38] It's the *knowing God* that informs our wisdom and this leads to making good choices. And making good choices from the right heart attitude will lead to a straight path. Not a simple or easy path, but a solid direction that's clear because you've layered the details of God's kingdom into your choices. Again, when you approach this verse with a need to know, you miss both God and the wisdom He's offering because all you're looking for is if it's Door No.1 or Door No. 2...

"I want what God has for me"

The idea: Since God has a perfect will and a plan for my life, I want it all. And it must be full of good things, so I want them too... Like, a man, parking spots, bargains at the store, or a place in a school that's hard to get into (despite my abilities). Oh please, oh please...

Psychosis: Built on the hippy expectations of the '60s (Jesus exists to make me happy), we've developed a sense that God loves us sooooo much that He has all this stuff in store for us. As the world gets more complex and painful, we escape into a happy place, a world of expectation, consumerism, and "claiming the promises of God". God, however, is not Santa and therefore does not deliver on the expectations. Regardless, we create a language of selfishness anyway, with a strong sense that God wants to bless us in everything. When something good happens, our self-fulfilled prophesies compound our notions and we praise God. Happy us.

The context: I'm not sure where the language of "what God has for us" came from. I know we've sort of been there and done that with the "name it and claim it" mentality of the 1980s, which by the way didn't work out that well (remember Jimmy and Tammy Baker?).

---

38 Young's literal translation. I've found that a little peek into the Hebrew or Greek or Aramaic often sheds a different light on the scriptures. Young's translation is a good place to find another facet of the diamond the scriptures truly are.

And yet it looks like it's making an indie-style comeback. Especially in the West, where we mistake our out-of-balance materialism with the blessing of God. If you look closer at the quality of life we think God's giving us, you'll see that it's largely been born on the back of slavery, ripped-off economies, and trade imbalances. It's pretty psychotic to call it God's blessing. I know that James 1:17 says that every good and perfect gift comes from God, but the general idea that God has loads of material stuff for us comes from a deeper root that's purely and satisfyingly selfish rather than biblical.

"Put it on the altar"

The idea: If you are good at something, like playing music or making money, you need to burn the guitar, lose the job, and do something completely different. You need to sacrifice anything that may give you glory instead of God.

Psychosis: A friend comes to you with this great idea about developing an iPhone app that would be awesome and probably make millions. Your response: "Have you prayed about that?" In the fearful world of God wanting blood on the altar, we assume that any of our ideas are naturally idolatrous and need a good knife in the heart. We then suppress these ideas and pour cold water over others, all because we think God wants us to die to EVERYTHING.

The context: Abraham loves Isaac and knows he's the fulfillment of God's promise, but before God releases a nation to Abraham, He tests him by asking for the sacrifice of Isaac. Fine. If God really does come to you (not you fearfully asking Him if your love of knitting is sin) and tells you to hang up your needles, then okay. But if He doesn't, why assume that anything you like is wrong? Do you think that when you come up with a good idea, the very first thing God wants is for that to die or be purified? And even if He did want to teach you how to balance your passions, do you think that happens by killing them? Wouldn't it be much better for you to start that business and learn as you go? Wouldn't it be God's kindness that leads to repentance and change versus the evil kill-it-all approach that keeps us afraid to even bring up a good idea? Our "sacrifice confusion" comes more from the controlling language of the institutions we serve than from a relational grasp of God's good character.

"Wait on the Lord... and keep waiting"
The idea: One should always wait on God before proceeding into battle – or business or any big decision. What one is waiting for is unclear, but the waiting is an important aspect in decision-making.

Psychosis: Our laziness kicks in on this one and we use "waiting on the Lord" as a form of procrastination. So while circumstances or opportunities may pop up all around us, we ignore them because we're waiting for a sign, or something. Sometimes we're not waiting at all; we just say we are as a way to delay the situation, or wait for God to do something we're not willing to do.

The context: There are lots of scriptures about waiting on God. Each has a specific context where someone is in the middle of something (they're engaged, not passive) and they need God to do something that only He can do. It's waiting for special wisdom (Numbers 9:7-8), for God's judgment (1 Corinthians 4:5) or for deliverance in massively difficult situations, like with Daniel or in Proverbs 20:22. In these sorts of situations, it's not a case of waiting for God to do everything while we go shopping. We're confused about what our part is in the waiting, or what we're waiting for. Effective prayer is asking for things we know God wants to do. If you're waiting on God, be specific and be clear that it's something God will act on. Then get busy with your part.

"Not my will, but Thy will be done" (Luke 22:42)
The idea: Even though this situation (dying on the cross) was unique to Jesus, we automatically adopt this thinking as a requirement to abandon anything that might have been our will. We also assume that faithfulness is synonymous with obedience to a specific will that God supposedly has for us, one we hope He reveals soon 'cause the waiting is leading us nowhere...

Psychosis: What if you're not supposed to die on the cross of the sins of the world. What if when Jesus said, "I only do what I see the Father doing" (John 5:19), He was talking about following through with the unique plan He and the Father had made millennia ago? What if God actually wanted you to use your intellect and identity and free will so that you could say something like, "My will be done, Your way"? Our psychotic world is one where we're always looking for something God does not want to show us (like what to wear or which friend to call today). Ask the wrong question and you will get the wrong answer or none at all. I've found that when I hear nothing in response to my question, it's God saying "wrong question". Odd as this may sound, we are not Jesus. And while we may always be asking WWJD, we do not have the same place in history and therefore cannot apply certain scriptures to ourselves. But if we do try, we'll be living in a world that God does not inhabit (the one where He tells us exactly what to do each day).

The context: Jesus had volunteered to sacrifice Himself for the sins of the world. It was His will in the first place. When it came to the crunch, and Jesus had to deal with the extreme pain of the coming "eucatastrophe" (Tolkien's word), He reminded Himself and the Father that it was the will of God that He chose to fulfill. Simply put, that ain't you. We are to carry our cross daily, and we do give our lives as living sacrifices, but these are metaphors put to work through our identities and passions, not despite them. When Jesus said He only did what He saw the Father doing, He was responding to attacks from others who were pissed that He was being the Son of God, or rather, Himself, in this case by healing the sick. So it wasn't Him saying "I'm a co-dependant who can't do anything unless I get a green light from Dad", it was that He agreed with, learned from, and was empowered by the Father. And that the work of the Father (healing, kindness, restoration) justified Jesus' actions even on the Sabbath. In our case, we could apply this by looking at the values of God (like His will to destroy poverty) and then do what we see the Father doing with the principles of Jubilee. We don't have to ask God if we should make micro-loans any more than Jesus needed to ask if He could eat dinner with Nicodemus. Instead, we start the business because WE ARE business people and can learn from our Father along the way.

"Not in your own strength"

The idea: We're not to do anything that comes from our own strength: "Let not the wise man boast of his wisdom or the strong man boast of his strength" (Jeremiah 9:23). So any effort or ability you may have to do a thing is leaving no room for God.

Psychosis: We end up doing very little for fear of doing things "our way". Or again, we disguise our laziness by saying we don't want to proceed in our own strength, and nothing happens. For example, we sometimes have an idea that we're really keen to try but feel like the desire to do it is so strong that it would be too much of us and not enough of God, so we put it aside, or wait for a sign, or do something opposite to what we want... all in an effort to make sure it's not "in our own strength". Doesn't that mess with your head?

The context: In Jeremiah 9, the prophet starts out wanting to cry streams of water because of how far the people have distanced themselves from God. And in the final verses of the chapter he warns them not to boast in their money, wisdom or strength, but that if any boasting is to be done, it should be in knowing God. Which by the way does not automatically make money, wisdom or strength a bad thing. In fact, all three are gifts from God and given to be used wisely. We need to stop throwing out the baby with the bath water. Jesus said it was *faith* in money that would block faith in God. It's the *love* of money that's the root of all kinds of evil. Resources, the wisdom to use them, and the strength to apply that wisdom are what God is giving us to bless the world. It's when we forget Him and brag about the gift that we're heading for a fall. Our confusion is in thinking the gift is evil or corrupt, which it's not unless you abuse it. So use your strength for the glory of God. Problem solved.

"Many are the plans of a man's heart, BUT..."
The idea: You have an imagination but don't you dare use it. I mean, it's okay to have your small ideas floating around your wee little head, BUT the Lord will direct your steps, so you just drop it right there mister, it ain't going anywhere. "Many are the plans of a man's heart" is seen as a bad thing, a negative glitch of creation which must be stemmed by God's controlling commands before your imagination gets the better of you and you do something crazy, like develop an alternative fuel or something useful.

Psychosis: Despite the fact that the possible connections your God-given neurons could make are near infinite, you need to suppress that activity because God wants to direct (control, manipulate, mold) your steps regardless. Your mind is only as good as its ability to hear the commands of God and blindly obey them. (Hmm, I wonder where we learned that, hmm, who would benefit from us thinking that?) If you do have a good idea, well, it doesn't really matter because "all such planning is evil" (James 4:13) so don't even bother. Just go to Bible College and learn what everyone else is learning... It's no wonder we continue to create an environment where Christians are mocked for our general stupidity and lemming-like behavior.

The context: Planning is not evil, and imagination is the gift of God. Having a clue is not the problem. The scripture, "In his heart a man plans his course, but the LORD determines his steps" (Proverbs 16:9), does not mean that the man planning his course was off the wall. In fact the plan gives God something to work with. Why do you think you were given an imagination in the first place? Young's translation puts it even better: "The heart of man devises his way, and God establishes his steps." There is no "but God" in this translation, it's "and God", which means your plans *and* the wisdom of God establish your ability to take care of the garden He's given us. God even ups the ante on this by saying in Proverbs 21:5: "The plans of the diligent lead to profit as surely as haste leads to poverty." So planning is actually wise in God's eyes, and He blesses us by helping us walk them out. Proverbs 19:21 says: "Many are the plans in a man's heart, but it is the LORD's purpose that prevails." Having many plans is not a problem; those plans can be the context for God's purpose to prevail, as again Young's translation highlights: "Many are the purposes in a man's heart, and by the counsel of God it stands." So you can see that your plans are not automatically in opposition to the heart of God, but that instead, God wants to work with you on establishing your plans, or the desires of your heart, and make them stand. Doesn't this sound more like the Father?

I've heard a lot of post-modern-style tidbits coming from pastors who take small pieces out of context, like Rob Bell's talk on the Israelites in the desert.[39] He maintained that the manna showed them they weren't to save up stuff, and the pillar of cloud showed how God would lead on a day-to-day basis and how five-day plans or forecasts were out... This kind of MacNugget teaching really adds to the confusion about planning because we only hear part of the story. Sure, God led two million people in an extremely unique

39 From a Mars Hill podcast. I must add that I think Rob is an amazing teacher and a committed community player, but like many in this institutional gig, his message is easily tweaked to keep the post mod kids happy, which keeps the engine running.

situation with fire and cloud, but what happened when they hit Canaan? They had to plan and develop their lives for the long haul. They had to be careful to understand all the ideas of God and not go looking for more pillars of fire. Again, it's a case of confusing the exception with the rule.

"The desires of your heart"

The idea: God puts desires in your heart. They're not yours, they're His. If they were your desires, they'd be evil, because your heart is evil. So it's okay to fulfill the desires of your heart if they're desires that God put in you, to fulfill through you, 'cause you're a clone. You got that soldier?!

Psychosis: Our crazy talk often focuses on this confusion about desires. We want to do something but we know that we can't tell our Christian friends, so we change the language. We say things like, "God put this desire in my heart" as a way to justify what we want to do or what we think God wants us to do. But since God rarely *makes people feel or think* in a certain way, we have to go through all kinds of hoops to either believe or make others believe the desires in our hearts are from God. It's a way to get permission. This can be as manipulative as a person saying God told them to marry you to something subtle like you'd really like a certain kind of car and you gotta find a way to make it "of God".

The context: Psalm 37 is talking about establishing yourself in the land, dwelling in a place where you "delight yourself in the LORD and He'll give you the desires of your heart". It goes on to talk about how God wants you to commit *your ways* to him so that your righteousness will shine like the dawn. It's important to note here that God doesn't say that if you delight in Him He will place His desires in you. He doesn't need or want to. He's okay with them being your desires, your ideas, your plans. In fact, I'm convinced He loves it when as His children we come up with creative stuff that WE THOUGHT OF, because that fulfills the original design of making people in His image – creators like Himself. He's actually so stoked about this that it also says in Psalm 20:4: "May he give you the desire of your heart and make all your plans succeed." Your desires, your plans... they don't make Him nervous at all. He can't wait to partner with something you came up with. The confusion comes when we don't accept that we have something of value to contribute or are so afraid of screwing something up that we don't even start the conversation.

In a lot of these examples, there's the real potential for screwing up. In using our desires or plans or dreams, selfishness could creep in and start ruining the party. So God gives us boundaries and warnings to keep this at bay. But the interesting thing I've noticed is that He's mostly about the positive potential we have and not the negative aspects of our possible failure. In fact, the positive can keep you from even wanting to be stupid. It's God's kindness that not only leads us to repentance, but also encourages us towards greatness, greatness of spirit and generosity which keeps us so fulfilled in doing good that we haven't got the time or the inclination for being evil, because despite the vehement warnings flung from lofty pulpits over the centuries, living in the kingdom is so wonderful that darkness loses its appeal. No need for indulgences, confessionals or other backward priestly offices. Just the proactive renewal of God's people doing good, being themselves.

Our psychosis is keeping us from the realm where God lives. Based on our own needs, we've combined so many *partial truths* that our view of God is now way out of whack. I think the sum total of the few examples I've given above has led to a psychotic fatalism in the church: If it happened, it was God's will. We interpret getting fired from work as something God is trying to say instead of the results of poor performance or a greed-based economy or an opportunity to reinvent ourselves. We interpret earthquakes in Haiti as God's judgment instead of a natural calamity on a shifting planet (where earthquakes in Chile and Turkey also hit in the same month), one where loving our Haitian neighbors and improving their next 100 years via permaculture techniques may be the real name of the game. We've marginalized our personal and corporate development by confusing each other with crazy talk and, as a result, we've been relegated to hang out in our padded cells (oddly called the local church) by a society that thinks we're insane.

The surrogates of calling

If in combining all these bits and pieces we've created God in the image of our needs, then we've also had to create a world and a calling that can meet those needs. When you don't know God and therefore your call, you survive by creating a surrogate call that replaces or substitutes with something else what you could be/do. Since God doesn't play the Santa or Control Freak game, we have to get our needs met on the sly and call it God in a subculture of our own making. I think this is where we as Christians are our most weird selves. For instance, the youth pastor, who feels compelled to obey God by doing his low-paid high-stress job also has to deal with the tremendous tension of relationships, a lack of money, and perhaps a young family to care for. Since God is the General, the pastors probably not getting much love from heaven and is therefore overly tempted by the 17-year-old girls in the group who adore him. He eventually has sex with one of them and the show's over. Somewhere along the way, he replaced his true call as friend, servant, and perhaps teacher with being "the youth pastor".

We're called into relationship, not service. But if all we have is service, then we'll look for other things to *surrogate* the relationships by serving in a weird, often controlling way. We substitute the sex for intimacy, or money for creativity. Our call shifts from being a prince to being a thief as we steal what we need to get by. It's what we do when as kings we don't go out to battle (like David in 1 Chronicles 20). We replace the real fight with something manageable. I understand why people pursue "casual sex". As shallow as I think it is, spending the night with someone you're very attracted to can be a pretty amazing thing. I think it's unkind, immoral and, in terms of commitment, cowardly. But I also understand the lack of depth perception involved. Sex at this level is as high as many people can see. They don't have the deeper perspective (and therefore self control) which comes from being called to create incredible relationships and living an unconditional lifestyle. Same is also true for food addictions or any other surrogate. When we're not fighting the real battles, we get enamored with the distractions of creation instead of its spirit. Here's a short list of surrogate calls:

- *In the absence of knowing the humility of God, our call to serve becomes a call to "lead", so we suck all the oxygen out of the room.*
- *In the absence of knowing the creativity of God, our call to innovate becomes a call to comply, so we build another orphanage... go home and back to our day job.*
- *In the absence of knowing the dynamism of God, we substitute our call to take risks with a safer life that eventually kills us.*
- *In the absence of knowing the real love of God, we replace our call to change the world with an average relationship that is fun for the*

first few months, but then we're back where we started – bored and condemned by our own souls – because our souls know we should be in Armenia training hip-hop dancers instead of being drained by some bum indie wanna be...

God does have a real call for us, and He wants to leads us, but into partnership and renewal. It's not the kind of leading we've been stupid enough to follow so far. God's leadership is as a warrior-father. Out in the battle with us, coaching us, sometimes behind, sometimes alongside, and, every now and then, ahead doing what only God can do. It's knowing the mix in this dynamic that'll keep us from creating a delusional world or succumbing to a surrogate call. It's knowing God and what He's really like that creates a reference for making choices. This kind of knowing helps us interpret with accuracy what God says in the scriptures, in nature, and through each other. For instance, in Psalm 48:14 the NAS says: "For such is God, Our God forever and ever; He will guide us until death." The passive will take that as a free ride until heaven. But for the seeker, you find Young's translation saying: "This God, our God – To the age and for ever, He does lead us ***over*** death!" (my emphasis).

Chapter meditation:

The cure for psychosis is a slow walk back into reality.

Our minds need renewing. We need to be transformed by the word and spirit of God instead of being conformed to the religious weirdness around us. In both biblical and psychological terms, there is a process for a slow and steady walk back into reality. In terms of psychosis, one form of treatment or healing is called Cognitive Behavior Therapy, which works "by gently leading individuals to question their belief, and inviting them to test it out in practice".[40] The few examples I've offered above can help you start to question some of the beliefs you might have held for years. But to test out a better way in practice requires some homework on your part. For instance, have any of the fears or lazy responses in your life fed into some of these beliefs? What would you need to do to address your perceptions with the help of God to test out a better way to choose or plan? I think each of us needs a customized approach to deal with the strange worlds we've created, look at why we've created those worlds, and discover how a better knowledge of God could help us walk out and into the light.

The biblical version of this process is found in Ephesians 4:22. I've mentioned this in previous chapters but I just wanted to emphasize that we can put off one form of thinking or behavior and try to be different. Ephesians 4:23 says that in the middle of this process we need to be renewed in the *spirit of our minds*. This is different from just trying to change your thinking. It's changing *why* you think or react the way you do. The spirit of your mind is where all the basic life experiences mold your core motives and beliefs. Like the time your dad told you to put down the paintbrush because you were never gonna make money doing art. This basic life experience speaks to the spirit of your mind and puts a damper on creativity until that experience is renewed by a better one. This is the slow and steady process of picking up the brush again and having a go. Or taking a risk to be yourself whether you make money at it or not. Each time you act as your true self and follow who God really is, you'll go through a new basic life experience which, over time, renews the spirit of your mind. After a while, you're not *trying* to be different, you simply are.

---

40 *Psychosis and Spirituality: Exploring the New Frontier,* Isabel Clarke (editor), Wiley, 2001, page 11.

The power of God is at its most radical strength when it changes our hearts and minds, because from there, our changed life flows into changing the rest of the world. Revival is the earth-shattering power of a father's heart being restored to his child and vice versa. True love is the revolutionary way a person lays down their life (or lame relationship criteria) for a friend that nobody else notices. Treating a person like you want to be treated is the pillar of the universe and worlds will change when it happens. These simple yet nuclear principles are our starting points. Work on this stuff with God and your internal, external, and psychotic issues will face the burning, purifying light of the Lord of the Universe. And that, my friend, is definitely God's will.

Chapter 8 • God's turn

The best way to deal with all this confusion about guidance and calling is to understand what part of the process is God's and what part is ours. I need to know who God is, what He hopes and expects, and what He will do to help me move forward. And in knowing this I should be able to determine what my response and responsibilities are. So the first step is to go back and listen to God, to hear what He hopes, dreams of, and expects. When I first became a Christian, I tried to simplify this process by walking up a smallish mountain overlooking the Santa Clara valley. I found a nice place with a view and made a relatively simple request to God: "I know that you can speak to me like you did to Moses and a few others – out loud. So I would like you to talk with me, today, in the same way." And I quickly added: "And I promise not to tell anyone that you did." I waited for around 30 minutes and didn't hear a thing. I went through a range of internal responses, like, "What in the world am I doing here?" and, "Maybe this whole Christianity thing is a crock, and I'm a sucker". But after reviewing the events leading up to my transformation, I knew that this was real and that God was God. And I eventually came to a place in my heart which said something like this: "Even if you never say a thing to me in any way, shape or form for the rest of my life, I will love and follow you because you are totally worth it." And right then, in my heart, clear but soft, I heard God say: "That's right. If you got to the place of needing audible commands, you will miss Me. I whisper, and it's those leaning into Me that will hear me."

I know there are many other aspects of who God is and that I got just a slice of the spectrum that day on the mountain, but I learned a few important things in those early days when I would also walk the streets of San Jose at 4am just asking questions and listening to God's responses. I started to understand what He sounded like, how His nature and character created the inflections and intonations of the voice I would learn to recognize in the coming years. As I learned who God was through the scriptures and through practicing those principles, I was able to get a bearing on how I should respond, on which part was His, and on which part of the process was mine. I guess the main lesson was that if I was willing to love and serve, He could be Himself and I could be myself. I could understand the intentions and the heart of God, but then apply those things through my own personality, identity, and intellect... I could co-operate with God.

During this time one of the main things about God that became clear to me was that He was not the Commanding General that some of my friends and those in the institution were making Him out to be. Sure, sometimes God was very militaristic, but this was only in the worst-case scenarios where His people were going so far off the wall that it forced Him to react in a command-and-control style. But even then, it was for the well-being of His children and usually to save them from some kind of disaster. When I explored the story of history and our place in it, what I actually found was a loving Parent; the Father and Mother heart of God. I discovered the familial nature and therefore the familial priorities of God. It became apparent that all His ways and ideas and even commands were there to bless and develop that family. This helped me see the word in its broad context, as a story about a very large and diverse family that I was a part of. Things started to make sense, like when the prodigal son comes back ready to be a slave for his wretched behavior, and the FATHER gives him a ring of authority and a cloak of honor instead. His dad wanted him not only back in the family, but also using his authority to create and grow that family. Instead of constant chastisement, he got a key role in the larger family development. This is what God is like.

The other thing that became clear was that God is dynamic. And therefore life, my life, is going to be dynamic. In terms of guidance, there were some scriptures that seemed to say "stop and wait" on God before proceeding, while others seemed to say God was waiting around to empower my ideas and goals if I'd only show up with a clue. Here's a simple chart showing the scale.

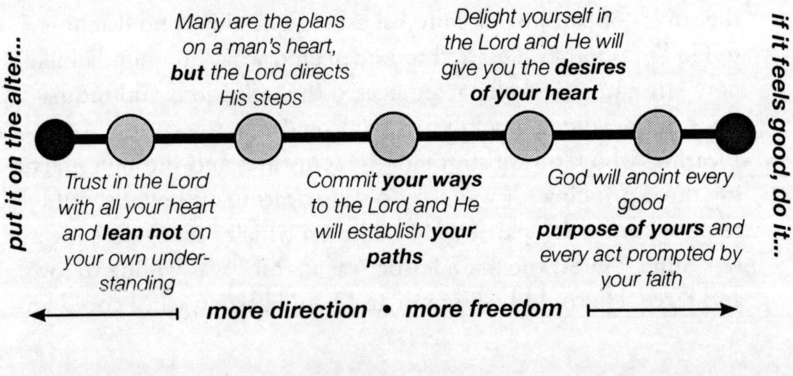

The point is that God's co-operative spirit is a dynamic one. In rare situations He will lead us step by step through certain processes (mostly to show us how, so we can do it the next time ourselves). And at other times He's sitting back watching and enjoying our being made in His image, as creators. The scale also shows that we live in tension. You can't polarize life and hide behind one pole ("God knows best and tells me everything I should do") or the opposite pole ("I do what I want"). The *relationship* with God calls for a dynamic walking out of these principles that are appropriate to the time in your life, the circumstances, and the needs of your community. See, God does have a plan of sorts and it's really simple. He's raising a family, and His priorities are to mature you and me as sons and daughters. Not slaves or soldiers, but preparing us to take over the farm kind of thing. This means He's more vested in our learning to choose than in telling us what to choose. He's more interested in our ability to take domain than always taking domain for us. It's only our laziness that's created an image of God that has Him in control and in charge of everything. If you go back to Genesis 1 and 2, you see right there that one of His first actions was to delegate the planet to us, to release control to us. That and free will reveal something essential about God's overall strategy, which is to co-operate and co-create.

All we need then is to know this Person in detail. Then, our part of the co-op becomes clear. Personally, I find that pretty exciting stuff. That I get to share domain with the Creator of worlds, that I've been delegated the astounding gift of both my person (which has all I need to do my part) and the world around me. I get to share in the care of that world and further develop it into the garden-to-city story we see in the Bible. I get to develop better permaculture solutions, spray-on solar technology, regenerative healing methods, and amazing works of art, and all that in my back yard. Imagine what we could do when we collaborate with an entire neighborhood or city?

So who is the amazing Person we get to work with, and how can we know Him/Her better and, in doing so, lose the lame religious image that's kept us bound? Here are a few starting points that I've found helpful, especially in working out the calling stuff:

God is relational

I know, duh, right? But if you take this seriously, it changes how you approach and work with God. The command-and-control view of God has led us to view our faith as task-oriented. Which makes sense when you think about how many white Western men, or men in general, there are standing in front trying to tell us what God's like. Mostly they're just telling us what they're like or what they've been told God is like from other men like themselves... But on closer examination we see God the Father always developing the family. For instance, there've been a lot of times when the choices I made were based on improving family relationships instead of improving my money-making abilities, because that family is where God's priorities were. I've also made choices, hard choices, to get into relationships that forced issues like commitment and responsibility to my kids instead of doing what would have looked like a "missions opportunity" across town or across the world. Most of this clarity of priorities has come from knowing God in a way that shifts the focus from the weird End-times God, who's only interested in saving the lost, to a Father who wants me to understand and heal the relationship with my father, 'cause that's pretty lost too.

Jesus challenges religious types by warning us about giving to God what could have been beneficial to our families. For Him, our faithfulness to the institutions was draining the resources and priorities of the center of God's universe; families. I think it's odd that our "spiritual homes" are some building across town instead of our kitchen tables. And that some guy calls us away from our homes to tell us what God's like. Which could be the same thing I'm doing right now, so how would you know better, or know God better, unless you ask? You gotta put the books down or take a break from the church and go for these long walks yourself and talk to the Father. Not about what you should do or how much money you need... These are things we talk about with authority figures now because we forget or never saw them as the relational beings they were created as. Most of us never had long walks with our dads or a great teacher at school just to shoot the breeze, to talk about life and beauty and the other foundations which would inspire us to know them and ourselves. It's the relationship that defines humanity and all its facilities. And this is all you need to make choices down the line. As I speak encouragement and life into my kids, they make up the rest as they go. Josiah is a game designer and Jordan directs film, not because I told them to, but because we walked together and talked of life and beauty – from their perspective. They built forts in the forest and board games. We went snowboarding together and they cut short films... It was the relational foundations that they needed, and the design of God (their identity and passion) took over from there. None of this developed in a church, but they were able to take the process to youth groups and other Christian gatherings to share what they were learning.

I can't stress how important this is, but I also can't define it. You really need to get back in touch with or go deeper with God at a purely relational level yourself. You need to define what a deeper relationship looks like and what you would do to make it happen. You need to practice it at home because that's the crucible for knowing God. I just know this family approach is a foundational part of the mix and it can't be found in a box with a cross on top.

The voice of God

It takes a few minutes to get someone's intonations and inflections down, but it takes a lifetime to understand their heart and priorities. I'm still learning this about God – and about everyone else in my life for that matter. And so while I've fostered the general ability to distinguish between God and my psychosis, I also know that this is a long-term project. But there's one simple principle that's helped me to focus in and not be totally confused by the things whizzing around my mind and heart: The voice of God sounds like Him. The things God is trying to communicate will sound like His nature and character. If I think God wants me to spend more time with my mom, I can measure that statement with what I know about God's nature as a parent. If I think God wants me to rush into a relationship or business opportunity, I can measure that tone against what I've heard of His character, in this case His patience, timing, wisdom or contentment. So the more I dive into knowing the intricate details of God's nature (who He is naturally) and character (what He chooses to be with that nature), the better I get at hearing and interpreting His messages.

There've been many times when I sought the wisdom of God in key choices or just casual inquiries, and in each case I've been able to test what I thought I was hearing with what I knew about what God was like. This is the relatively easy part. The hard part is applying the wisdom, because often I just wanna have that thing faster, or make a rushed choice, or run from a problem, or have God fix whatever. This brings me back to the relational side of God, which reminds and comforts me by revealing the bigger relational picture. I am slowly learning that living in God's kingdom, by His ways, is so much better than the lame place my selfishness would lead me to. And this is becoming more natural, so there are many times when I don't ask God at all. I just act in a natural way because I'm becoming more and more like a son – the ring on my finger and the cloak over my shoulders.

What we already know

So while we're working all the nature and character stuff out, we can start immediately on what we already know God is saying to us. If you look in the word, the whole word (so stop ignoring the Old Testament or treating it as a type of Christ, or cruising through the genealogies, bored, looking for the red ink so you can get back to familiar territory), you will find the key things on God's heart. I mean butt-obvious priorities that we don't even need to ask about. For instance, God has said over and over again that "there should be NO POOR among you" (Deuteronomy 15:4). He goes into detail about how to destroy poverty and presses the point with around 2500 scriptures on business, resources, and management. Man, you'd think we'd get the point! But instead we keep throwing aid at people instead of doing some godly development work like Bill Gates, who I think is a world-changing genius.[41]

We don't have to ask God things He's already told us. We just need to apply *our hearts* and *our identities* to the issues we already know He's keen for us to engage in. For instance helping widows, orphans or the elderly. Or honoring your parents, loving your neighbor as yourself or visiting those in prison. No-brainer, right? Just get out and do something and figure it out along the way. There's so much we already know about God's priorities. If you started with that, in combination with your skills and passions, you'd be well on your way.

---

41 Check out this site showing all the amazing project the Gates Foundation is working on. Talk about a godly application in working key issues in the world. http://www.gatesfoundation.org/Pages/home.aspx

Chapter meditation

This one's easy. Pick one of the issues you already know God wants you to develop (a family relationship, old folks in your town, foster kids...), ask God how He views the issue, get some scriptural tips, and then go and apply that at an old folks' home or mow your neighbor's lawn or whatever. Anything. Just get off the couch, eh? There's something powerful in loving your neighbor as yourself. It's interesting how in Matthew 22 Jesus reminds us to love God with heart, soul, mind, and strength, and immediately after this, to love our neighbor as ourselves. It's like our relationship with God gets activated or deeper when we take our selves (heart, soul...) across the street to practice the flow of love through simple acts of kindness. Our faith gets real and our knowledge of God's thoughts gets real when we bring these two most important commands together.

Finally, journal what you've learned about God, about your neighbor, and about yourself. Rinse, repeat...

part 2

calling

The call of God is essentially expressive of His nature; service is the outcome of what is fitted to my nature.
Oswald Chambers

Chapter 9 • Vocatio

You have been called by name. Your calling is built inside of you and it has a name, an identity. God has breathed a dynamic and unique mix of identity, intellect, personality, and DNA *in you* that creates a huge range of possibilities depending on how you bring it all together. Therefore, God's "plan" is that you would be yourself. In other words, you are *called to be yourself.* Which, given your range as a person, would be super dynamic and therefore kinda scarily exciting for both of you. The thrill for God is to see how you'll put all this together to create a new thing in the garden you've been given. This calling does not come from the clouds, or from a voice from above, or from the outside at all. You're not some robot pre-programmed to perform factory Christian functions, nor are you a pawn on God's chessboard. There may be times when God asks you to do something specific, but this is not your calling; it's a project and it's extra ordinary. Your call is not a geographic location (that's also just a project) or a person to marry (those are called relationships). Your call is the magical potential that comes from being made in the image of God, a co-creator, which God eagerly waits to see unfold before a world in need. That potential, or the possible combinations of the ways of God and your identity, is your sacred calling or *vocatio*.

Vocatio is Latin for the word we commonly use as *vocation* or calling. But unlike our modern term, *vocatio* isn't something you do, it's something you are; a dynamic mix of mind, soul, and heart made by the hand of God. Until recently *vocatio* had always carried a sacred meaning, as in Virgil's *Aeneid,* where Aeneas is "the man / whom heaven calls", or in Luther's idea of a "priesthood of *all* believers". *Vocatio* evokes a sense that human beings are "summoned or invited" (the literal translation) by their Creator to something special, something holy. In regaining the everyday holiness of vocations, Luther was also quick to point out that this calling was not just to be for church workers. God's calling was much broader, more dynamic, and spoke of the unique qualities of each individual and how they could make their work a sacred activity – whether they were butchers, bakers or really cool candlestick makers.

Today, vocation simply means your job or somewhere between your job and your career. You go to "vocational counseling" to get placed in a position that may suit some of your abilities, but the focus is all wrong. Our modernist view of life has not only dehumanized our vocation (paving the way for the industrial revolution), it has created a secular approach that erodes the very soul of work and, therefore, of creativity (which is why I think there's very little innovation in most people's jobs). It took hundreds of years for Luther, Calvin, and many others to develop the sense that everyone has a sacred calling, a calling that gets to unfold the mystery of God and of life. Mystery was the driving force behind Pascal's and Einstein's passion for science, as it is for many artists. This call into mystery then leads to creativity, which both the scientist and the artist well understand. This is what Luther was trying to explain, that the painter's work is as holy as the pastor's.Taking it even further, William Romanowski claims that when a Christian artist is not creating art or music, "that [...] is secularization".[42] But as modernity drained spirituality and thus meaning from the world over the past two centuries, we lost that hard-fought understanding, and now people have either a "ministry" or a "just a job". We live in a world that Regent Professor R. Paul Stevens calls a "post-vocational society".[43] So now we open the paper and look for a career, a career that has taken the place of what Shirley Roels calls a "divinely derived vocation". [44] Instead, we go with the meaning derived from the Middle French origins of the word – "giving the horse [...] an open field in which [it] could run freely" – that eventually became "self-chosen occupations for which people trained and progressed on their own initiative".[45] No God, no more mystery, and no real purpose outside of paying the bills. In the place of God then, we worship stuff and try to find value in what we do and, by extension, what we own.

While the secularist pounds this soulless message home from the outside, the inside Christian view of work and calling has added confusion to the problem. Our religious institutions have created what Os Guinness calls "distortions": "Whereas the Catholic distor-

42 *Eyes Wide Open: Looking for God in Popular Culture*, Brazos/Baker, 2001, page 81.

43 "Calling" in *The Complete Book of Everyday Christianity*, Robert Banks and R. Paul Stevens (editors), InterVarsity Press, 1997, page 98.

44 "The Christian Calling to Business Life" in *Theology Today*, 60, No. 3, 2003, pages 363-4.

45 Ibid.

tion is a spiritual form of dualism, elevating the spiritual at the expense of the secular, the Protestant distortion is a secular form of dualism, elevating the secular at the expense of the spiritual."[46] In both cases, our dualistic (split) thinking has created a secular/sacred world-view in which we compartmentalize our work as secular and our "ministry" as sacred. This is a tragic loss of God's dream that every walk of life could be a holy combination of His wisdom and your identity. It's the loss of our sacred calling.

But I think the real tragedy here is the loss of value – God's and ours. On one hand, our split thinking reduces our view of God and His priorities down to a few roles in the church, based on the assumption that all He really cares about is getting people saved and, um, yeah, I think that's about it. So our worship and "ministries" become dry, repetitive expressions of this myopic goal. On the other hand, our soul loses its value by being boxed in to thinking God's only interested in a few job descriptions like pastors, teachers, candlestick polishers... And if this is all God values, and we're not one of those things, then I guess our abilities in glass blowing or landscape design are kinda useless? We elevate the typical "ministry" professions and denigrate everything else as "secular", which ironically actually makes them secular because, in the end, we've lost our ability to integrate God into the things we love.

As Christians, too many of us have bought the modernist view that work is a machine, and since we long for heaven and the world's going to burn, we've formed a subcultural sacred/secular lifestyle. This is why we're so confused about work and our place in it. But even more, we're confused about what God wants because we're not sure if He's interested in our jobs, if they're holy or not, and if our identity even matters. It's obvious (to me anyway) that it does, which is why I think we really need to restore a godly view of calling, or our sacred *vocatio*. The rest of this book will focus on this issue.

Calling and identity

We'll unpack this in the next chapter, but I just want to mention here that God presents different levels of calling in the Bible, all of which are relational, by the way. The first calling is by name, which carries depths of meaning and identity, like when Abram's

46 *The Call: Finding and Fulfilling the Central Purpose of Your Life*, W Publishing Group, 2003, page 38.

name was changed to Abraham, or "the father of many nations" (Genesis 17:5). The name defined *what God thought* of the person and *how He saw* them. Another kind of call is our familial, tribal or national calling. As with Israel, God speaks to our cultural and ethnic identities and to their connection to other nations. And again, as a relational being, He is concerned with how our families treat other families ("a foreigner with you shall be to you as the native-born among you" Leviticus 19:34). In terms of redemption, the Bible uses two words to describe our calling back to the original relationship God desires. Professor Stevens points out that in the Old Testament, the Hebrew word *qara* ("summon") is used to invite us "to participate in God's grand purpose for the world [...], to salvation, holiness and service"[47], while the New Testament use of the Greek *kaleo* also "calls" us to discipleship, holy living, and a corporate way to serve those in need. Again, these are not callings primarily to the priesthood or even to a job, but to the community, as relational people of faith.

There are biblical examples of extraordinary calls from God on people's lives. For instance, a call to action in desperate situations (Moses freeing the slaves) or to projects that God wanted certain people to use their gifting for (like Jonah in Nineveh). These exceptional callings were given in times of extreme danger or some pending doom. But even in each of these extra-ordinary calls, God still worked with the identity and gifting of Moses, Jonah, Deborah, Paul... This kind of special call may happen to you a couple of times in your life. But to God, the core element of calling is not a historic task or a project, it's your name, your identity. As Stevens says: " Our call is to belong (*family*), to be (*identity)* and to do (*creativity*)."[48] It's from this foundation that you can first be, and then create all kinds of wonderful things which, to God, is where the party is.

So calling is not about what you should do, it's the opportunity to know who you are, to know your name. It's about taking that identity and anointing it with the ways of God so you can bless the world around you. The pursuit of knowing yourself outside of this context (that of God's ways and meeting needs) leads to the lonely existence of self-searching hedonism. But if you search out the

47 *Vocatio Magazine*, January 1999, page 15.

48 Ibid., page 16 (emphasis mine).

design of God through your identity, and place all that goodness to work in the service of meeting real needs, then you'll understand *vocatio* and its sacred intention. On top of all this, calling draws out the potential of who God imagined us to be. As Os Guinness points out: "Calling is not only a matter of being and doing what we are but also of becoming what we are not yet."[49] Even in our fearful, lazy, and selfish confusion, God is drawing us into *what we are, but not yet*. He knows our name and that it's way better for us to focus on our *vocatio* than for him to simply tell us what to do.

Finally, in being ourselves with God, we also get in touch with our part in "destroying the works of the enemy" (1 John 3:8). Jesus came to restore our souls, but that wasn't the ultimate goal. To God, it was to reconcile all things back to Himself, and that means dealing with the destruction caused since the fall. I'm not the center of the universe and my identity is not the only game in town. I think identity is essential to understanding life, but my life is not fulfilled simply in being myself. It's in being myself in the work of God, and the work of God is to destroy the work of the enemy. That's poverty, loneliness, nakedness, injustice... all the concerns of Jesus in Matthew 25. Understanding this gives me free rein to develop my identity because that's the weaponry I've been given.

49 *The Call: Finding and Fulfilling the Central Purpose of Your Life*, W Publishing Group, 2003, pages 29-30.

Chapter meditation

The tragedy of not knowing

First, there are three people I'd like you to look up. They are Dr. Paul Brand, Flannery O'Connor, and Abraham Kuyper. Three stubbornly devout people who knew who they were and the God they loved. It's their fierce determination that first caught my attention, and after seeing what they had to go through to achieve the things they did, I could see the importance of *vocatio* in their lives.

Seems to me that a person needs to be very clear about who they are and extremely passionate about the things they're doing in order to get away with great exploits. What's amazing about these three people is that they knew God *in* their identity, not despite of it, meaning that their knowledge of God did not negate or invalidate who they were. They didn't have to put their soul's gift on the altar and serve the world as clueless clones. Instead, they purified and freely gave that gift to enhance and challenge the world. I'm convinced that God was thrilled with who they were as well as the work of their hands.

The fourth person I'd like you to look up is Branwell Brontë. The only brother of the remarkable Brontë sisters (Anne, Charlotte, and Emily), Branwell also had tons of talent in his own right and was a gifted writer, painter, and speaker. But as James White points out, while Branwell "was considered the most brilliant, the most talented, of them all" he was "also the most tragic".[50] In his life (and often in our own), the failure to value a soul worth more than the whole world was a quick path to a slow death. He drank too much and created too little. What he did make was tarnished through his obsessions and broken relationships. He could have left a legacy equal to that of his extraordinary sisters, but instead he died young, leaving very little behind. These cautionary tales are an important reminder that we can't afford to get this wrong, and while we may have been discouraged, rejected or just plain confused, we have to get back on the horse.

---

50 *Serious Times: Making Your Life Matter in an Urgent Day*, InterVarsity Press, 2005, page 127. This book is well worth reading. Packed with great examples of calling through the lives of people like William Wilberforce and Dietrich Bonhoeffer, White's book explains, way better than I can, the historical nature of calling and how people of faith wrestled with this huge issue.

I wonder how the prodigal son woke up after the party his father threw for him. Perhaps with the stone-cold realization that even though he totally screwed up his life and that of his family, he was now looking at a new ring on his finger. A ring that represented authority, place, and destiny. It reminded him that he was still important, but now humbly so. He is us.

Chapter 10 •

The general call of God

So far we've spent a lot of time talking about our confusion, or how we see the will of God from our point of view or point of need. What I would like to express in this chapter is how God may see the issue. Not as a strategist (team A goes to this people group and team B goes to that country...) or as a nervous caretaker ("DON'T TOUCH THAT!"), but as a Father who has billions of children placed in a world that they tend to screw up daily, like in a massive – really complex – pre-school.

In order to see calling from God's point of view, and to answer my own questions over the years, I've learned to look at the biggest possible picture. I'm looking for the rule from Genesis to Revelation instead of the exception. I look at history to get a sense of the timing of God's interventions and thus His priorities. And after the guy in front tells us the big story and then sits down, I wander over and ask what his Monday morning looked like... In this way, I'm not approaching guidance with an agenda to validate the stamp of God on a certain choice I wanna make, but rather to see what God is like so I can know what to expect in the relationship and discover how we might walk together in the years to come.

What I've learned through all this is that there are three kinds of calling or invitation that God offers us.[51] The *general call of God* shows His heart and purposes but is intentionally shy on details. The *extraordinary call of God* is very clear on details but extremely rare, like a project He may send us on from time to time. And the third but most important, dangerous, and radical aspect of calling is the *call to be your self.* This third one is huge and will be introduced in this book, but covered more fully in another volume I hope to

51 What's with that number three, eh? Is that just :"Christian teacher retardation"? Like we can't think of a fourth point? I dunno. Anyway, I wanted to add here that, yes, this is my limited perspective on what little I know of how God works. I offer it to you not thinking it's the full truth of God, but a valid world-view that may just be helpful.

write next year about identity.[52] As a gentleman, God is always inviting us to respond to these three offers. And yes, one day "the Judge of all the earth will do right" and hold us accountable, but for now we're being invited into the will of God. The great thing about this call, though, is that it's an amazingly balanced and intelligent approach to our humanity and our potential, which comes from both the humility of God and the wisdom of God. He knows so much about the depth of our potential that He's keen to push it forward and help us meet the world's challenges with that potential.

Note: I have included a long list of scriptures at the end of the book so you can have a look and then dig through the Bible yourself and be like those intelligent Bereans in Acts 17 "who searched the scriptures to see if these things were so".

The general call we've already heard

The bible is incredibly vague when it comes to the specifics of calling. Jesus says "follow me" but He doesn't tell you where. The ten commandments tell us to honor our father and mother, but does that mean washing the dishes or calling every Tuesday at 7pm? Our lives are to be "living sacrifices", so do we burn the guitar or our algebra book? Which one is it? WHICH ONE??? We don't know because He doesn't tell us. So I say, torch the algebra book (unless you're an engineer in which case I guess it's the guitar, sorry).

Maybe God doesn't add the details because that's not the point. Maybe all He wants His kids to understand through these scriptures are His heart and His intentions. Maybe overly defining these things would not only suck the soul out of our response, it would kill our ability to actually love. God can command angels to level cities, or rocks to cry out praises to Himself. So in terms of getting His will done, there doesn't seem to be a problem. Therefore, we gotta ask why the very agents He's left in the world to manage and co-operate with Him are us free-will beings bent on our own hippie independence. Why do you think He would do that? Would you do that? Would you give some general instructions and toss the

52 Identity can be discovered in a number of ways, and my angle is simply one of those ways. What's essential right now is that you get moving, and that's the point of this book. The identity piece is about refining and directing that movement once you're well on your way. I also have podcasts about this if you're interested right this minute:
www.patrickdodson.net/Podcast/Entries/2006/3/25_Processing_Your_Future.html

keys of your new pimped-up Hummer to some big-eyed pubescent? You would if you wanted them to learn how to drive that sucker.

The reason I think God gives us *His general call or will* (heart and intentions) is twofold. Firstly, He knows that we learn by doing. Even though He could walk us step by step through every decision and process in our lives, the net result is that we would end up retarded. Literally, our growth would be stunted, because what moron walks through anally detailed instructions in order to teach us how to live (oh wait, that's our public school system)? God's idea was to give us an intellect and a heart that could learn by doing, making mistakes, and constantly improving. And not just us as individuals, but nations as well. I mean, look at the last century. Even though Richard Dawkins and Sam Harris whine about the insane Christian effect on the world, the real madness happened in the name of modernity and progress as evidenced by the unprecedented killing of millions by Stalin and Hitler.[53] But the truly amazing thing is that as powerful as God is, He let it happen. Which means one of two things: A. He's not God and can't stop stuff like that, or B. He chose not to so we could learn how to take domain and steward the world. I guess you could also dodge the complexity by saying God used all that as judgment, but that would just make Him tyrannical and us weird for being okay with that. The truth is we're free agents who are not under the control of God, but rather His tutelage. In His economy, He would rather let us nearly burn down the store than close it.

Our ability to learn is one of His top priorities. So, the innocent suffer because we haven't learned to take care of them. Kids will be trafficked around the world until we learn to stop it, punish the pigs involved, and build better economies to stop the demand itself.[54] In these situations, God has limited Himself to either shutting it down and judging the whole thing or teaching us how to improve the situation, because He will not step in and control everything. It's not an option and it never was. The only reason we

---

53 Dawkins et al are not wrong in their assumption that Christians, too, can be nuts, but what they're missing is that insanity is a human problem. The problem is not a delusional church, it's our capacity to be evil, and being evil will work with any genre of humanity – Christian, Muslim, Despot, Scientist...

54 A woman I know here in Auckland runs an organization called "Stop the Demand". Check it out at www.stopdemand.org. It's exactly what I'm talking about.

would even want Him to control all this pain is because we're too lazy to end poverty ourselves. But like it or not, it's our job. When God said, "there should be no poor among you" (Deuteronomy 15:4), He fully intended that we would be the ones to make it so. His part is the blessing of multiplication and the wisdom to facilitate us, but He will not do the work by Himself. God gives general instructions so that we will learn to be like Him, as sons and daughters and not as robot slaves.

The second reason God's will is largely general is that in filling in the gaps, we get to create unique loving responses. If He had to define exactly what He wanted, or His "love language" (choke), then our response would simply be obedience (boring). In fact, maybe it's that whole Book on *Love languages* that makes us think doing what other people want is how we show our love. Not that the author who invented the term is to blame (I'm sure he's a very nice person), but I think he's tapped into this command-and-control spirit. Namely, if God is demanding our love via obedience, then we show love to each other by telling people *what we want* and having them obey our desires. All I have to say about that is eeuuw. No, the real reason we've been given a brain, a heart, and opposable digits is so we can create a loving response *our way.*

When God says to love our neighbor, He gets joy out of how we choose to love them. When He tells us to honor our parents, His pleasure is in seeing the unique way each one of us will do just that. When He says to take care of widows and orphans, He loves how our hearts respond to His and their needs by serving them either in primary health or entrepreneurial business developments. And, yes, His heart also grieves when we completely miss the point, but He will not step in and force a response. If He has to define the details, it's no longer love or creativity on our part, unless you're still stuck on "obedience equals love". Now, sometimes it does. Jesus said that if we love Him, we'll keep or obey His commandments (John 14:15). But if you look at the context, He was about to leave and wanted them to remember what He had said about loving their neighbors, honoring their parents, treating each other as they wanted to be treated... again, all general stuff. It wasn't a warning to ask what color of shirt to put on each day, it was a reminder that our love reflects the general heart of God as expressed throughout Jesus' life and the Bible in general. So when you look at the whole

Bible, you see an expansive story about our relationship with God. Not just the mission of God or the church, but the complex connection between the sovereign Lord of the universe and His astonishing design of free-willed sons and daughters. In His wisdom God chose to mature us through the process of sharing domain. In His love God chose to teach us about kindness by allowing us to be kind our way, or not.

And in all this, God's justice finally prevails through a clear moral will that's mapped into our psyche and the physical world. Because at the end of the day, there will be a judgment and an accountability whereby we will be measured according to how we responded to what we all know in our hearts to be right. This ability to judge us is in direct proportion to the free will we've been given. And that free will has an internal standard called "eternity in our hearts" (Ecclesiastes 3:11). Our conscience is the means by which God calls us to account, so that even if we abuse all this free rein, we will not escape the cost of that abuse either in this life or at the time of judgment. God's general will is an opportunity to respond, but that same will has moral implications that cannot be ignored.

For instance, if we don't apply our specific response to God's call to alleviate poverty (like through micro-finance or improved agriculture), then we'll have to deal with the short- and long-term implications of not loving our neighbor. Our lack of action may explode in our faces immediately, as in the case of disenfranchised individuals blowing up themselves at a local restaurant. Or it may have devastating long-term effects on families and the economy in the form of indentured servitude exacted from nations like India (and its people working in the Middle East). There is a cause-and-effect kickback that we have to look at because this is the real lesson and responsibility God's trying to share with us. The general will has moral implications which will affect our souls and then our world. These general commands are not really optional in terms of *if* they should be fulfilled; our privilege is *how* they get fulfilled. One way or another, we're responsible for them happening, and God stands ready to help us.

And this is the cool thing about the general will of God. It's not complicated. These priorities are so clear that if you stopped reading the Bible today, you already know way more than you could ever apply in this age. You don't have to ask about how to love your neighbor – you just get on with it. The other cool aspect is that God is eager to help us with the wisdom and means to make these things come about. So you don't have to ask *if* you should visit people in prison (Matthew 25), but you can ask God to give you wisdom about the process of renewal or rehabilitation (which most prisons suck at). In this way, you put your heart and creativity to work with God's, and good things happen. However, the bad news is that if you're waiting at home to be told what to do, you're gonna end up as a goat (also in Matthew 25).

The other thing I love about the freeing nature of God's general will is that anyone can do it. You don't have to be a seminary graduate (in fact, that probably just makes things confusing) or have a clairvoyant ability to hear the guidance of God. Everybody can see it plain as day and respond. You could spend your life just building up an amazing family and neighborhood like our friend Dave Andrews in Brisbane.[55] Or you could be working on the destruction of poverty like the indomitable Jacqueline Novogratz.[56] And when I say "anyone can get it", I mean anyone. Because when I look at the people who are truly engaged in the priorities and values of God, I see A LOT of "non-Christian" people. I've followed the social entrepreneurship movement for quite a few years now, and the two astounding things I've noticed are, firstly, how these initiatives align with the heart of God and, secondly, how they're mostly manned (or womanned) by people who would not call themselves Christians.

In Matthew 25 Jesus echoes six values that are repeated throughout the scriptures. Basic things like visiting the imprisoned or clothing the naked. Which is exactly what a lot of these social entrepreneurship initiatives and the people behind them are about, which is kind of surprising. For instance, Muhammad Yunus won the Nobel Peace Prize for his life-changing work in raising millions out of poverty through microfinance in Bangladesh ("when I was hungry, you fed me"). And then there's the Bill and Melinda Gates Foundation, which is channeling both wisdom and truckloads of finance into health care needs around the world, especially working on the big killers like malaria and dysentery, which can easily be treated,

---

55 en.wikipedia.org/wiki/Dave_Andrews

56 www.gsb.stanford.edu/news/bmag/sbsm0705/feature_novogratz.html

or getting micronutrients into the diets of billions of people so they can live, work, and develop their own lives ("I was sick and you looked after me"). And I *know* Bill's not a Christian, I mean, Microsoft? (Just kidding. Bill's not there any more, so I guess he's not evil – now.)

I'm not saying that the only people creating systemic change with the true values of God are "non-Christians". I'm just saying that anyone can understand and apply His general will. But since we're having so much fun, let's look closer at the question of who's "saved". Not that it's any of our business, but since we kinda think it is, check out the not-so-hidden message of Matthew 25. The sheep (those who are inheriting the kingdom) are surprised that they're sheep. It's as if they didn't think they deserved to be there 'cause they didn't go to church or "see Jesus" in the typical ways. And the goats (the ones who thought they were "saved") are really surprised that they're goats because *they were in church...* or were saying the right things but didn't even recognize Jesus in human need. So the only thing separating these two groups was how they responded to the most basic of the Father's intentions, namely that His children (and by extension creation) would be looked after in the worst-case scenarios. He never judged them based on their ability to hear His voice, but rather on their conscious response to basic needs.

This shouldn't be dismissed as humanism without God. There is no human response to basic need that does not have the heart or intentions of God attached to it. There is a form of humanism that rejects God, but its adherents are not working in the refugee camps of Kampala, they're just scratching out lousy poems in some hip cafe in Tribeca. In fact, most of the truly caring entrepreneurs of today have not rejected God, they just don't wanna be like Pastor Ted. My point though, finally, is that there's a beautiful simplicity to both perceiving and acting on the general will (heart) of God. Jesus said that the kingdom was so simple, children would easily understand it. God's will is not complex. We've made it so with our selfish smoke screens or complicated institution-speak, but knowing the will of God is as simple as looking at what He already said. The only real question is what you're going to do about it, and how you'll apply your *self*.

Chapter 11 •
The extraordinary call of God

Imagine what the world would be like today if that garden of Eden episode went down differently. If Adam were still around to show us how to create the most delectable fruit salad (sans that knowledgy tasting kind) and Eve was teaching us about fashion (sans the clothes)... I mean, if sin had not crippled our relationship with God and the planet, would He need to tell us what to do all the time? Would our mind and heart be free to create alongside the master inventor and, if so, what kind of things might He talk about with us? And would we be asking the most basic of questions about relationships or college if we had a pure connection to God? Guess we'll never know until we get restored back to that state. Oh wait, didn't that already happen? I think it did, but in the meantime God's had to work with a fallen world and with billions of people under messed-up conditions.

So from the time of Adam until Jesus, and every now and then after that, God has been forced to step in, in order to keep us from ruining everything. He doesn't like doing it, but these special interventions have been necessary from Moses to Ruth to Daniel... mostly to keep us from total disaster. I call these special interventions *extraordinary callings.* For instance, God speaks clearly to Abraham: "Leave your country, your people and your father's household and go to the land I will show you" (Genesis 12:1). God basically interrupts Abram's life because He was developing a nation. It's a very direct piece of guidance that can give us the impression that God will speak to us in the same way. What we usually miss, though, is the fact that Abraham was going to directly affect millions of people, and that he only got these special words two or three times in 187 years. With Paul it was around 2.5 times in 40-something years. These situations are extra ordinary and not the rule. An exception to the exception is Moses. God called Moses very specifically via burning bushes, all kinds of wonders, and other people for most of the latter part of his life, because he was being called to save millions of people from destruction. God was also preserving the nation He started with Abraham. In Moses' time God didn't speak this way to the rest of the people because, for them, the ordinary call of God (which we'll explore in the next chapter) was already in place. But for Joshua, Ruth, Jonah, David, and a few others, God gave extraordinary calls for extraordinary times.

Confusing interventions

The confusing thing about these special and wonderful interventions is that we mistake them for the rule. I mentioned this before, but when the people in front speak only about the extraordinary guidance they received, or we skim through the Bible looking only for the "moves of God", we get the sense that extraordinary is how it's supposed to be. But when we normalize the exceptions, we feel we lack faith if we're not being saved from cancer or seeing God do something supernatural *all the time*. When we mistake the exception for the rule, we raise our expectations of what God *should* be in our life, and this skews our view of God. The truth is most of us will live our entire lives without God dropping a pillar of fire in our path so we can turn right just in time. And we need to know that that's okay. I mean, sure, it would be pretty cool to have a donkey or a dog suddenly tell us how stupid we've been and which direction we should go in, but remember, that was an extreme situation involving a very obstinate person. You want that? God wants us to be the kind of people who don't need carrots or honey trails or pillars of cloud placed in our paths to get us to do something. In the first place, all that fire and cloud stuff was the result of a lack of faith, not an example of how God wanted to walk with His people, so why do we exemplify this stuff? In fact, most of the times God intervenes in extraordinary ways, things are going badly. His interventions are not the model, they're the fire alarm.

Nobody wants to use the BatPhone, but every now and then God has been forced to go against His own design because of our hardness of heart or stubborn resistance to that design. For instance, even though He told us to choose wise leaders, He's had to step in occasionally and get a guy like David to deal with a guy like Saul. And even though He taught us about preventative care throughout Leviticus, He still steps in and occasionally heals us even though He told us pigs are, well, pigs and we shouldn't eat... pigs. Now, God is able to intervene in any way He wants, but He only does so when it's the best for everyone. Constant healing of our sicknesses would not teach us about preventative care or nutrition, so He rarely heals us in extraordinary ways. Putting "the right" people in political office would not teach us about justice or servanthood from the grassroots up. Telling us what to do through words, signs or wonders would stunt our ability to grow up and run the business, which is why He rarely talks to us in those ways. Doling out resources like an ATM would never allow us to create value or learn how to save and plan, so He rarely answers these requests. It's just not good for us.

Note: Again, when things are going bad on a more personal scale, asking God to fix everything is not good for us either. So when we ask for an easy answer to patch a hole we've created and don't hear anything back from God, it's His way of saying "wrong question, try again". A better prayer would be for wisdom and the understanding to apply it. God's ways are more sustainable than God's interventions because that's how He designed things to work in the first place. Seeking first the kingdom of God does not mean abdicating your part, it means you seek the ways of the kingdom and apply those ways, and that's where you see the natural hand of God.

The conditions of extraordinary

Looking over the larger story of God's interventions in the Bible, and in history, I've noticed there are some conditions involved in extraordinary callings. It seems God kicks into special action when things get to a certain point, or when people need something beyond the systems (including relationships) He's already put in place. God's interventions are not limited to these conditions, and one of the mysteries of who God is, is that He will heal whom He chooses to heal and bless whom He chooses to bless. It's not arbitrary of Him, because these actions are always based on His wisdom and love. There's a consistency to the special moves of God which gives us a framework and a clue to put the extraordinary into perspective. These conditions do not limit God, but they do remind us that extraordinary really is just that, and that we don't lack faith or have problems hearing God's voice if these things are not happening to us.

Scale: Most of the times God steps in or across the flow of our free will, something big is about to happen, and I mean nation-sized big. When God spoke to Abraham and Moses and Daniel, it was for millions of people. God's special call to King David was huge because He was reforming an entire nation and creating a platform for Jesus. Sometimes the scale is about the sheer number of people that God wants to bless, and sometimes the scale is about what God wants to do over time among groups of nations. But it seems He's willing to step in only when the scale is worth overriding the natural systems He's already put in place.[57] I think the same thing was true with Luther and Calvin and their crew. God was speaking to them and through them to reform the religious weirdness that had built up for centuries, a move that would then go on to affect millions of people.

Crucial change: The best example of this is the extraordinary calling of Jesus and His transitioning us from the law to grace. Jesus came at a crucial time in history and was given an unprecedented task that would change how mankind related to God. Another example is God's special call on Deborah's life. Because of their own stupidity, the people of Israel had been abused by the Canaanites for 20 years. God heard their cries and called Deborah to rescue them as both judge and warrior. She did most of the work both politically and strategically, but Judges 4 shows a special intervention by God in routing Sisera and his 900 chariots of iron. God acted in a supernatural way on Israel's behalf to restore its sovereignty. But we should note that He didn't often save Israel, and more often than not, He let its people be defeated and dragged into exile as a cause-and-effect lesson. He gave them many opportunities to change, and spoke through the prophets about the crucial stages they were in, but even then, it was a co-operative process with the people, because at the end of the day, He's trying to teach us more than He's trying to lead us.

Nations and kings: If you look at the times when God intervenes specifically, you'll notice that it's almost exclusively about a nation or about those leading a nation. In the Old Testament, prophets gave God's guidance and warnings only to either the nation or the king. It's not that God is too busy for the little guy, it's that He has

---

57 I can't stress here enough that the real wonder and work of God are right in front of our noses. They are in the relationships that can build both families and nations, or in a natural world that ALWAYS has enough resources to feed every community in that world. The built-in ways of God in the universe are always "pouring forth speech" (Psalm 19:2), and we often miss it by looking for the skywriting. In fact, it's when we ignore the natural processes (like taking care of the environment, or respecting family relationships) that we get into trouble in the first place and then foolishly call on God to fix it for us with something supernatural. That has to be sooo frustrating for Him.

a better way to walk with the average person. But if you piss Him off by screwing up a whole nation of His people, He's gonna send a guy like Nathan to a guy like David to tell him a thing or two, and it ain't gonna be pretty. I'm not sure I want guys like Nathan showing up in my life. If we knew how this really worked – that God showed up in extraordinary ways to bring massive correction – maybe we would stop asking for a personal visitation.

Projects, not a life: In Jonah's situation, once he finally got around to answering the extraordinary call from God and went to Nineveh, he was done. That was it. Nothing else was recorded anyway. In fact, aside from the prophets who tended to have a longer-term string of special words from God to give to the people, most of the extraordinary calls from God were a spike in the history of a person's life, then it was back to work as usual. This was the case with Gideon, Rahab, and even Mary, who got an amazing visitation and calling, but we don't see God repeating this throughout her life. Some of these projects take a while, like with Daniel, but for most people the extraordinary call is a project that God needs help with now, and then it's over, and back to the original call which is our response to *His general will* and *our call to be ourselves.*

The reason this is an important distinction is that we have to realize that these projects are usually huge, God-chosen moments for the benefit of others. So asking for a sign or a special word so I can know which job to choose is unreasonable and unnecessary. Instead, God could give me advice about how certain work may line up with my skills or my ability to bless people.

Maturity: When God came to Moses, he was 40-something years old. Same with Paul, and Abraham was much older still. Being able to handle the extraordinary means we need to be at a place of maturity in our lives. We need experience with God, time to have processed our own issues, and an understanding of the world in general. These pre-requisites help us cope with the scope of the extraordinary. In some exceptions, God gives certain people an extraordinary call very early in their lives (like Samuel or Jeremiah) because of the special nature of that call and how it will affect a nation. But for the most part, God's special projects are given to those who are ready for them and at a time when they're absolutely necessary.

God initiates: One of the most freeing aspects of the extraordinary is that God ALWAYS initiates the conversation. In each of the situations I've mentioned, it was God who showed up with the plan and was clear about what was going to happen. When God visited Abraham, Samuel, Moses, Paul... there was never a question about whether it was God or what He wanted. There were other times when the people initiated the process by crying out for help, and God responded, but the timing, communication, and facilitation were all God's initiative. You can ask for special help like Daniel did, or just commit your ways to God in a general prayer, but you don't have to wait around to be told what's next. This should alleviate all the riddles and confusion in our heads, the wondering about which circumstance God may be causing as a response to our questions, or the expectation that we should wait on God to tell us something extraordinary. If there's something special He wants to tell you, He will, and He'll make it very clear. You don't have to hang out in your truck all year (as a friend of mine did), asking for God to speak to you and tell you what to do with your life. The extraordinary call is God's business. Ours is to follow the general will of God and the call to be ourselves. Simple.

Extraordinary calling, normal identity

Daniel goes through 70 years of political involvement in Babylon without an extraordinary call. He was dragged there as a teenager, forced to go through one of the hardest universities in history, and then continually finds himself in challenging situations without a "word from the Lord". In fact, aside from getting a dream interpretation (which *is* pretty extraordinary), Daniel often finds himself facing problems where he's not really sure what God will do. Like with the lions or that fiery ordeal. His take: "I'm not sure what God is going to do, but I'm not going to bow down." What Daniel does know is what God is like, and it's on this basis that he makes most of his choices, prays for assistance and wisdom, and goes to work every day slowly changing the world of Babylon.

Paul is kinda similar. He was an apostle before Jesus got his attention. He knew God, was passionate about teaching and discipling others, and was willing to go anywhere to make that happen. So when Jesus appears to Paul, giving him an extraordinary experience and call, He simply redirects the target while still working with Paul's identity. He gives Paul a better context in which to be himself. God knew who Paul was, as He did with Moses or Ezekiel, and chose them because of *who they were,* not despite them.

This has been true throughout history. When God shows up in an extraordinary way, to work on some huge issue, at the right time... He always works with the identity of the one called. Even if the one being called doesn't yet know they have the ability to be what God is calling them (like Moses and his self-confidence issues). God knows what "fearfully and wonderfully made" means for each of us, and calls us by our diverse and gifted names. God spoke to Newton through the laws of nature (physics), a language both of them were very fluent in. God spoke through passion to the passionate Francis of Assisi, and strategically to Jeanne d'Arc to be the warrior she truly was. And on a less dramatic scale, I once worked with a man who was given extraordinary words from God to bless the world with alternative energy. Gilman Hill was an engineer who would get dreams from God revealing either the location of natural gas or how to drill for it in difficult geographies. He would wake up, draw out the schematics, and hand them on to his drilling teams to create another breakthrough in energy development. Mr. Hill was an extraordinary engineer, and God spoke His language, or the other way around...

In each of these examples, God does extraordinary things through the identities of His children. He knows who they are and does not call them to burn the gift or do something so abstract that they're simply acting as clones in the process. He's not afraid of our effectiveness, He's banking on it. He also knows that the encouragement of connecting our identity to His larger plans will give us a feel for blessing others *with our strengths*, and this encouragement becomes a sustainable force in our lives. We don't need Him to *keep telling us* how to drill for energy or how to serve a nation; we learn from the extraordinary and pick up the ball from there. And I guess that's the point. To God, the extraordinary is simply a way of either rescuing us from our own mistakes or modeling something we can pick up and run with as the royalty we truly are. Maybe if we saw the extraordinary in this light, we might stop expecting things God knows aren't good for us. There is a better way, a daily way, to walk with God that's not full of riddles and a pseudo-faith that acts all supernatural but at the end of the day can't even balance a checkbook, or a life for that matter. I think that instead of always looking for the spirit to do something amazing, we should walk with and in the spirit, and anyone can do that.

Chapter 12 •
Called to be yourself

Remember the story Jesus tells about the three guys and the talents they were given? Remember how He said the master gave them these resources *according to their abilities* (identity)? And then how the master went on with his own journey (no micromanagement)? And how the two guys who weren't afraid *immediately* went out and doubled what they were given (taking huge risks)? And how they debriefed (celebrated) and did it all again? Well, this is the story of our lives, of your life. Welcome to the real party.

If you can deal with the three internal filters confusing the issue...
- *fear*
- *laziness*
- *selfishness*

and the three biggest external pressures adding to our confusion...
- *fatherless*
- *choice anxiety*
- *lack of encouragement*

...then what you're left with is a clear and simple view, a pure, natural relationship with your Father in heaven who is the master in Jesus' story.

- *God knows who you are and what you're capable of ("according to their abilities").*
- *You know what the Master wants (His general will), which in this case is multiplication.*
- *God knows He doesn't have to define how you invest because you'll work that part out yourself, which is the unique gift you get to give.*
- *God knows that you'll learn from the experience and constantly improve, because to God, learning is more important than initial success. By the way, He has this kind of patience because He's working on an eternal time frame.*
- *And finally, the Master knows that the real celebration is the co-operation between the two of you, which is what He enjoys more than anything else.*

The only way we can get to this kind of understanding about calling is to view it from our Father's perspective. To Him, it's all about maturing the core stuff He's created within us, like our heart, soul, mind, and strength. This growth or maturing is our calling. We are called, summoned or invited to "be perfect even as your heavenly Father is perfect" (Matthew 5:48). The original Greek for "perfect" here actually means "complete" or "mature". And what God is maturing is our selves. This is why I say *we are called to be ourselves.* We've been given everything we need for life and godliness through our knowledge of God who called us (II Peter 1:3), and I think identity is a key part of the "everything we need".

Just look at the soul. Jesus said this was more valuable than the whole world. What does that mean? Have you ever unpacked that outside of the typical evangelical approach that souls are worth saving because they're eternal? Of course they are, but is that all they are? What's a soul made of, how did God design it, and why, as far as we know, are we the only thing on the planet and maybe even in the galaxy with one? The soul is completely beyond my (and Richard Dawkins') comprehension. Its spiritual function in connecting the spirit of God to that of man, its capacity for wonder, its recognition of beauty, its ability to create worlds in the mind and in the physical domain... none of this can be explained by any science we have to date. Why would any sane person want to set all that aside and follow the cold path of religious obedience? Jesus came to redeem this soul and set it free from the sin that corrupts its true nature. God's calling us to life again and we can't live without our souls. You are called to be your self.

God's perspective: you're called into *designed spontaneity*

In Paul's letter to the Thessalonians, he mentions a crucial principle that we need to get ahold of: God wants to "empower your good purposes and acts prompted by your faith" (II Thessalonians 1:11). This is amazing because it shows that God's heart is not to control our every action, but to empower and facilitate our purposes and faith. As I mentioned before, the *general will of God* leaves a lot of room for you to figure out and create ways to bless your parents or love your neighbor. The reason He doesn't "micromanage us", as Os Guinness puts it, is because He's more interested in our creativity. It's remarkable how the master in the story actually goes in the opposite direction to the talents so his guys can work it out for themselves. This is not the only biblical mention of this kind of room to fail. Remember the garden? God gives clear instructions about taking care of the stuff, and then He backs off. If you were God, would you have sat back and watched some seedy character push your kids' buttons to destroy the future of your world? And yet He does. He gives His children room to blow it. So if God was willing to allow Adam and Eve to change the course of the planet, don't you think He'll probably want you to choose which instrument you might want to play?

God designed the spirit of man and the physical world to be spontaneous systems that respond to each other in a cause-and-effect way. This is a brilliant design by the way, because it creates so many possibilities. God's joy is in watching us grow up to be like Him and in the creative use of all this potential. He meant for you to spontaneously respond to the possibilities around you, creating new possibilities. For instance, relationships respond to each other and multiply new relationships. The planet responds to crop rotation and multiplies food (30-, 60-, 100-fold...). In the same way, relational or agricultural mismanagement can create destruction, a risk God was obviously willing to take. Instead of locking creation down to a robotic construct, He chose the awesome potential of spontaneous interactions.

Take the possibility of marriage. The old-school way of looking at this was that God had "the one" all planned out for you. All you had to do was find them, and they had to make sure they didn't die, 'cause if they did, you got God's second best, which would have been horrible because every relationship (for you, your children, and their children forever) would have also been second best, which pretty much would have created all kinds of messed-up eternal ramifications. Fortunately, we now know that's psychotic thinking. Right? You do, right?

I (sign here)________________________________ believe that God having "the one" planned for me (and if I don't meet them at the mall, at the perfect time in history, I will eternally screw up the universe) is a psychotic concept and I promise not to put said psychotic mind-freaks on my friends or my family (including my children and theirs) or some stranger at a bus stop. Ever!

Okay, so anyway, the possibility of choosing someone in marriage... If relationship or love isn't something you find, but rather something you create, then you could choose from a million different people (not a billion, but probably a million). Imagine the possibilities in connection with your respective diverse abilities, DNA combinations, histories, and futures... Just you and another person getting together would unleash eternal ramifications (your children). From God's point of view, this dynamic spontaneous power is the only thing worthy of His true design and creativity. To imagine that God would want to puppet-master these relationships into existence and map out their every step is the worst form of idolatry, because it reduces God to that bald little man in the *Wizard of Oz* pulling all the levers with his sweaty little hands. Where's the wonder in that? Truth is, we're created to interact and develop this dynamic and volatile world. While we keep trying to *interpret* circumstances as signs from God (from parking places to an acceptance letter from school), He keeps hoping we'll *create* them. He knows our choices will affect our children's children just as your grandparents' relationships and jobs affect your life today. I know it's kinda scary to own all this and take on the responsibility, but like it or not, you already have it. So the best thing to do is figure out how to use it and co-operate with the design of God's spontaneous systems. And in time, we can learn the ancient wisdom of debriefing and partying with the Master, as stated in the first question of the 1640s Westminster Shorter Catechism: "Question: *What is the chief end of man?* Answer: *Man's chief end is to glorify God, and to enjoy Him forever.*"

You're called to use your *delegated authority*

God has put a lot of faith in us. He gave us the planet (Genesis 1:26), free will, and the shared calling with Jesus to reconcile all things (Colossians 1:20). That's a huge amount of authority. But since, as Michael Schluter says,[58] the kingdom of God is a relational

58 In an interview with *Christianity Today*, Schluter also had this to say about the kingdom of God: "I had become interested in relationships as the underlying and unifying principle of biblical law while working with the World Bank in Kenya in the 1970s (see Matthew 22:37-40, where 'love' is a description of relationship). The whole idea of what we call Relationism, or Relational Thinking for wider society, came out of a biblical reflection in which we looked at biblical laws talking about land, capital, the state, criminal justice, and what holds them together. Well, Jesus says it's all about love. When we asked what's love got to do with land tenure and the ban on interest and so on, the common theme of course is relationships."

kingdom, all authority in that kingdom is about relationships. Our authority to "rule over all the earth" is about our stewardship connection with the planet. Our free will is the freedom to bless each other in relationships, and not to dominate. And, as I mentioned before, *exusia*, the authority the Father gave to Jesus and Jesus gave to us, is basically the power to serve. Get this right and the world flows under the law of love. Mess it up and everything breaks down, from families to businesses, as Schluter also explains:

> I think the main symptom of relational distress is the breakdown of marriage and what is happening both to children and older people. Malachi 4:6-7 comes to mind. I think there are six or seven major drivers behind the breakdown in marriage and the family and they include long and unsocial working hours, debt – because debt breaks up families like nothing else – the tax system, and corporate structures which mean that the people running companies have little connection with their employees. They therefore have little idea of what the daily life of their employees involves, and therefore what the effects are of their decisions on those employees. They just have to satisfy the needs of their shareholders.[59]

There's a relational connection between our working hours, our family lives, our neighborhood involvement, and our nations. The strength or blessing of the relationships in our lives is based on how we use our primary authority as individuals and how we share, delegate or abdicate that authority. For instance, the dad who works long hours has largely given the authority of his schedule to the company. Sometimes people have no choice because of a complex set of financial circumstances, but most people are making a very specific choice to have more stuff and less time for family relationships. This is an abuse of our authority. Most dads in the West are living under the myth that they love their children by giving them stuff (mortgage stuff, food stuff, and big flat-screen TV stuff). They have largely replaced their role in the home with stuff. So the computer teaches the kids and the dad keeps bringing home more bacon, all the while complaining about the long hours and demands at work as though he has no real control over it. Curious.

"Dr Michael Schluter on relational thinking and transforming society", *Christianity Today*, posted on Friday, September 26, 2008.

59 Ibid.

Authority can never be taken from you, it has to be shared, given or abdicated. Have a look at your civic or political involvement. Do you make knee-jerk civil decisions by either not voting or voting in a uniform manner? Like voting for either of the Bush Clan thinking that's going to stop abortion,[60] or pandering to the fear-mongering right in the 2009 California vote to ban gay marriage.[61] So many of us have never thought through the issues and therefore scratch our big ugly "X" exactly where we've been told to. We share or give away our authority to a political process that often bites us in the end, making us feel disenfranchised so we get even less involved next time around. And in the absence of light, all you get is darkness. The result, in the USA at least, is that our relationship as Christians with the general public has been hurt. They know that we've given our minds and authority to an insane pseudo-conservative agenda, which makes us look like brainwashed clones. But if we used our authority in an appropriate way, we'd create a blessing for everyone involved. We've been given authority by God and He will not take it back. Now it's just a matter of what we'll do with it. This is why God gave human beings the planet, the ability to start and redeem families, and the chance to build cities and nations – He's hoping we'll learn how to do justice, love mercy, and walk humbly...

You're called to *diverse areas of influence*

I think one of the reasons we all feel like we can do 20 or 30 things is that, because we're wired in such diverse ways, we actually can

---

60 Presidents don't legalize or penalize abortion. It's not their job. They can promote something and veto a law a couple of times, but that's pretty much it when it comes to supreme-court or senate decisions. So voting for a smiling right-wing kinda guy who keeps his thumbs up while decrying abortion and knowing full well he can't really change the law (which Bush didn't, during his eight years in office) is being led down the garden path. When we give our authority to someone who promises to do something *we should know they can't deliver on,* it's a form of civil laziness. Or worse, a spirit of control. Check out the Rick Warren debate between McCain and Obama for an interesting discussion on this subject.

61 This is a tricky question but, again, most of us have not worked through the real issues or created a law that's appropriate to the need. We've confused our feelings about homosexuality with the rights of our neighbors. For instance, should a person have rights to visit their partners in hospital after hours? Why should or shouldn't the government allow the full benefits of marriage to a couple that can't have children? What's the difference between a civil marriage and full marriage rights? When we look at the real legal issues, we can use our authority to create humane responses. This might help Christians to not look like the new KKK.

achieve more than just the traditional career approach to life. We have a huge range of interests and talents, intellect and physical abilities. Plus, we're exposed to just about everything under the sun through a ubiquitous media machine. It's kinda daunting actually, but it does feed something inside of us that knows we can do more than just one thing.

But before I get into this, I want to say that we need to know the difference between an interest and an ability. When you don't know who you are, everything's possible, but everything's also confusing. Mainly because you're not sure if your interest in music is a possible future in the field or just a simple liking for music. It's a hard call, because a person who LOVES music may not have the ability to play a violin, but they might make an amazing sound designer or musical director on a film. On the other hand, a person may really like music, but it goes no further. The difference between an interest and an ability is usually a nuanced mix of talents and passion coming together under the clear guidance of a soul obsessed with creativity. Which is in direct contrast with the person who simply daydreams about something, but never gets off their ass to do it. I'll discuss this a lot more in my next book on identity, but for now, you could start by reading Sir Ken Robinson's *The Element*, which goes into a lot of encouraging detail on this subject.

So, as you discover more about your identity and therefore your possibilities, you see that there's still a lot of diverse option for work, civic roles, creative ideas... One of the reasons for this is that God did not design a bunch of *Brave New World*-style clones with specific jobs like elevator operator. He made you diverse so you could engage in a world of possibilities that needs that same diversity. For instance, your business talents are not enough to meet the needs of your community. You need to be strong in both business and relationship at the core, but you may also have creative solutions for civic issues that put you on the city council (including the youth city council if you're younger). Or you may need to use some of your bass-playing skills to play in local Jazz clubs to enhance the artistic side of the neighborhood, like Me Without You (sans the Jazz of course). As time goes on, this same diversity may be just what's needed to deal with regional or international issues.

All this diversity is an opportunity to influence the world around you by taking the nature and character of God and applying it in the areas that already influence society, the key ones being family, government, media, science and technology, health care, the arts, education, and business. You have natural abilities in a few of these areas and need to find the connection between your talents and the ways of God in the fights you choose to pick. Like taking your heart to heal people and applying God's principles of regenerative care. Or matching your entrepreneurial skills with God's ways in customer service (i.e. delivery over expectations = customer satisfaction). I guarantee you that God has wisdom for any chosen field of yours, because that field was designed by God in the first place. My friend Landa Cope taught me this a long time ago and I have seen it to be true throughout the years, namely that we have business because God is a provider, we have education because God is wise, and we have science and technology because God is a creator. The main areas of influence in the world have their roots in God's nature, which is why I know we can find wisdom and purpose in any of these fields by applying God's original thinking to that field.[62]

We can use our diversity by working as an electrician by day, band member by night, and big brother to local kids all week. Or any mix you choose to create. But we also exercise our diversity by "choosing wise leaders from among us" (Deuteronomy 1:13) in the political domain, or by engaging our conscience and buying only fair-trade goods. In other words, we can use our influence wisely, learning from the ways of God and applying them to every facet of our lives.

We are called by name, in our diversity, to plug the goodness of God into the world via our own talents. And the world needs it. We're facing all kinds of huge challenges in population explosion, financial mismanagement, and the breakneck speed of paradigm shifts that seem to come every few weeks (like booting up stem cells to bring dead hearts back to life).[63] And while all this is swirling around our sheepish heads, we're oblivious to the fact that no one's gonna hold our hands through this and make it all right, an

62 For more info about this, have a look at Landa Cope's *An Introduction To The Old Testament Template*, The Template Institute Press, 2006.

63 Check this shizzam out: http://speakingoffaith.publicradio.org/programs/2009/stem-cells/index.shtml

oblivion that always leads to crisis. We have to wake up and use the diversity we've been given, call God into the fray with us, and link our film-making skills with His story-telling principles. Or add His wisdom to stem-cell possibilities, better nutrition in schools or any health care issue you choose to engage in. The ironic thing is that while we're waiting around for God to "show up", He's been waiting for us to re-engage our childhood dreams.

You're called to *reconcile all things*
There's a wonderful French phrase, *noblesse oblige,* which the Oxford English Dictionary translates as "privilege entails responsibility". Spiderman's uncle said something similar. The point is, if you take all this *called to be yourself* stuff seriously, then the next thing to understand is that being made in the image of God is a divine blessing that comes with responsibilities. The original French concept was that if you were blessed with noble birth or rank, that gift had an implicit calling attached to it, namely, that you should care for those less fortunate than yourself. The Jesus version is to love your neighbor as yourself. But through the story of the good Samaritan He defines our neighbor as those in need. He goes even further in Matthew 25, defining six areas of need and saying that it's our response to these that proves whether or not we know anything about God. If we know God, we're with Him in battling the sickness, nakedness, poverty, loneliness, injustice, and hunger of His children.

Now, a lot of people I know have (admirably) taken this seriously and jumped into meeting basic needs, but without much thought as to who they were or how they could be more effective, or what the systemic issues are and how the deeper ways of God might actually alleviate poverty. It's all very well to hop on a plane and go to China, but what are you going to do once you get there? I mean, holding babies for a while at the orphanage is cool and all, but that on its own doesn't change anything. So while they're to be honored for their commitment, there's another level to our calling that needs to be added here. Basically, our noble obligation is not to patch problems with a disconnected monetary effort, or short-term school-building excursions, or brief orphanage visits. We are called to something much deeper, something that Colossians 1:20 describes as "reconciling all things back to Christ". And "all things" does not mean "get their souls into heaven 'cause the rest are going to hell". It means ALL THINGS, which Tom Marshall once told me meant the reconciling of souls and the structures those souls inhabited. Our responsibility is to take the massive range of our own abilities and put them to work in meeting the systemic challenges of the world. For instance, how can we possibly reduce the massive numbers of street kids in the Ukraine or teen suicide in Japan without bringing into play *all of your abilities and the wisdom of God's ways.* A short-term outreach just won't cut it.[64]

No, we need to realize that reconciling all things is the ministry of Jesus, and the blessing He gave us (forgiveness and restoration) means that we get to seek God for the specific wisdom for and solutions to these issues. Issues which, as I said above, can be resolved only when you put your whole mind, heart, soul, and strength into action. Which is also why it's essential that you know who you are and are committed to applying your soul to decades of local effort. There are a lot of examples of this happening around the world through people like Jeff Skoll[65] who, by the way, will never show up at your local church, but I don't think God really cares about that, because he's ticking all the right boxes (basic needs, systemic change, holistic development...). I pretty much wanna be like Jeff when I grow up.

Bottom line is that to achieve what I'm talking about here, we have to come back to our place as sons and daughters. A slave does not know what his master is doing, which is the perfect picture of a clueless, chained, religious understanding of calling. We've seen ourselves as worms while He says we'll judge angels. We've seen ourselves as having "no good thing within us" while He knows that the truth is that there's "no good thing in our flesh or corrupted nature". We keep trying to throw the baby out with the bath water, and He's trying to restore our souls. Not only are we called to be ourselves; the world will not be saved, reconciled or redeemed

64 What a short-term outreach will do is provide exposure to the issues and needs beyond our own comfort zones. This is well worth the time as long as you have a follow-up plan. Way too much time and money has been spent on tourist-style outreaches with zero long-term effect.

65 Jeff Skoll helped eBay as its first employee and president. He then sold his shares to make movies with a conscience. Participant Media and the Skoll Foundation have gone on to address major issues in the world from oil and indentured servitude to sexual harassment in the workplace. Using media to share values via story, Skoll takes issues further by promoting aid and entrepreneurship to create sustainable responses to the problems he tackles.

unless we combine our selves (identity, passion, ability) with the power and wisdom of God, and work on the problem.

Over the years, some people have cautioned me that if we really let our selves be free, it would end up badly. That we would become prideful, selfish or idolatrous in the process. That unless we followed strict instructions from God, we would go astray as did someone's cousin who delved too deeply into the arts... And it's not that there aren't stories of people who have left the church or God by following their passions. I know people like this. But what most of them have drifted from or left behind is the controlling spirit of religion. Something inside of them popped because one too many people told them to stand up in worship or bow their heads in prayer or give to "the Lord"... The God presented to us often drives us to the confusing point of desperation, where we feel we either have to become a total drone or just do everything our way. We don't really know the Father who calls us by name; all we've heard is the institution's controlling chants. We've barely spoken to our Father about this because we've passively taken the spoon-feeding. And I don't blame pastors or church "leaders" for this. But we gotta break out of this sense that if it's your idea, it's a bad idea. That if it's in your strength, God can't be involved or get any credit. This Christian subculture BS has got to be challenged by a better conversation between you and God. You will go off the wall if you can't reconcile the fact that, while you have been corrupted, you also have a soul more valuable than the whole world. If you pendulum between these two poles, you will stay confused the rest of your life. If, however, you have received the grace and forgiveness of God, then you are not hanging on the cross, you're back in the garden. I suggest you live like that.

Chapter 13 • Teleology

I'm not sure that this is a necessary chapter, so if it sticks, fine, if not, sorry for wasting your time.

After hearing about the potential of a calling to be yourself, you may think it's a bad idea because it means leaving God behind. And He won't get any glory from a person who is in charge of their own destiny. Our faith can sometimes confuse loyalty to past ideas with loyalty to God. For instance, if you've been told your entire life that God knows the future and has it all planned out, then agreeing with the last few chapters would seem like being unfaithful and way too independent. But I think there's another problem we should be looking at. Jeremiah warns us that "the heart is deceitful above all things and beyond cure. Who can understand it?" (Jeremiah 17:9). I think we use the "It's all about God" and "WWJD"-speak as a subtle way to stay conveniently disengaged. If I'm "waiting on the lord" and He isn't saying anything, then I don't have to do anything. Our problem with "called to be yourself" is not the fear of losing a radical commitment or a sacrificial understanding of God's plans, because if that were the case, our lifestyle and choices would be a lot more hard core than they are. Our real problem is the deceitful nature of our own laziness, especially when it comes to taking responsibility.

Our fearful hearts could be hiding behind a strange version of God's knowing what's best for us. We think that because He knows the future, He can therefore predict the best possible plan for us, one in which we won't fail or be hurt. But does God really know the future? And if He does, do you think Him planning your life in detail is good for you? Or is it just a convenient belief that keeps us happily stuck in the same boat? Most people repeat what they've been told but never make the effort to verify it. It's too much work, and those other people went to seminary (or write books ☺), so why bother checking their facts...

There's another part of our world-view which now comes into play (introduced in Chapter 1 as what's real, what we then believe, which forms our values, which predicts our choices). It's called our *teleology*. Based on our existing world-view, we then project our futures. For instance, if I think God is real and believe He knows everything (including the future) and has planned my steps, then my values and actions will follow that same thread. In other words, I'll wait around for that future to reveal itself. My teleology is waiting for God. Now if my beliefs were true, this would be pretty sweet because all I have to do is listen closely. But what if my belief system is wrong, or I've been listening to partial truths which don't give the bigger picture, and therefore my waiting is getting me nowhere fast? Well, I'll spend most of my life partially confused because those partial truths (God loves you and has a plan for your life) will be manipulated by my lazy heart to keep things at the pleasant temperature of the status quo.

The last 12 chapters have been trying to help you avoid this convenient theology, and I hope that's been effective. But I know that, at the end of the day, our hearts will look for any loophole they can find to avoid the massive responsibility involved in being human.

Biblical teleology

So let's ask the question:

1. *Does God know the future?*

Maybe. I'm not really sure. I've heard the argument from a lot of directions and it's not really clear to me. What I do know is that if He wants to predict something that He will do (like dropping a plague on Egypt or calling the day of judgment), then that's exactly what'll happen. God can speak out what He wants to happen and make it so. (Funny thing is, we can do pretty much the same thing. We can speak out what we want to see happen within our abilities, and make it so. It's called planning.) I also know that God's relationship with time is really different from mine, so there may be mysteries I won't quite fathom until I can have a nice long chat with Him (hopefully over a nice long dinner, 'cause I hear there'll be a bunch of sheep laying around up there).

But there are some other situations which cause me to wonder. For instance, when God interrupts Abraham killing Isaac, the angel tells him to stop because "now I know you are a God-fearing man" (Genesis 22:12). What? *Now* you know? You didn't before? Was that just the angel who didn't know? So the angel goes back to God to report, and God's like, "yeah, I knew that", and the angel's like, "well, why didn't you tell me?", and God's like, "because, I'm God and I don't have to". And the angel's like, "nah, you didn't know, did you". And God's like, "I knew, I'm God, right? I know everything". But the angel's just shaking his head, so God's like, "I knew, I did. I just wanted Abraham to know that I knew that He didn't know what he would do but I knew that he would have killed him, but, that it was important for him to, you know, go through all that. But I knew."

So, yeah, whether God knows everything that will happen or doesn't is an open question for me because there are some things that point either way. But the real question is:

2. Does it matter?
I'm not so sure it does. Even if God knew the future, would telling us be a good idea? Or would planning each step of our lives according to that knowledge be good for us? I mean, I know it would make things a heck of a lot easier for us, but would *that* be good for us? Believing He does know often stops us from doing something proactive, which I think is a central part of the problem; the belief becomes a kind of distraction. We talk as if He knows our plans, but we ourselves don't know what those are, so we make choices anyway in this kind of limbo, "trusting God" doldrum.

What we have to do is cross-reference the omniscience of God (which we barely understand) with the parental nature of God. So while the all-knowing part of God may see exactly how your marriage will work out, the parent part of God knows you still have to make choices that *create* the best possible relationship you can. Likewise, if the omniscience of God sees that you'll make a ton of mistakes choosing the best job, the coaching part of God isn't fussed because the lessons will be well worth it. Him knowing the future doesn't affect most of your life. The even wilder notion is that you can change the future, like Abraham arguing with God over the number of righteous people required to save Sodom. See, I'm not totally sure about what God knows, but I'm convinced He's created us to create the future. Which means that whether He knows what I'm about to do or not, it's not predestined to happen. It's not fatalism. I was given a free will to choose and create and to bless. I get to invite the wisdom and power of God back into the world God delegated to me. So I'm not looking for a road map, I'm pioneering new country.

I guess at the end of the day all we really need to know is that if God has a plan for your future, and thinks it's best to tell you, He will. But for you to assume this about Him, and wait around for it, and not take action in the meantime, is to misunderstand your relationship to the all-powerful and all-parental God. But even more importantly, you gotta keep your eye on the deceptive nature of a heart that's just looking for an out, looking for some loophole in God to avoid taking risks, using the partial truths about God to sit on that treasure. And while I said that I would stop hitting you with stuff a couple of chapters ago, I just need to finish with this last warning before we go on to the really encouraging (and responsibility-building) part.

The third guy in Matthew 25 sat on the investment the master gave him. Now, the master knew this guy was tentative and gave him only one talent so as to not stress him out too much. But the servant still just buried the thing, sat on it, and waited for the master to return. This is just like us; maintaining, surviving, and being status quo in church – all outward activity (or not even that) but no real growth or multiplication. So when the master comes back, the scared servant repeats partial truths about him being a hard man and reaping where he didn't sow. Partial truths paralyze us. It's a case of being willing to believe enough of God to stay comfortable ("God's in control"), but not looking deeper into the parts of God that may require something of us. In this way we take only certain pieces of the picture and weave them into a tapestry that conveniently hangs over our hearts, protecting us from the challenge of ruling the world.

But the master won't have it. He calls out the lazy man for what he really is. He identifies the sloth's inability to begin to love, take action, and risk something – anything. And this, to the master, is wickedness. It's not that the poor guy didn't have a good investment strategy, or that he wasn't as good-looking as the other two Wall Street types. The issue is that he didn't even try. And similarly, as in the other two disaster stories in Matthew 25, we are too often *unwilling* to act (like the goats) and unprepared (by not keeping the lamps trim) to do what we're capable of. Now, God can help us with the preparedness part, and that's what I'd like to focus on in the coming chapters, but neither God nor I can help with unwillingness, especially the kind that hides behind a partial theology of riddles and half-truths. You're the only one who can put that dog down.

As encouragement, though, I will offer this reflection from Oswald Chambers on Galatians 1:15.[66] I think he sums up the whole context of calling from a relational standpoint:

> The call of God is not a call to any particular service; my interpretation of it may be because contact with the nature of God has made me realize what I would like to do for Him. The call of God is essentially expressive of His nature; service is the outcome of what is fitted to my nature [...]. Service is the overflow of superabounding devotion; but, profoundly speaking, there is no call to that, it is my own little actual bit and is the echo of my identification with the nature of God. Service is the natural part of my life. God gets me into a relationship with Himself whereby I understand His call, then I do things out of sheer love for Him on my own account. To serve God is the deliberate love-gift of a nature that has heard the call of God. Service is expressive of that which is fitted to my nature: God's call is expressive of His nature; consequently when I receive His nature and hear His call, the voice of the Divine nature sounds in both and the two work together. The Son of God reveals Himself in me, and I serve Him in the ordinary ways of life out of devotion to Him.[67]

66 "But when God, who set me apart from birth and called me by his grace, was pleased to reveal his Son in me..."

67 *My Utmost for His Highest*, Discovery House Publishers, 1992, page 17.

Your reflections so far:

part 3

creating the future

When YAWEH brought back the captives ...
we were like men who dreamed. psalm 126:1

Chapter 14 • Restoration

To many of us, the years have not been kind. The negative development of our souls at home, school, and church has taken a toll on our sense of self. For a lot of us, living in a fallen world has eroded our courage. Most of us have not been living in the environment God imagined for us, like with a loving dad who apprenticed our skills into action or dynamic teachers who could unfold our distinct mix of intelligences. And most of us have not been part of a dynamic spiritual community capable of equipping us for our unique ministry. Instead, we've been programmed to maintain the program. All this has cost us dearly, and even while we may want to re-engage and break out, we need to start by restoring the years the locusts have eaten.

Restoration happens to be one of God's specialties. He knows how we're wired, what we've gone through, and exactly how we've been affected. He also knows how to heal the deep neurological trenches we've dug. He knows how to renew our souls and revive our core strength, hope, intelligence, and spirit to not only change our own lives, but to drag our friends, kicking and screaming, into a better future. Towards that end, I'd like to share some of the things God's been restoring in me.

Restoring a spirit of boldness.
At the age of 13, we didn't care that much about failure, or money, or the opinion of others. We were ready to write an amazing story or take the black run on the slopes without over-analyzing our motives or the results. This kind of boldness is natural to us and was meant to build up over the years until it eventually matched our abilities, resulting in a confidence that could build cities, or spaceships... In fact, Richard Branson left school at 15 to do just that. He knew he couldn't learn in that scholastic environment, so he maintained his boldness and entrepreneurial spirit by taking risks and starting businesses (selling everything from Christmas trees to mail-order music). Today, among the many businesses he owns, he runs Virgin Galactic, an airline to space.

Branson developed his spirit of boldness by following his heart. It's a good method, but I would take it further and say we need to know and follow the heart of God first, so that we can put our own heart into perspective and to better use. I did this in the early years by spending hours talking with God about everything I could think of. At 23, I was on a relief ship sailing from Los Angeles to Fiji. I would get up at 4 each morning and walk the decks, exercise, and talk with God about life in general. I didn't know it at the time but, in getting fresh perspective and the occasional revelation, I was being restored. The values of God and the ways of God started washing over my spirit, slowly changing me. The important thing was that I pursued God, asked questions, and listened long enough to hear really helpful insights. It wasn't a passive experience, like sitting in a pew waiting for someone to "enlighten" me. And I didn't grow up in church, so there wasn't a lot to unlearn, but for some of you there may need to be a desert or mountain-top experience where you go off and ask some questions directly to God.

I needed to know what I was really capable of, and how God saw me, both as my Father and as a partner. I needed to have my confidence restored, which meant that I knew my name (or what God calls me), what He expected of me, and what I could expect of Him. So most of the questions I would ask or study in the scriptures were about knowing His original idea as the Father of sons and daughters. I asked how He intended to share the business with me, co-create with me, and hand over large chunks of responsibility to me. I would ask how I was uniquely designed to handle my part through my passions, intelligence, and abilities. At first, I would just ask these kinds of questions and not hear anything back. But God was listening, and I found that, by asking, I developed a kind of spiritual radar that was sensitive to seeing the answers as they popped up in my reading, or in conversation, in teaching, or through nature. He showed me in tons of different ways what He thought of me and how He intended to walk with me. (And hey, it only took a few decades altogether.) The prayer and communication was only one part of the restoration of boldness. A lot of it happened when I took the risk to relate and get married. A lot happened by placing myself in situations where I needed to be bold and see God come through on His part. So overall, by prayer, meditation, and action, this clarity of God's purpose and my identity slowly rebuilt my sense of confidence so that I was growing in faith (which comes by hearing from God) and not just in religious thinking. I also grew a sense of mission and a better understanding of my part in it. This is how I dealt with the fear I mentioned in earlier chapters. I had something bigger than fear itself.

Boldness is something dads instill, and being re-parented by God is a central part of discipleship. He's apprenticing our spirit and reminding us what we should have heard in the home or school – that we are fearfully and wonderfully made. Our part is to agree and put the wisdom to work in some kind of baby step until it feels natural again. Our Father in heaven is also preparing us for a pretty massive battle up ahead which we've been uniquely equipped to enter. I don't know what it is about dads and learning how to fight, but it seems to be a natural thing. Maybe God's intentions were that our warrior sides were part of our father-son/daughter training. But the battle God's called us into requires using our creativity and meeting basic needs instead of trying to Christianize or democratize other nations or passively waiting for Jesus' return while hiding in the bunkers of gated communities.

Restoring this spirit of boldness is central to all other restoration processes. We need a raison d'être to get out of bed, off the couch, and into the fray. God does this by showing us who He is and then showing us who we are. But this needs to be a personal conversation. You have to ask Him yourself about what He calls you. You have to listen and apply what you hear. When God has a chance to really speak into our hearts, unfiltered by institutions and invited by our own desperation, the restoration draws out our boldness and we get back to that 13-year-old spirit. We become "as those who dream" again (Psalm 126:1).

Restoring your strength

There's a discipline to having good health. The small, everyday decisions we need to make in order to keep this machine of a body functioning create a kind of structure in the rest of our lives. Using self-control to manage calorie intake versus output, or making the effort to shop locally and take the time to cook/eat in a leisurely way with friends add a level of maturity and ownership to your life. In fact, I've always been amazed at how the simple things (like the discipline of walking or considering the food you're eating) add depth to our lives. I think this is because God's placed us in a material world that teaches us through cause and effect. We're tactile learners and as we interact with the beauty and function of the natural world, we learn about its creator. As we learn about God through the material creation and co-operate with His ways in diet, health, and managing the garden, we get in tune with a deeper strength and wholeness. I think this is the foundation of *shalom.*

In order to have the energy to take risks and get on with your life, you need to be healthy. That means you need to eat what God made for food (seed-bearing plants, fish with scales, certain kinds of meat), don't eat the stuff that wasn't meant to be eaten (like shell-fish, sorry), don't process God's food to death (like white flour), and don't get addicted to any one thing (like coffee).[68] It also means you need to be exercising regularly to get the machine working well. I know this is simple stuff, but when I've been the most depressed or unable to take the next step, next to serving others, the redemptive wisdom of God has been to work on my health. I mean, how can I love Him and others with all my strength if I have none? So find a rhythm that suits you, develop some discipline, and grab some friends to help if you need to. It's hard to do this kind of stuff by yourself, and I'm sure they could use a good kick in their flabby abs too.

Our spiritual condition and our health are intertwined. Once you've got your nutrition and exercise sorted, you need to look at the deeper connections between your relationship with God and your physical life. Loving God with all our strength has incredible ramifications, which some mystics have understood for years, but we're only now starting to see the cellular reasons why. For instance, researchers at the UC San Francisco (Elizabeth Blackburn among others) found that tiny units of DNA called telomeres protect cell functions and regulate cell aging. If you're stressed, telomeres shorten, which shortens the life of the cell.[69] Cell researcher Dr. Doris Taylor found in one test that meditating for just 15 minutes in-

68 Dr. Rex Russell wrote what I consider the best book on God's idea of health and food ever. *What the Bible Says About Healthy Living: Three Biblical Principles That Will Change Your Diet and Improve Your Health* goes through every scripture on food and measures them all from a scientific perspective resulting in the three principles I just mentioned. It also shows what an amazing dietician God is and how for thousands of years He's been giving us detailed advice.

69 Elizabeth H. Blackburn, Carol W. Greider and Jack W. Szostak won the Nobel Prize in Physiology for their discovery of "how chromosomes are protected by telomeres and the enzyme telomerase" nobelprize.org/nobel prizes/medicine/laureates/2009/press.html

creased the positive stem cell count in blood, the very cells that heal your scratched knee or inflamed arteries.[70] Restoring our health is as much about rest and meditation (the proper kind, where stretching, breathing, and mental focus are involved) as anything else. It may seem like a small thing, especially if you're young. But developing a healthy lifestyle also means getting in touch with God's design and priorities. And by the way, you'll probably appreciate the added years later on, when you really need them...

Restoring your mind – all eight parts of it

If your local school didn't kill off most of your brain's activity, the local church quite possibly finished the task. Many of us have been numbing ourselves to death by sacrificing our minds on the altar of religion. We've been drilled with the mantra "if you thought of it, you need to kill it" so God can take over your mind and body to speak *through you* because He wants to *use you...*

Not on my watch, dammit. I'm so sick and tired of these partial truths controlling and killing the creativity of the body of Christ, leaving us cold and numb and fleeced by an institution that profits from our inertia because we got nothin better to do with our time and money. When we look at the wonders that are our minds and intellect, we have to assume that they're some of the most precious gifts in the universe. Our intelligence is to be cherished and developed to its beneficial potential. Restoring our minds is a top priority for any Christian who wants to be salt and light in a world that desperately needs some godly wisdom, "wisdom that comes from above" (James 3:17) but goes through our intellect as a co-operative synthesis creating appropriate solutions. That's the Father-and-Daughter/Son business we're in.

Years ago Heather and I came across a book called *The Unschooled Mind,* and later, *Frames of Mind,* in which Howard Gardner presents the idea that all human beings have multiple intelligences and we use two or three of our strongest ones to "solve problems and make things" (his definition of intelligence). Gardner explained that our typical view of intelligence was limited to math/logic skills and language, but that true intelligence is a much broader combination

70 Dr. Taylor discusses this and her work in general with stem cells with Krista Tippett on speakingoffaith.publicradio.org/programs/2009/stem-cells/transcript.shtml

of at least eight main areas functioning in our brains. He listed them as math/logical, lingual, spatial (like an architect), interpersonal (like a teacher or counsellor), intra-personal (like a poet), kinesthetic (like a dancer), musical, and natural (like a botanist). In pointing out the dynamic nature of intelligence, Gardner and many others in the growing field of cognitive neuroscience are challenging the narrow results of typical IQ tests – namely, that if you have math logic and language skills, you're smart, but if you don't, you're not.

Temple Grandin has added to the conversation on thinking and intelligence by adding her brilliant views from the autistic/Asperger spectrum. As an insider (Temple is what would be termed a high-functioning autistic), she has identified three types of "specialized" thinking:

- *Visual thinking, or photo-realistic thinking*
- *Pattern thinking, like in math or music*
- *Verbal thinking, where language tends to obscure the first two types*

Grandin says that recognizing types of thinking (and their variables and combinations) is crucial to help "build on the child's area of strength and appeal to their thinking patterns"[71] so they can be more effective. Acknowledging the diverse and dynamic forms of intelligence is a freeing prospect for people judged by arcane systems (IQ tests) and measured by standardized curricula. Freedom from this trap comes as we understand and recapture the use of our minds by understanding the depths of God's design – which should also speak forcefully against the negative words and rejection of an education system formed in the industrial revolution.

Heather and I started to use this broader framework to assess and understand ourselves and our kids so that we could all learn along the lines of our strengths and not always be beating our weaknesses to death. We developed a customized curriculum for each child so they could focus on what they loved to do in a way their intelligences naturally worked. We still covered the basics of math or history whether they liked it or not, but for the most part, we facilitated their strengths. Which is exactly how God works with us – through encouragement and a "kindness that leads to repentance" (or "change of mind", Romans 2:4). We learned that it's not that

71 *The Way I See It: A Personal Look at Autism & Asperger's*, Future Horizons, 2008, pages 14-15.

hard to change a mind or develop it when it's being encouraged along the lines of its own natural neural pathways.

I suggest you review the use of your mind in relation to God. Learn to love Him with ALL of your mind, and not just the part that can hear and obey. A lot of us have grown up in education systems that divided "hand-minded" kids from the "abstract-minded". The hand-minded kids went to "vocational training" (which in the early days meant an inferior curriculum), and if you were math/logical, you went towards a white-collar education. What this social division wrongly assumed is that an electrician is not using his mind when he or she problem-solves a short in your home, or that my sister, who loves working in her cafe, is not using all kinds of social and lingual intelligences in managing the orders and relationships of her domain. Mike Rose, a professor at UCLA, mentions that a lot of his ground-breaking educational techniques stem from witnessing "the intelligence of the waitress in motion, the reflective welder, the strategy of the guy on the assembly line".[72] We usually extoll these skills as the sheer hard work of the blue-collar class, but we fail to see the deep intellect involved in these nuanced tasks. Loving God with all of our minds needs to take this kind of thinking into consideration because that's part of the restoration from rejection or demeaning systems. Everything we do can be a diverse expression of intelligence and all of it can bring glory to God. Today, vocational training can be a solid way to build your intelligent skills, but if you have a stigma hanging over your ability to learn, some renewal may be in order.

In order to do this, I want to encourage you to go through three phases of mental restoration, which you may be doing already, in which case this is just a pat on the back.

1. Assessment: You need to know what you're working with. Your learning styles, ways of processing, intelligences, and natural preferences need to be mapped out in such a way that you can understand and practice your strengths. There are a lot of "learning style" or "multiple intelligence" assessments online, or you can just get a

---

72 *The Mind at Work: Valuing the Intelligence of the American Worker*, Penguin, 2005, page 1. I haven't read the whole book, but heard an extensive interview with Mr. Rose regarding intelligence and education on "Speaking of Faith" with Krista Tippett, an amazing podcast that I highly recommend.

book or two on the subject and dive in. You probably already know a little about how you tick but haven't necessarily been validated in that area, so this would be encouraging.

2. *Education:* The next step is to review what you've been learning and why. It may be that you started a course of study or a way of studying that is now unhelpful for you. Once you have a clue as to how you learn, you should take steps to facilitate that learning. And don't be passive here, thinking that someone else should make your educational life easier. I'm convinced that we need to design our own curriculum and co-op that process with people who can meet our standards instead of the other way around.

3. *Application:* Romans 6:17 says we fully change when we *apply* the education we're committed to. Knowing how you learn is good, and getting education along those lines is also helpful, but if you don't find a way to *do something* beneficial with that, it goes nowhere and you're in art school for life...[73]

There's tons more you can do to develop your mind and heart, like reading classic literature, meditating, or learning how to rebuild an engine. I guess we just need to be reminded that to God our minds are still amazing and therefore worth the effort.

Restoring your soul

In a sense, this one should have been first because I think it's the most important. But I also know that if we're not bold, healthy, or validated in our minds, we won't have the ability to go through the long-term process of restoring the soul. I've been working on understanding and developing the soul for decades, and while I feel like I've learned a lot, I'm still scratching the surface of this eternal faculty. But I guess the main point I want to make here is that while we've been brainwashed into placing our souls (passions, dreams...) on the altar for God to demolish and give fragments back, the truth is that Jesus went through heaven and hell to restore our souls to their full potential. I want to understand why the soul is "more valuable than the whole earth", and engage in a personal restoration so that I can also understand the broader mission of my neighbor's

73 Robert Louis Stevenson says art isn't a vocation, it's a temptation. Check out his essay: "Letter to a Young Gentleman Who Proposes to Embrace the Career of Art", 1888.

soul. This would not lead to a heartless evangelism that attacks their life, but rather to a thoughtful appreciation for who they are (mind, soul, heart, and strength) and what's important to them. Maybe then I can co-operate in their reconciliation back to God...

In 1975 Tom Marshal wrote a really helpful booklet (it's kinda hard to find today) called *Free Indeed,* in which he explains that the soul is the intersection of the spirit of God and our body. That when God breathed spirit into our physical being, all the eternal attributes of will, intuition, passion, the ability to dream and therefore to create were forged into a life that God called *very* good. The soul is kind of hard to get your head around from a scientific (or empirical) point of view, but the actual process and product of the soul is simple to grasp. For instance, your intuition may be a matter of rapid cognition, as Malcolm Gladwell points out in his book *Blink.* But the synthesis of intuition, spirit, and passion can inspire fantastic architecture or a brilliant piece of music. In fact the word "inspire" carries with it the sense of being filled or breathed on, as the Oxford English Dictionary defines it:

> ORIGIN Middle English *enspire*, from Old French *inspirer*, from Latin *inspirare* 'breathe or blow into,' from *in-* 'into' + *spirare* 'breathe.' The word was originally used of a divine or supernatural being, in the sense
>
> [impart a truth or idea to someone.]

The soul, from my point of view, is the creative meeting point of our hearts, minds, and strength. It's where we assimilate and process and create from. Of course, a lot of that process happens in our brains, but the place where those neural pathways jump the circuitry into the ether of our essential being is the magical domain of the soul. The trick is to know how this all works and to facilitate it. For eons this has been the domain of poets and scientists or anyone who could tap into that magic, like Einstein playing the violin until the penny dropped. Most people who understand inspiration will acknowledge their own hard work, mental processes, and sometimes sheer luck, but they will also speak about the muse, or genius, or spirit of inspiration that cannot be empirically accounted for. That it can't be measured and tagged is not a big deal to me, because I don't think we need to be able to track the soul through diodes taped to our heads (or stomachs I guess, wherever that soul thing is). What we do need to know is what the soul is, how it works, and how to listen to and co-operate with this gift from God. Which has also lead me to the conclusion that putting our soul on the altar, for any reason, is treason with heaven.

There are of course many elements of our soul to consider, but in terms of calling, I want to focus on identity. Identity in its fullest context is a dynamic mix of all the parts of who we are physically, psychologically, and spiritually, but the root of all this expression lives in the soul. I think we're born with an identity, at the cross-section of our spirit and body, named by God to call us into being. These *names* then develop into physical and psychological expressions as we grow into maturity. But they're placed there from birth, and our lives then unfold them into concepts and words. I call these "I am" statements, because they're who we are at the core. (Another commonly used term is "identity" statements.) I like "I am" statements because they are not job descriptions or Myers Briggs terms, they're the dynamic building blocks which you could forge into hundreds of creative expressions. Here's a quick view of my identity expressed in "I am" statements.

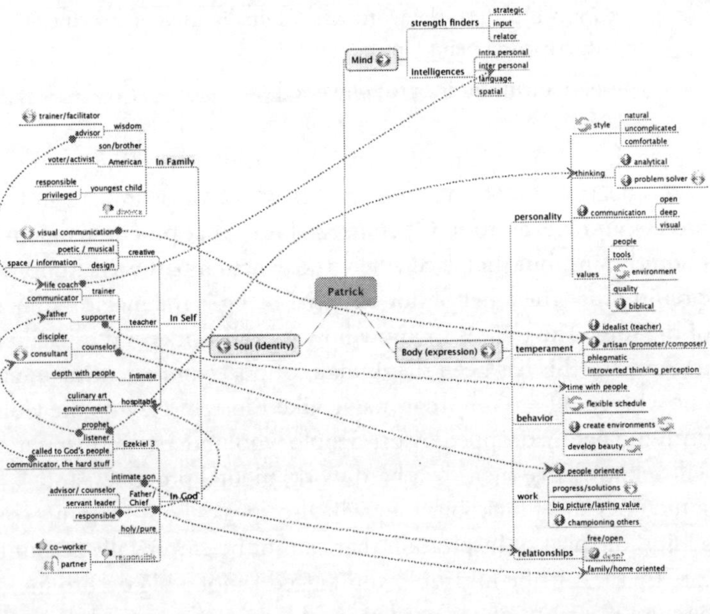

From this basic identity map, I can thank God for what He's called me, I can see themes and connections with various parts of my soul, and I can synthesize various identity statements into creating something completely new – or I could just pick a better job. This is the stuff God's given me to work with. These names are what I'm called and, therefore, my calling.

As I've said a few times, this is a huge subject and one I will write more fully about in another book. But identity and restoring yours is probably the most important aspect of understanding your calling and thereby having a closer co-operation with God in the expression and partnership of that call. The really important stuff for life (conscience, identity, free will) is already mapped into our hearts and souls. And we need to look at our soul and the identity within to start living from the *inside out.* We need to see our calling as the personalized expression of that soul, coupled with the ways and principles of God. And we need to creatively use our soul to bless our neighbors and nations because, despite popular demand, Jesus has left the building and is not coming back to save us from our own work.[74]

Another aspect of our soul is our passion and the resulting creativity. Passion is a remarkable gift from God that activates these "I am" statements in the real world. Passion helps me take these raw elements and call them something great, something potentially amazing. Passion helps me start the process of becoming that musician or architect in spite of the hurdles in front of me. It gives me the grace to overcome all the obstacles I'll face, or cope with the down time between successes. Learning to listen to and develop passion is part of our soul's restoration. And this is where we come back to inspiration and intuition. Most of us have become intuitively deaf. As a result, our passions are largely stifled. We've lost the ability to hear intuition through the droning language of professional pastors or the obnoxiously loud noise of a soft-porn-obsessed media. And any other space we might have had left in which to meditate and get in touch with our souls, we've given to the internet. In effect, we're numbing ourselves out of intuition by searching for identity

74 I'm convinced Jesus will return, but "soon" is a relative term to a guy who lives in eternity now. And the saving (or reconciling) that God wants to do today involves the co-operation of all your identity and gifting. So don't wait around in some bunker looking to the clouds. Like Jonathan's armor-bearer, God's in the bunker with you waiting for you to move it.

outside of ourselves (via work, relationships, stuff). We've lost the ability to rest, to cease from the rat race long enough to hear the still, quiet voice of intuition (which, by the way, is also how God speaks to us). Fostering the voice of your intuition will also help you get back in touch with your passion. Restoration then requires that we learn how to seek and study and listen closely to the spirit who whispers.

In the coming chapters I'll try to give some practical advice for making choices based on your identity or your call to be yourself. For now though, I want to suggest that you take a break. Restoration is rooted in rest, ceasing from labor or the way you've been operating (at least in the unhelpful ways). If you're really gonna work on your health, your mind, and your soul, you may need to get into a new space, both mentally and physically. I've done this a few times over the years, taking six months to a year to get ready for the next season. Your version can take any form you can make happen, but I suggest you make it happen. No one hands you rest or the option to break out; you have to create this. But imagine how cool it would be to get some spiritual boldness back while reinventing your diet and health regime, or to take the time to talk about and map your identity so you have a clearer picture of what you're really working with. For some of you, it will mean a short period of time in which to regroup. For others, it may lead to a new place to live, study, or work within a new community. In either case, work on the basics I've mentioned above as well as other areas you think are important, because in doing so, you're taking your life and your call seriously.

Chapter 15 • Recovering your call

As children, we grow up passively receiving from others. We really don't have much choice as we can't fend for ourselves for quite a while. Somewhere around the age of puberty though, we need to transition and take initiative for ourselves. The way we make that transition is largely based on our fathers walking us through a knowledge of our identity and potential (our value), and of how to use that in the real world (our destiny).[75] If they do this, we develop a sense of confidence in who we are and what we can do. From there, you start making educational, work, and relational choices that facilitate the direction you want to move in. If, however, that father is not present or doesn't take on this role, which is the case for a lot of us, then we stay stuck in a receiving pattern for the next 10 years until we get another chance to transition (at around 21 to 23 years old). In fact, most of us go from the natural state of a child's ability to receive and learn, to an unnatural passivity where we start to expect other people to wash our clothes, cook for us, pay for everything, and drive us around forever.

If you look at the key environments in your life, places where you were meant to grow up (like home, school, church or work), you'll see that they all have an authority component. Your parents at home, teachers at school, pastors at church, and bosses at work all represent authority in the kingdom of either light or darkness depending on how you've related to each other. From God's point of view, the servant-leaders in these places were meant to speak out your identity and therefore your calling so you could grow up, bless the world, and serve others. But this is rarely the case for two reasons. One is that if you don't transition from passive to active at puberty, you've probably brought that same childish passivity into these other environments. At home you do what you can to get by, but you don't share the mortgage or cook meals for the fam. At school you fulfill the curriculum instead of expanding it. At church you never raise your hand and ask questions or encourage dialogue.

75 Mothers obviously have a role in developing identity, but it seems to me that moms have the primary role of nurturing a sense of unconditional love and provision from 0 to12 years old, and fathers have the primary role of fostering a sense of value and destiny from 12 to 30.

And at work you probably clock in, do what you're told, and live for the weekend instead of innovating and developing new products and services... The second reason is that people in authority usually don't serve and release others because in terms of "leadership" they're functioning in the kingdom of darkness. A spirit of control or fear undermines God's intentions through them, which then plays on our passivity, creating an environment of co-dependance.[76]

Bottom line, we've maintained a passive attitude in most of the key places we were meant to grow up in. The home was meant to speak out and encourage our identity and calling. Schools were meant to educate the raw material of our souls, adding skills to "I am" statements. Church is meant to develop a theology around those skills. And work is one of the places we were meant to create new things from our own nuclear potential. Now some of us may have had the opportunity to do just that, but for those of us who haven't, we need to be re-parented by God and go back through that 13-year-old transition into taking initiative. We need to move from passive to active and recover our call.

Rites of passage

Growing up, I think I had the typical kind of life where my parents loved me but never really spoke directly to my identity. School was a bore and work became a way to pay for my car. The only thing that changed in becoming a Christian was that I got put into a different box. I never really understood what my place was, although I was 100% clear about what was expected of me. After years of getting to know God, I finally came to the point of understanding His desire and ability to re-parent me. Most of this happened in my 20s and 30s, so be encouraged if you think you're behind the curve. You're not, and the power of God's blessing is a thousand times stronger than any curse you've endured. Just look around and notice the slow-motion pace of most people's true development. You're doing just fine.

Okay, so most of us didn't transition from child to adult with a great party where our dads took us on as apprentices and helped us

76 I know I've been very critical of people in leadership positions. Ironically, I've been blessed with many fantastic, releasing people who sought to serve (and challenge) me in my development. I'm not bitter. But I am observant and I've seen a lot of controlling types messing with people's destinies.

know ourselves and our place in the world. And yes, a lot of us feel retarded that we're 20-something or whatever, and still don't know who we are and what we can do with our lives. But the reality is, we are pretty much all in the same boat. I say this because, in order to recover your call, you've gotta be able to say, "Hi, my name is Patrick and I'm retarded". If I'm not willing to acknowledge that I've missed a key transition in life and that, as a result, I'm still acting like a child (playing WoW and calling it a life or watching chic flicks thinking, "Oh please, let it be so for me"), then I won't see the need to be re-parented, to go back to that 13-year-old position before God and rework the process.

What God wants to do, I believe, is to take us back to that point of transition. Together (us and God), we need to acknowledge the end of our childhood and its dependencies, speak out the truth about our selves, and start an apprenticeship that develops our raw identity into a living, creative reality. Which is exactly what we did with our kids. We noticed that in the West we've dropped rites of passages, like the Hebrew Bar/Bat Mitzvah, and replaced them with teenagers having sex and a cigarette as a way to grow up. And we knew that in order to take this *passive to active* transition seriously, we needed a formal process that we could apply to the entire family. Heather and I have done this with our kids (and learned the idea of re-parenting in the process) and then personally with God taking us through a slightly different process. It's been an amazing revelation and journey, especially with my kids. The simple power of the following three actions has changed their lives and mine:

- *speaking out identity*
- *educating their raw material into skills*
- *apprenticing those in real-world scenarios (work, relationships)*

I'm sorry to tell you that this is another story I'll fully describe in another book when my youngest (Levi, now 16) gets a little older. You don't need instructions from me; we all just need encouragement to start the process in a way that suits where we're at today. Which is what I did by going to God and asking Him to help me walk through the three steps above. There wasn't a lot of literature or models around for us to learn from. So we just asked basic questions, looked at Hebrew culture and biblical history, and had a go. I suggest you ask God to remind you who you are – in detail. For me, God spoke in a number of ways; some quietly into my heart, and others through scriptures that normally would apply to all of us, but since I asked, I was able to personalize them, so where Psalm 1 says I'm like a tree planted by streams of water, I took this to mean that I am a covering, strong, rooted...

The next step is to start educating or developing the things He says to you and then put them to work in the service of others (through business, education, the arts...). If you give yourself 10 years to develop the raw material of your soul, you're gonna do fine. And even if you're 23 now and just starting out, at 33 you're gonna be way ahead of the curve because most of your peers are *still* going to be stuck in jobs they hate and relationships they've rushed into.

Identity

There's a ton of material – books, courses, teachings – on the subject of identity. I say, the more the merrier. This is such a crucial and underdeveloped area in our lives that we need to unfold it by all means. We need to see the layers of complex identity each one of us has been blessed with in as much detail as possible. So whether it's looking at the psychological perspectives of the Enneagram or an internet algorithm breaking down our Strength Finder, we need to recover, journal, and develop an understanding of who we are. My only criticism of some of these otherwise helpful tools is that, in knowing our desperation to figure out what's next, they tend to jump to job descriptions or applications that are kind of canned. What I understand about identity is that it's a dynamic, complex set of raw truths about you which can be synthesized and reformulated in many possible combinations. Personality or identity testing typically tries to describe and quickly place you into a pre-existing role, for example as a secretary or administrator, simply because you can organize well. Figuring out your life has become figuring out your job, which is still coming from an industrial revolution mentality.

Recovering the call by knowing your complex identity also requires that you continue to connect with the important people in your life (especially your parents). Our families could be encouraging and speaking out identity statements that only they can see. Our teachers could be assessing and facilitating identity through customized or adaptable curricula. Church could be a place that acknowledges and gives room for our gifts and their unique expression in the body. And our workplaces could be opportunities to constantly invent and improve based on our unique contribution. But whether this is being offered or not in the contexts above, God is ready to re-parent and establish a better sense of identity in each of us right now.

I started out by asking Him to speak into three main areas of my identity:

1. *Who I am in God, which I understood by looking at what He said to me or called me (like "friend and son", "father", "prophet", "warrior").*
2. *Who I am in my family and community, which I could see by knowing my name or place in those social groups (like "wise advisor", "challenger", "provider").*
3. *Who I am in myself, which I could see by simply asking what it is that I love and what's natural to me (like "chef", "designer", "trainer").*

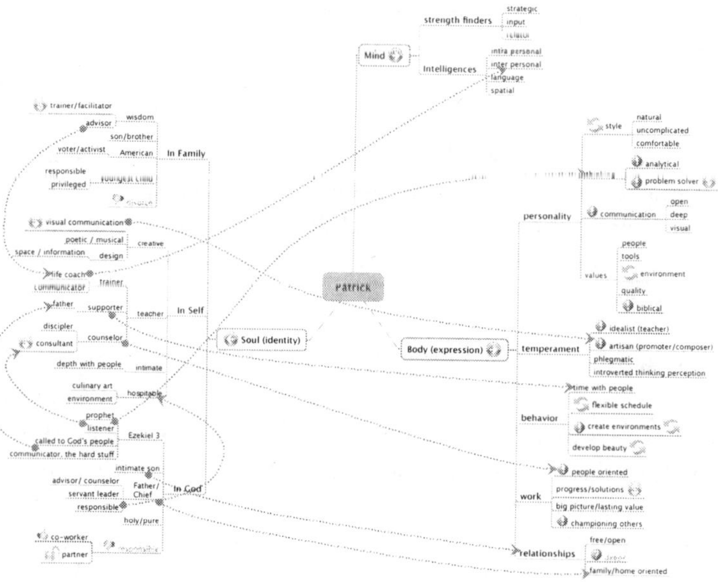

I have a podcast online[77] which goes into more detail on this, but what I want to say here is that if you start asking, journaling, and processing in your own way, with God, family, and friends, you're

77 http://www.patrickdodson.net/Podcast/Entries/2006/3/25_Processing_Your_Future.html I would also encourage you to read Sir Ken Robinson's book entitled *The Element*, as well as Os Guinness's book *The Call*.

going to start recovering what's been in you since birth – your name. And from that name, you create your future with God.

Relationships and collaboration

Whatever happened to identity development in your early relationships at home or at school, you've probably gone on to extend that community or developed a new one. Don't try to "move on" or look past your family, because they always have a place in our lives and in encouraging identity, but wherever you are, I would encourage you to take the relationships around you more seriously. For instance, make it your business to give specific, substantial encouragement to those in your life. Speak out things that are true about who they are in God, in family, and in themselves. Have *identity parties* where you invite a group over and speak out detailed truths about each other and brainstorm possible creative futures you guys could build on.

With those really close to you, you may want to map out your identities together and see what kind of collaboration you could form with your strengths. Or, approaching this from the other side, in knowing more about who you are, you can better seek out your tribe, the ones who will best understand and co-create with your unique set of skills. God said that it's not good for us to be alone, and in terms of recovering our call this is especially true because we need that shared sounding board to help resonate and encourage the fledgling ideas we have of ourselves.

Creativity

As you move into the freedom (and risk) of being yourself, the next part of recovering your call is recovering your creativity. Most of us have lost this or, as Picasso famously said, we've been educated out of it. In remembering who you are, you also need to remember how you create. All of us are born creators, not necessarily artists, but creators. Some create in labs, others on canvas, but we all have the capacity to take our identity, mix it with inspiration, and bring new things into being. When you were a child, this was the most natural thing in the world. Before you were told about making money or why what you made wasn't important, you knew how to create. My suggestion is that you find that place again. Most of us can pinpoint the negative word, rejection or internal decision we made to leave this part of us behind. God can speak life back into that area if you give Him a chance to help you remember what you may have forgotten or given up on.

I can't stress enough the importance of this step. Creativity is the raw ability to synthesize your various identity statements and perspectives into a new expression. If you've lost this, or aren't willing to risk developing it, you'll loose the ability to forge your identity into something meaningful. What you'll be left with is a monotone view of self which turns you into a secretary instead of the entrepreneur – or the construction worker instead of the furniture craftsperson – that you really are. Being a secretary or a construction worker is fine if that's what you truly are. What's not cool is being a writer stuck in an administrator's job. You don't have to be creative like other people, you just need to be *your creative self.* Which is totally do-able. Go back to where that ax head fell into the water and ask God for help in raising it back up again (see 2 Kings 6:5 to decode...).

Risk and failure

You have to know that as you move forward in all this, you'll have to take some big risks and you will fail. You'll make mistakes and try things that will not work out how you'd like them to. And you have to be okay with this. Not moral failure of course – that you can avoid. But you have to be okay with not knowing God's perfect will, because He's giving you resources and then walking the other way. He wants you to take whatever you have and multiply it.

I spent nine years on one project that I'd have to say ended in failure. But what I've learned from that, and from a lot of little things along the way, has been huge. Because the whole time, I was unpacking and refining and using more of my identity. Eventually, this stacks up into a form of wisdom and perspective that makes less mistakes over time and actually becomes an anointing, blessing the next thing you touch. You just have to be okay with the process. If not, you'll rush through things or not do anything because you don't want to blow it, or lose money, or miss another opportunity – all fear-driven motivations.

Working out the ways of God

To me, the most exciting thing about restoring our call, or identity, is that when I know who I am and what my part in the mix is,

I can seek God along the lines of that call and add amazing new dimensions to what I'm doing. (*Again, you gotta know that He loves this. You can't see this as God-less independence simply because you're driving the car He's given you.*) For instance, as a story-teller, I want to know the God of story and learn from His wisdom in the field. As I seek the nature and character of God in this way, I also see the details of His wisdom in how He tells stories, how they're usually hard core, relational, and inspirational. I start to know God in deeper ways, ways I can apply in my own work via a screenplay or short story... Basically, I'm learning a theology, or the ways of God, in my own craft.

This is a true partnership: My identity, anointed by the ways of God, and put to work in blessing my neighbors. This is a missional life and a sustainable one at that. It's loving our neighbor *as* ourselves and it's really effective versus, say, door-to-door evangelism where no one is being themselves. God gets the most joy out of seeing us grow into our full potential, the design of His thinking and creativity. It's a win win.

The way I approach knowing God's ways in my craft is by asking five specific questions. They are:

1. *What is the nature and character of God (for instance, in story-telling)?*
2. *What does the word of God say about this area?*
3. *What can creation (or "the book of God's works"[78]) teach me about this area?*
4. *What has history revealed and what can I learn from it?*
5. *What are my personal perspectives and revelations about this area?*

The following page shows an example I've been working on in the field of writing...

---

78 Bonaventura, Newton, Pascal, and Bacon all had a common view that God had given us two clear references to know Him; one was the scriptures, and the other was nature or, what they often called, "the book of God's works". Romans 1:20 also states that God's invisible qualities, divine nature, and eternal power can all be "clearly seen *through what has been made*" (my emphasis). For a good primer on the subject, check out http://www.templetonresearchlectures.com/winners/bar_ilan.asp

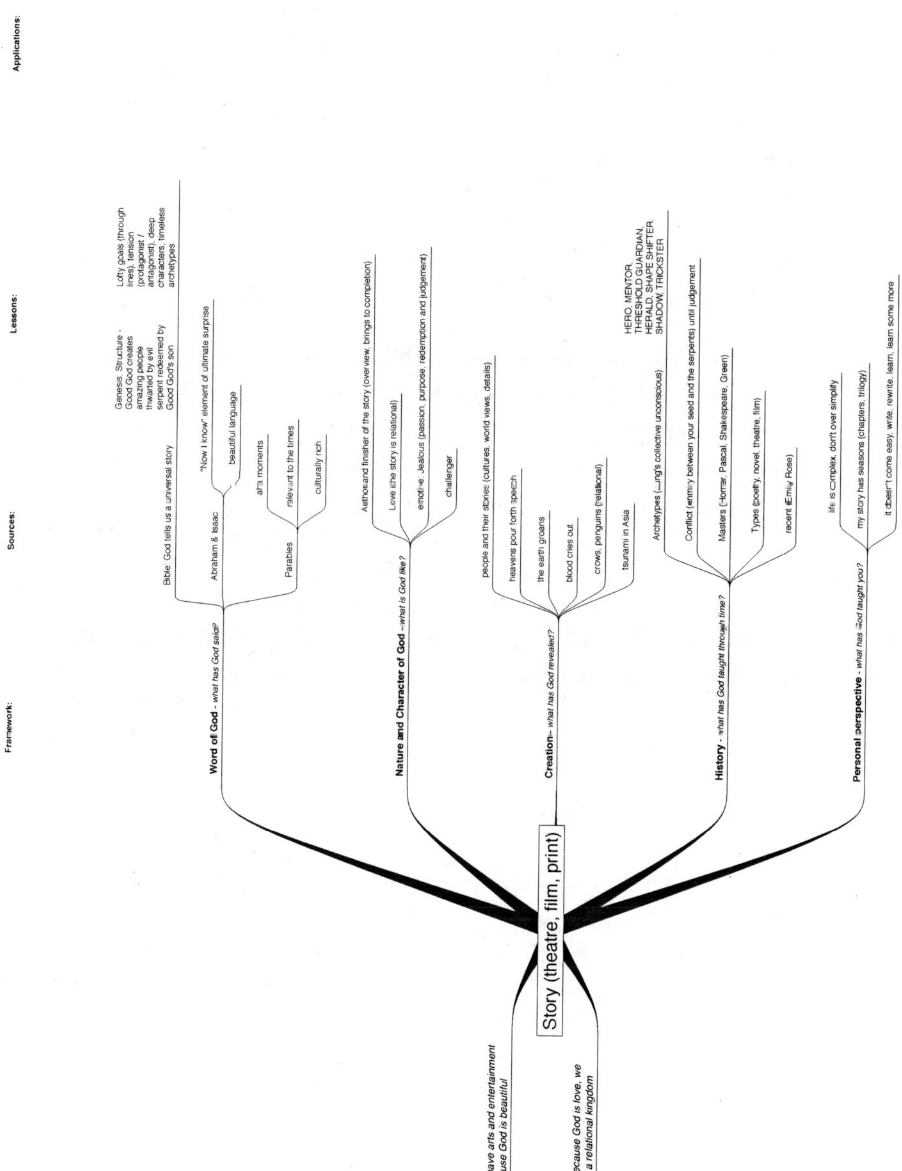
Framework:
Sources:
Lessons:
Applications:
Story (theatre, film, print)
We have arts and entertainment because God is beautiful
and because God is love, we live in a relational kingdom
Word of God - what has God said?
Bible: God tells us a universal story
Genesis: Structure - Good God creates amazing people thwarted by evil serpent redeemed by Good God's son
Lofty goals (through lines), tension (protagonist / antagonist), deep characters, timeless archetypes
Abraham & Isaac
"Now I know" element of ultimate surprise
beautiful language
Parables
aha moments
relevant to the times
culturally rich
Nature and Character of God - what is God like?
Author and finisher of the story (overview, brings to completion)
Love (the story is relational)
emotive: Jealous (passion, purpose, redemption and judgement)
challenger
Creation - what has God revealed?
people and their stories (cultures, world views, details)
heavens pour forth speech
the earth groans
blood cries out
crows, penguins (relational)
tsunami in Asia
History - what has God taught through time?
Archetypes (Jung's collective unconscious)
HERO, MENTOR, THRESHOLD GUARDIAN, HERALD, SHAPE SHIFTER, SHADOW, TRICKSTER
Conflict (enmity between your seed and the serpents) until judgement
Masters (Homer, Pascal, Shakespeare, Green)
Types (poetry, novel, theatre, film)
recent (Emily Rose)
Personal perspective - what has God taught you?
life is complex, don't over simplify
my story has seasons (chapters, trilogy)
it doesn't come easy, write, rewrite, learn, learn some more

You know, if you were to spend time and journal/apply even a small percentage of the stuff you would learn in doing this, you would be way ahead of the curve. Some of you would even change the world, because that's what happens when we tap into the ways of God. And also, there's no real competition for the anointing you would develop in applying His wisdom to your identity. There are not that many anointed story-tellers or engineers out there (in the sense of them tapping into the wisdom of God in their craft). You would be operating at a completely different level. I think one of the reasons we fear failure is that we compare ourselves to people who may be good at something. But imagine looking past that and to God as the model of interior design or medical research. It would blow the lid off the equation.

Recovery takes time. Building on the restoration I mentioned in the last chapter (which also takes time), you need to give yourself the space to become you again. If God designed our lives in a way that would take us around 20 years to get up to speed, you may need another 10 to get going again. Not 10 passive years of waiting to be told what to do, but 10 active years of developing identity, educating it, and sharing it with others. In that way, God can restore and recover what you've lost. But even better for you, you will know God in a way that will change your possibly stale relationship with Him, your world, and that of your children's children.

Chapter 16 • Free will

You make decisions every day and all of them are important. Every choice you make has a ripple effect on your friends, the community, and even future generations. Whether you make small choices like taking your bike or the bus, or larger ones like where to live or which job to work in, you're creating a unique set of circumstances that'll largely determine who you'll relate to (your future family?), the resources you'll have to work with, and a million other tiny but significant things that get set into motion. You may meet someone on that bus or run into someone else on that bike which could create a lifelong relationship. When you choose a place to study, you may be choosing a city which the next five generations of your family will call home. *Every decision* you make is important. And you're already making them pretty much on your own.

I mean, you may pray for wisdom or guidance every now and then, but for the most part, the everyday choices you're making are yours. Even if God gives you wisdom about the matter, the choice is still yours to make. And God wouldn't have it any other way. Even in times when God seems to be guiding more visibly, like when He chose David to be king, the decision has to be ratified by His people. (And, as discussed earlier, the few direct interventions of God in history – like the Red Sea parting – are rare and not examples of what we should expect or even want, since most of them were worst-case scenarios.) The whole idea of giving us free will was to allow us to be partners and fellow creators, to learn from the cause and effect of our choices, and to apply the wisdom He offers along the way so that we learn to *choose well.* The reason I'm stating the obvious is that we often talk about God's leading and guidance as "what God told us to do" here or there, but for the most part we're the ones making all the calls, and I just think we should own it. Let's stop saying God's in control of free parking places and who I just met at the cafe, and own the fact that *we create circumstances* because that's what free will is all about – the creative ability to bring together random people and opportunities and make something good of them. As I said before, we don't find our future, we create it.

If we own the fact that we choose, two good things can happen. First, we get to approach God from a better angle. Instead of asking Him for the parking place or the wife, we can ask Him about how to schedule our days[79] or learn God's ways in developing friendships. When you see yourself as a co-creator, you ask partner kinds of questions, and the wisdom of God starts flowing. When we don't own our decisions, we end up asking God all kinds of lame questions from a co-dependent world-view. The second benefit of owning our choices is that we can answer questions like why the innocent suffer or why, after so much praying, our friend still died. We can see the cause-and-effect relationship between what we do every day and how we affect the world around us (like how the consumption of meat and fuel among the relatively low populations of the West has a disastrous effect on the rest of the world).

If we own it, we can do something about it, with God's help of course. And if we own our choices in the simple things like nutrition and well being, we probably wouldn't have to pray for God's healing as much as we do. It's ironic that we think supernatural healing is more godly or special than a healthy life lived through the preventative wisdom of God (think seed-bearing plants and healthy relationships... = less stress = less disease). There may be things like MS or certain forms of cancer that we don't have any personal control over (as far as we currently know), but we still have a corporate responsibility to figure out the cause and effect of health in a fallen world. Research is just as godly as prayer.

At the end of the day though, we have to acknowledge that we make most if not all the important choices in our lives, and that these choices affect our health, relationships, economies, etc. There may be circumstances we can't control, like a car accident or unforeseen financial disaster, but even then, we have to see that it's our corporate choices that create most of these issues and not God. For instance, a person who's speeding still affects a person who's not. Or a greedy loan officer can affect a person who has worked hard and saved all of their life. These disasters are not the hand of God. Some may be the cause-and-effect "punishment" of God (as in, He allows these things to happen so we'll learn), but they were not initiated

79 Gordon McDonald wrote a fantastic book called *Ordering Your Private World*. In it he discusses, from a godly world-view, how to use your time and the seasons of your day wisely. Have a look.

by God any more than that parking place opening up right by the front entrance.

Choosing wisely

So if we are destined to choose, let's choose well. Let's identify the various choice architectures that affect us every day, and *understand* what we're doing. According to authors Cass Sunstein and Richard Thaler, "a choice architect has the responsibility for organizing the context in which people make decisions".[80] They're people we may never meet, but they've designed the ballots we're voting on or given our doctors various spins on the drugs we're being prescribed. They're the sound, color, and even scent designers in major retail outlets who're trying to influence our shopping habits. They're pastors, teachers (or *authors* :-) the ones who construct and present information in such a way that influences us to make "the best" choice. Sunstein and Thaler also point out that most choice architects are benevolent, but in any case you make choices every day which are affected by these presentations. Being able to see behind the curtain and being responsible for our own biases will help us improve on the everyday responses we make.

Choosing well means we own not only our everyday choices but also the fact that we've been given the farm and need to start taking better care of it. Free will is a beautiful thing, and while you may not be super happy about me leveling more responsibility on you (like for, say, the PLANET), you have to give God credit for the brilliance of His idea. Because free will and our taking responsibility for our lives/the planet is probably the wisest possible foundation for the relationship between a loving Creator and His children. The antithesis, as far as I can see, would have been to create a robotic people, pre-programmed to do the bidding of the programmer. Instead, God chooses the loving risk of giving us control, because that's the best way forward.

Daniel Pink, a career analyst and former vice-presidential speech writer, says that if you want compliance, the general command-and-control structures of management will do. But if you want creative thinking, you have to have:

80 *Nudge: Improving Decisions About Health, Wealth, and Happiness*, Yale University Press, 2008, page 3.

- *Autonomy (self direction)*
- *Purpose (ownership)*
- *Mastery (the ability to pull it off)*[81]

He goes on to cite a number of studies in which the typical incentive (carrot on a stick) approach actually had worse results than when people were empowered by autonomy. Mr. Pink mentions one experiment in which Karl Duncker gave two groups of people a box of thumbtacks, some matches, and a candle, with the task of attaching the candle to the wall. This problem literally requires some "out of the box" thinking, because one solution is to empty the box, tack it to the wall, and place the candle in it. Duncker found that the group that was rewarded for finding the solution took three times longer than the group that was simply timed. What Pink has discovered in this and other studies by Dan Ariely, the London School of Economics, and companies like Atlassian, is that incentives actually dull thinking and block creativity. We're not wired to be told what to do or be motived by rewards. We're creators, and you simply can't create without autonomy, purpose, and mastery.

Note: What I love about the developing fields of social science, neurology, and even career counseling is that slowly but surely, they're finding the ancient ways of God. What I don't like about most institutions of Christianity is that we're still stuck in the dark ages, waiting for Jesus to come back. But it's not just us. Pink also points out the mismatch between what science proves here and what businesses (who are still largely stuck on incentives) do to motivate people. Command and control is a human problem, not just a religious one.

I've found this to be true in my own life. When I became a Christian, my friends stuck me in a series of "missionary training" programs. I got all the apologetics and strategies. I could tell you how many people groups there were in the world and exactly how to reach them bla bla bla. What I noticed after a while was that, at least at that time, the predominant thinking around "strategic mission" was all coming from a white, Western, older male point of view. It was as though a bunch of accountants got together and decided how Christianity could spread around the world in order to bring Jesus back as soon as possible. What I also learned over time was that this was not going to work.

81 http://www.ted.com/speakers/daniel_pink.html

Fortunately – wait, that's a bad word, right? Um, okay, let's try... Happily, I had a number of really wonderful, diverse, and gifted people in my life who modeled something very different. They didn't see "the strategic mission", they saw communities and basic needs. They also saw that one very effective way to meet the basic needs of dynamic communities and their various cultures, was to approach them with our diversity. I was encouraged by these very cool people (ex-hippies I think) to start employment schemes for designers who were losing their jobs to emerging technologies. I was given resources to develop ad agencies and bless the community with a rare form of marketing: telling the truth about products and services. I was given a platform to develop university courses that trained people to line up their abilities with the ways of God in various fields of communication.[82] It was a blast because I got to follow through on my heart to serve God – but as myself. And because I was in an environment that encouraged autonomy and responsibility, I got to innovate with a group of people who couldn't live any other way.

Autonomy – (self direction)
God knows that for us to learn, make things, and serve the planet, we have to have a high degree of autonomy. Without this, we'd be the archetypal government worker; slow, unmotivated, and tied up in red tape. So He's designed our souls, minds, and bodies to think and work for themselves. It's a gift, not a curse. The curse isn't the freedom, it's the temptation to selfishly use our autonomy in destructive ways. As I've said many times, putting your ideas on the altar is throwing away the very thing God gave you. Throw the selfishness (or abuse of self) away instead. A healthy independence helps you know your part in working with God and others. In fact, the studies mentioned above have shown that people who are autonomous work best when they're co-creating together in a team of out-of-the-box thinkers. You can't be *us* without being your self.

There is an exception to this rule. In the candle experiment, researchers found that if they took the thumbtacks out of the box (therefore *simplifying* the task), the group with incentives actually did better than the timed group. So when a task is dead easy (like

82 Landa Cope was one of these wonderful people, and if you ever get a chance to read something she's written or attend a workshop she's giving, I suggest you take that opportunity. She's changed my life many times over.

when you think God is saying, "Go to China" or, "Be a teacher"), then the rewards-based methods work fine. So with basic mechanical tasks, we'd all be fine with a Santa in the Sky. But Dan Ariely found that whenever real cognitive issues were involved – i.e. "tasks that demanded attention, memory, concentration and creativity" – more reward equaled worse performance or, as Ariely puts it: "Dangling a very big carrot led to poorer performance."[83] In other words, the reward mechanisms actually overwhelmed the creative process and distracted the teams. So if this is true, why do we think a heaven (reward) or hell (punishment) approach is God's motivation for salvation? Why would the idea of getting God's "second best", which is a form of anti-incentive, be how God warns us? The simple answer is that we've been weaned under control structures that incentivize performance, which is just poor kingdom-of-God management practice, and just another reason I'm not big on religious leaders.

Incentives do motivate people, but for the wrong reasons, as these researchers found out. They tend to distract from the right motivations, like creativity for its own sake, or the reward of being in the flow. You can't pay for or force people to get into that space. Add a clear purpose driven by your passion and the mastery to fulfill what's on your heart, and you have a heart on fire. I'm convinced that God knows this and, therefore, has given us free will, autonomy, and an internal motivational system which responds more to creativity than anything else. It's the joy of being like our dad in heaven or, as it says in Nehemiah 8:10, "the joy of the Lord is your strength".

I think most people would take the job they love over the money to do something they hate. And I'm pretty sure this is you. You can't work for the man because it goes against the grain of your soul. This isn't rebellion, it's being a child of the Most High God. You think that kind of creativity and authority is supposed to be wasted on something cookie-cut? You're an ambassador, called out to be your unique self representing the God of the universe. There isn't enough money on the planet to pay what you're worth. So stop

---

83 http://www.wired.co.uk/wired-magazine/archive/2010/03/start/dan-ariely-bonuses-boost-activity,-but-not-quality.aspx
Dan Ariely is the James B. Duke Professor of Behavioral Economics at Duke University, North Carolina, and author of *Predictably Irrational*.

pursuing it. The money that you need will show up when you start creating some value, and that happens when you're running the shop.

Purpose

Free will was not meant to create an independent separation between us and God, it was meant to give us ownership, which creates a spirit of co-operation. In order to even want to co-operate though, we need an internal sense of purpose. And by the way, obedience and purpose are not synonymous. It was never God's idea to motivate us into action by giving us a string of commands to obey. This may work for a while, especially for the compliant or confused, but I've noticed that many people who got a general command to "Africa" or some project in a Romanian orphanage never stuck around or brought lasting change. When calling becomes a job (and a super-low or no-paying one at that), it loses a sense of purpose because it has shifted from an internal value to an external religious command.

I mentioned earlier that a lot of God's calls are *general expressions* of His heart or, as Oswald Chambers said: "The call of God is not a call to any particular service." His will for us to take care of widows and orphans or to eradicate poverty are general calls, because if He has to define the specific application as a command, it's no longer a family operation. Specific commands lead to missions by committee or whatever. Aside from the extraordinary call mentioned earlier, God doesn't call us to China, He calls us to the nations (or *ta ethne,* which is Greek for ethnic groups, families). He doesn't send us to South Africa, He shows us the value and power of reconciliation. As He expresses these values, concerns, and principles (like Jubilee), He hopes that something in our heart, our identity, and passion will respond with a creative solution. When we see the world from God's point of view and then tap into our creative potential, we discover purpose; a unique motivation that aligns our *self* to the known heart of God.

Anything less than this is not love, and love is the only thing that can bring change. We've seen hundreds of years of "strategic missions", where thousands of people obeyed a call that often came more from the institution than from the heart or the ways of God. The results aren't that pretty. There may be more people calling themselves Christians today than at any other time in history, but they're also killing Muslims in Nigeria or leading huge corporate scandals in the USA (like Enron). When you show up at the train station, tracks in hand, one of God's angels dies (or at least, their heart is broken). When you make any knee-jerk response to go door-to-door or across the world to "evangelize" because "that's what God wants", you disconnect your heart from the issue and things get strange really fast. But when you see the world and its needs from God's perspective, and you connect that with something inside of you (like your ability to build community, teach, or be an entrepreneur), the response you make will not only have the power of your unique self, it will have love at its core, and that's the most powerful, sustaining thing in the universe. You will bring lasting change when you're operating from a heart of purpose.

I think everyone really wants to live like this. Some feel they need permission, while others may feel they need more money or better circumstances. But to put the horse in front of the cart, having purpose creates open doors and resources. If you consider people who're determined, like the revolutionary school chef Ann Cooper, they create the environment for their purpose. This woman almost single-handedly changed the Berkeley School district's lunch program from a highly processed, diabetic-inducing diet of canned crap and microwave burritos to salad bars and fresh organic meals. She's a preacher chef, and she has a clear mandate which others have to take notice of. I think living with purpose is a God-given right, but you have to kick it into action for others to co-operate with.

In the absence of this kind of purpose, God may get you moving from time to time with a command or a reminder, but what He really wants is for you to share in His passion and world-view. He knows that if it's a "good *purpose* of *yours* or an act prompted by *your faith*" (II Thessalonians 1:11, my emphasis), then it's gonna stick. He's not looking for hirelings. Cold, sterile obedience leads to dull and ineffective programs. No matter how much some guy in the front drums up the idea, it's a program unless people's hearts, souls, minds, and strengths are engaged. God wants to empower people who love what they're doing, people with their *own* sense of purpose.

Designed to choose

As I've reiterated a number of times, free will is the foundation of God's co-operation with us. But the actual design and capacity of that will is astounding. When you look at our capacity to choose – our wiring – you see an intricate and complex gift which, when understood, becomes a powerful tool to love God and our neighbor. There's a neurology to our decisions that I don't have the ability to unpack but want to acknowledge, because this God-given combination of reason and emotion in our various cerebral cortices (anterior cingulate cortex, orbitofrontal cortex, and ventromedial prefrontal cortex) is the hardware behind all the "soft" choices floating around. Our brains are crunching all kinds of data to make choices based on what's advantageous, what's likely to fail, where the cool kids are... When we understand what the tendencies are in decision-making, we make better decisions. It's being self-aware in our will. Here's a quick audit of a few approaches to decision-making, just to show the range we're dealing with:

Heuristics, from the Greek for "find" or "discover", is a method of choosing or problem-solving which involves your experiences (educated guesses, intuition, rules of thumb) as a trial and error process. Basically, it's making choices based on past experiences, which becomes a way to trial the next choice.

Advantage listing, where you itemize the advantages and disadvantages of the option so you can weigh up your choices. This is a form of optimizing, which is cool, but it's usually stuck on optimizing just one option.

Alternatives mapping, where you look at all the possibilities and weigh up each one based on its highest utility. The formal term is Decision Analysis, which is a highly complex model for graphically mapping the utility of each choice. You may use this kind of logic for large projects (like designing a hospital) but not for choosing your wardrobe for the day. I mean you could, but you'd never leave the house...

Satisficing, where you accept the first option that may *satisfy* you. The lazy man's approach to decision-making.

Acquiescing, where you follow the "expert" opinion or people in authority on the assumption they know better than you.

Flipping, where you make decisions on random circumstances from flipping a coin, cutting a deck of cards or, the Christian version, "I saw her standing there, it must be God".

Incremental choosing, where you take a small step, assess, take a few more, keep assessing, and create an overall path based on this gradual build-up of choices.

Myers-Briggs, where you look at your "type indicators" and choose based on your personality strengths, such as *thinking* or *feeling*. In this way you may move away from logic-based choices to more intuitive or even emotional ones.

I wouldn't place a value on any of these ways of choosing. The idea is to show a small part of the dynamic range of the ways we decide. What I would encourage is to look at how you make decisions and see if it's lop-sided. Alternatively, is there a way you could extend your natural process in order to make more rounded, long-term-oriented choices?

Biases to watch out for:
This next short list (again, we're just scratching the surface here) is a set of biases we may have in making decisions. Have a look and see if you tend towards one of these, and why.

Selective evidence, where you choose the "facts" that support what you want and neglect other evidence which may support what you don't want to do. Also called "choice supportive bias", it's when we remember only what we want to, or distort those memories to form the image of the past that supports our next choice.

Choosing too fast, where you accept the first guy that says he likes you instead of giving it time to see what he's really like. This can also be a form of inertia, where you get stuck in a way of doing things and make knee-jerk decisions because you always have. Related to this is making choices based on the first thing we hear instead of looking around to see what other options exist.

Romanticism, where you make up facts or situations in your mind that create a reality or, rather, a fantasy you wish existed. Not bad in itself, as passion and dreaming are similar strands, but if this is based on a selfish intent or just plain psychosis, then it's an unhelpful bias.

Status quo, where you go with the flow in an effort to not be left alone. Out of fear then, you make choices that the crowd validates. Also called a herd mentality.

Wishful thinking, where you see things in such a positive or optimistic light that you disregard evidence that shows the downside. In relationships, this "uninformed optimism" usually constitutes the first few months. In the workplace, it can be imagining how great your new job is going to be until you actually meet your boss...

Repetition, where you go with the information most often repeated to you. So in advertising or church, for example, you hear the same thing said so many times that it becomes true, or more important than it really is.

Prejudice, where we reject evidence or advice from people we don't like for any reason, and then too readily accept advice from people we like or trust. This "credibility bias" isn't a bad thing unless we're accepting bad advice and rejecting the wisdom of those who actually have something worthwhile to say to us.

Role fulfillment, where you fulfill the role others expect you to play, and make choices according to what's expected of you.

Most of these terms and patterns have been deconstructed from observable behavior. You may tend towards one style or another. But if your decision-making process is half as complex as your identity, then we can't really peg you to one of these ways of choosing or to a certain bias. What we can acknowledge is that "fearfully and wonderfully made" means you've also been given a very diverse set of choice tools to exercise. But you may not feel that you have any control, and that this is just deep-down stuff that you simply *are.* I mean, it's hard enough to get people to the point where they realize they have a free will and are responsible to use it. Now we need to look at the way you use your will, and for a lot of people it's like going back to pre-school. Our choosing facilities have generally been so ignored, they feel dormant and rusty. Using your will is the most natural thing in the world, but using it well, as an adult, takes some effort.

For instance, if you lean towards the Myers-Briggs idea that we make decisions based on our cognitive style, say *judgment and perception*, then you may tend to make choices that don't have emotion attached to the consideration. That's fine if that's how you tick, but emotional intelligence experts would say that when emotion is disconnected from the decision-making process, we often lack sound judgment. So any one slant, or giving too much credence to one way of choosing, may not be healthy for us, especially if that slant has developed as a result of some dysfunction in our lives. And this is where it gets tricky. For instance, I can remind you that most of the decisions in your life are going to be your call, but how do you make those decisions if the very reason you deferred them (or have not been making them) was that you felt incapable in the first place?

This, too, is part of God's restorative work in us. In the same way that He's reviving our identity as the core to calling, I think He also wants to restore the function of our free will so that we start to exercise it properly. In the chronology of God, taking care of the garden (Genesis) depends on our using our will, just as judgment (Revelations) calls that use to account. So teaching us how to use our will wisely is part of God's plan to mature us. What I appreciate about His input though, is that He doesn't define four bi-polar dimensions (the MBTI's) or peg us to any of the styles above, but instead gives us principles to draw from so we can continue to learn by doing. By the way, I think that, as with identity, knowing as much as we can about choosing styles helps us broaden our views and applications. So while I do think simple algorithmic assessments like Myers-Briggs et al are limited in themselves, I know that the composite (putting various assessments together) will help us get a clue to the complexity of our creation.

Principles, not paths

Here are a few of the "choice principles" God's given us:

- *If it's a tough call, seek wise council (Proverbs 20:8 says, make plans by seeking advice)*

- *Make decisions that bless others instead of creating more problems (Romans 14:13 says don't make choices that create stumbling blocks for others)*
- *In conflict, decide/judge as family (1 Corinthians 6:1 says, don't take each other to court)*
- *Use common sense (1 Corinthians 10:15 says, assuming you're reasonable, decide for yourselves)*
- *Your judgment plus that of a couple of others equals wisdom (1 Corinthians 14:29 deals with judging whether God has spoken or not)*
- *Use your heart (2 Corinthians 9:7 says, when choosing to give, use emotional and rational judgment together)*
- *When it affects everyone, the people have to choose (Exodus 18:22 deals with the political decision-making process)*
- *Sometimes, God decides (1 Samuel 16:1 describes God choosing a leader, but notice that he doesn't become King until the people ratify him)*
- *Sometimes we choose simply to support the choice of others (1 Samuel 14:7 tells of when the armor bearer ties his choice to Jonathan's)*
- *Don't choose based on outward appearances (Isaiah 11:3-4 says, choose based on what's right and just)*
- *Try something and decide on the results (Daniel 1:13 says, trial and error is okay)*

Note: These are just a few principles drawn from the overall story God is teaching us, and I want to encourage you to find at least five more and write them below. What I've learned here is that the wisdom is in the story, or the principle, and we get to contextualize and customize it. Aside from the 10 commandments (or "how not to destroy each other") and some clear guidelines on preventative health or destroying poverty, there are very few places where God actually outlines how and what we should choose. The reason is found in the relationship (or "it is *the relationship, stupid"), which is how He coaches and we learn/discover. Outlining our choices for us would be a one-way relationship. And it's dumb, which God is not. Not dumb. Nope. Okay, so list five more principles from God about using your will and choosing wisely.*

Now imagine how cool it would be to combine our various decision styles according to the ways of God or the principles of God. I think we'd develop a broader, more holistic way to choose because, at the very least, we'd move past our simple approaches and be a little more circumspect. We'd stop being so WWJD and start looking at the complex set of circumstances we're juggling and turn them into art. We'd stop being reason only, or choosing based on feelings all the time, and round ourselves out a bit. It's gonna take time though, and a lot of trial and error, but the end result will be wisdom, which I once heard described as *the loving application of knowledge.* And to God, the process would be well worth it because wisdom and maturity is what He's been developing in us all along.

Finally, the act of owning your free will and refining your ability to choose moves you from the oppression of living from the *outside in* to the freedom of living *inside out.* You get to define the priorities of how you'll work, whom you'll relate to, and what your home will look like. You may already be doing this, perhaps in a half-hearted way, but as a son or daughter of God you need to start kicking up some action that better defines your identity, priorities, and how you'll love your neighbor as yourself. If you don't define the way you want to live, someone else will. I'm hoping you're kinda tired of that.

Chapter 17 • Collaboration

I've spent a lot of time talking about your identity, your free will, and the calling to basically be yourself. I know this sounds like swinging away from inter-dependence with God and the body of Christ, but, at the risk of being repetitive, I believe you have to know, love, and understand your self in order to have something you can share with others. And I don't think God's nervous about you going on this journey of discovery. Having said that, I think the process needs to be shared with others in a collaborative way. In fact, I'm pretty sure you can't develop your self by yourself.

I think most of us have a go at developing who we are in our families, schools or churches, but mostly we end up conforming more than anything else. When we catch ourselves doing that, we usually make one of two responses. Some of us move into the center of the group and become like everyone else, losing our self and soul in the process. Others drift away or reject the status quo and end up pretty much alone. Going back to that developmental problem I mentioned with our dads not being present, I think most of us really don't know how to collaborate because we never learned to make that transition from child to adult. So our efforts to break in or break free are usually kind of stilted and awkward.

If we're allowing God to re-parent us though, we can address this by figuring out how to share our process of growth and change with the right people in the right way. Under the care of a loving father, we'd learn how to move towards people who understand us, challenge us, and facilitate us. We'd also learn to not waste our time on people or situations that aren't working our strengths. In essence, we need to learn to move towards what Sir Ken Robinson calls our *tribe,* "connecting with other people who share [our] passion and a desire to make the most of themselves".[84] Robinson describes how, despite her extreme shyness, Meg Ryan discovered her ability to act by getting involved with actors who loved their craft, and how Gillian Lynne (choreographer for *CATS* and *The Phantom of the Opera*) discovered her ability to dance by going to a dance school at

84 *The Element: How Finding Your Passion Changes Everything,* Viking Adult, 2009, page 103.

a young age. Moving towards your tribe unlocks something in you, something both natural and powerful.

Robinson maintains that there are two elements to a tribe. One is the *domain* of the tribe, which is "the sorts of activities and disciplines that people are engaged in – acting, music, business, ballet, physics, rap, architecture...".[85] The other is the *field* of the tribe, which refers to the kind of people engaged in the domain, like actors, scientists, musicians... When we get close to these domains, we light up. When we spend time with people in our field, we grow and develop key elements within our identity. In this way, we really unfold as a person, because we're part of the tribe that best suits that unfolding. Finding your tribe is essential to understanding your calling and making the incremental choices that develop that calling into a full-blown life.

Who's in your tribe?

From my experience, I've learned that the domain of my tribe is found in my identity. Meaning, we pursue tribes that are doing *what we are* as people. I'm a trainer, cook, father, and communicator. So I pursued tribes and activities that suited my identity. We'll talk more about this in another chapter (and another book). But I've also learned that I need to pursue or connect with different members of the tribe, because each type of member has a helpful role in the unfolding of my part and of the domain altogether. Here's what I've found:

- *Passionate early adopters.* These are the first people to try something out. They're the first ones with an 8-mm camera making short films, or the ones ripping new sounds with a busted, cheap guitar they bought at a garage sale. They aren't looking for recognition or acceptance, they just can't help being themselves. These people are collaborators at the grass roots, and they're happy to figure it out as they go – and they're happy to have others like them along for the ride. People like Jack White (of White Stripes) who pushed the bed out of his teenage bedroom so he could make room for another set of drums (he already had one in there). They're looking for something, a sound or a look or a better mouse trap. You know when you've found them because you're looking for that something too.

85 Ibid., page 111.

- *Obsessed craftsmen.* These people are the ones who've put in their 10,000 hours (or close enough) to master the thing they're passionate about. They've learned how to take what was once an interest and make it into a beautiful skill. These people help you see the long road you've started upon and what it will take to walk the distance. Like Dr. Paul Brand, who pioneered leprosy treatments and reconstruction surgery techniques. He worked for years unpacking a theology of health care based on the similarity between *shalom* and homeostasis (all the cells of our body in harmony and following a single rule of health). He dug so deep into his science and into God that he developed new pathologies in leprosy, based on God's wisdom *in* creation. He then trained many others in the craft that he so passionately and faithfully developed. We need to find people like this that help us see the really big picture, how much work is involved, and what we're capable of.

- *Mentors.* I've found that we don't need one "all-knowing" person in our lives That usually leads to a kind of monotone advice. What we need is a diverse set of people who can help in the following roles. By the way, our mothers and fathers, God, and other key figures can help us get started, so maybe these are the people we should be looking for first? Anyway, Robinson defines four roles for mentors that I totally agree with, and they are:

A. *They define the difference between an interest and a passionate ability.*

B. *They encourage that ability (give it heart).*

C. *They facilitate our forward movement, which also means they allow us to falter and learn by doing and failing.*

D. *They stretch us and push us past our limits.*

Sometimes mentors find us, but mostly we need to find them. The trick is to not wait around. If you don't have people like this in your life, call it out of those around you or go looking for it in a new place. Mentors usually don't have time for us, and we need to make them see why we're worth their precious hours.

- *Friends.* All through the process of developing our tribe, we need the friends who'll be with us come hell or high water. People who will love and be loved by us regardless of how our calling or gifting is developing. They may be collaborators in our revolution, or just willing to make lunch, but true friends are an invaluable part of our tribe. Having said that, be careful not to get stuck with a group of friends where all you're doing is making lunch and nothing else. I've said many times that this generation of people hangs out like an olympic sport – you guys have it down. What you typically don't do well is take that friendship to deeper levels of activity or challenge so you actually go somewhere together.

The tribe's Chief

We just looked at the people side of collaboration. The God side is kind of similar in that you want to move towards God, particularly towards aspects of His nature and character that align with your strengths. There will be plenty of times when you have to change diapers, wash dishes, and clean toilets, but in the main, you want to serve God with your strengths. Plus, there's way too much to know about God anyway, so you might as well focus on the parts that align with what's natural to you. One way we do this is by studying and meditating on those five questions I mentioned earlier, where you take your interest in graphic design and ask what God's nature is like in this area, what the scriptures say about it, what creation reveals, what you can learn from history, and what your personal perspectives are. In developing a theology of your domain, you're specifically inviting God and His ways into the tribe and your activities.

Matthew Sleeth did this as an emergency doctor-cum-health environmentalist. At first he couldn't stand the sight of blood, but he knew he was a healer, or health care something... During his years in the emergency room, he kept noticing the increased rates of diseases, like certain kinds of cancer. After doing some research he found that huge amounts of carcinogenic substances (like Red Dye No. 4) were being dumped into diesel fuels in his area. He quit his job, sold his house, moved into a new one the size of his previous garage, and became an environmentalist for Jesus. He now lives a healthier life and practices health care by teaching people (mostly Christians who still think the world's gonna burn soon) how to take care of their health and the environment. Over time, Matthew Sleeth found his tribe and calling by moving towards his passion and his people. He then took that agenda to God and learned creation management from the Master.[86]

So, yeah

It's not good to be alone. And it's a bit of a paradox because, in one sense, we need to have the space to develop our selves – alone. We need to know what we have to share, or what our part in the tribe actually is. But the only way to do that well is to manage the tension between being "us" and being "you". Your personality may lead towards being more introverted or extroverted, so you'll have to manage that. You may be the eccentric poet who can express heavenly thoughts but can't have a decent conversation over lunch, so you'll have to work on that too. You may be all about people but never take the time or effort to develop your own craft (...master of none), and yes, you'll have to work on that.

God looked down on His creation and said it was good, but then quickly noticed that it was not good for us to develop in a vacuum. The answer to this need started out in relationship (Genesis 2) and built towards making cities (Revelations). Collaboration is thus best built on a relational foundation that makes great stuff. As you get more clarity on your own calling, make sure you draw a crowd.

86 Check out Sleeth's book *Serve God, Save the Planet*. It's saved us all kinds of money while it also taught us about creation management.

Chapter 18 •
Putting it all together

I hope you're now at the point where you've taken the car keys in hand and are ready to drive. God's provided the car (your life) and given you a road map (His general will), but you definitely need to head out on a road trip. The adventure is to create meaning and blessing for you, your neighbor, and the nations. As you get ready to take this journey, I'd like to offer some gear to help you along the way.

I'm going to give a broad outline of what I've seen on my own trip, and some tools to equip you for yours. In some areas, we'll look back at the ground we've covered, but only to highlight what's available for you to move forward. The following scriptures, Harvard recommendations, books, and decision-making maps are all ideas that you can customize, take, or leave. At the end of the day, if we've done our job in clearing the confusion about calling, then the rest should come pretty naturally. I'm not trying to be too prescriptive here, as in, "these are the things you must do to build on your calling...", because I know that all you really need is already in your heart. Instead, this will be some recommendations that you can slot into your own path, which I'm okay about sharing, because we both know it's your life and ultimately your responsibility.

Note: By the way, if you are still stuck in fear or laziness, then you may need more time with God or in counseling to work on past issues or things that may be anchoring you to the couch. But even still, making small choices with the tools below may be a healthy part of the process to get some action started, which can then encourage you to start taking bigger risks.

First: The horizon

I've found that in knowing the bigger picture of both God's heart and what I'm capable of over the span of my life, I've been helped in making the micro decisions it takes to reach that potential. So despite my hippie-self-promoting-independent-sounding approach in this book, I'm actually 100% dedicated to God and His ways.

And I base my life's goals and decisions on fulfilling His heart and applying His wisdom to my steps. Knowing what that big picture is, from His perspective, has given direction and meaning to the application of my identity and abilities. Knowing my Father gives me direction as a son, but the direction is still general and full of opportunity for customization. Here's the big picture from my driver's seat:

Domain: God has given us charge over the earth (Genesis 1 and 2). I therefore look at all the resources available to help me take up my small but significant part in managing the world I've been given. I read five news sources every day to keep my eye on the garden.[87] I read and apply books on organic living (like Matthew Sleeth's *Serve God, Save the Planet*), and I study the scriptures and other teachings on God's broader call to manage the earth. For instance, if you read the Bible for 15 minutes each day (I listen to it on biblegateway.com) over the years, you'll have gone through the whole thing multiple times, which gives you a much better overview. There's also an unprecedented number of really good podcasts and teachings available online to broaden your horizons, like Greg Boyd's mind-and and-soul-stretching stuff on why we're here (www.gregboyd.org). Basically, I make it my business to see the long view so I can make choices each day that facilitate my calling.

Family and community: All of God's big ideas focus around our extended family, which of course includes our neighbors. When we're working on restoring or building our own complex families, we're doing God's will. Knowing that He wants to restore our hearts to our fathers, and vice versa, gives me a road map for my activities in my own family, which I then extrapolate into my community. For instance, a distributed network of Christians in Portland calling themselves Imago Dei (www.imagodeicommunity.com) have a fantastic ministry to kids without dads in their community. They combine the artistry of their crew with the real needs in the neighborhood and come up with relevant ministries. Look around your own area and see who's doing solid stuff at this level, and bring your own unique gifting as a designer, carpenter, salesperson... to

87 I suggest you pick five or six things to track your own interests and region. Mine are the BBC's International News site, my local news (*The NZ Herald*), WIRED News, *The Huffington Post*, Google Flip (an amazing combination of 30 or more news sites in one window), and Macintouch (a Mac technology site, 'cause Macs rule, PCs drool).

the need. Sometimes this will be a local church, but more likely than not it will be a few randoms working under the radar, like The Global Cafe in Auckland (www.zeal.org.nz), who run a music studio and event location to get kids off the street and into their creativity. You could do that. Or at a larger scale, you may want to pursue a course on counseling or social work, or develop a family business. These kinds of "ministries" take years to develop, and the time is well worth it. They also translate into the nations. If we're working on the systemic problems in our families and neighborhoods, then we can safely assume that people in Tokyo or Cape Town are working through the same stuff. As we learn about and work on these home-based issues, we're being prepared to minister to the whole world, a world of families and neighborhoods.

Reconciling all things: On top of the first two foundations, God's general call throws out this huge opportunity to share the ministry of Jesus, which is the reconciliation of all things (Colossians 1:20). The big-picture calling of God includes everything. Reconciling marketing practices, city planning, game design, health care simulation techniques... the rabbit hole goes down into every detail of life. This means everyone has a ministry, but none of them necessarily looks like "ministry" in the stereotypical sense. They're living expressions of God's detailed wisdom, walked out through your unique identity in every aspect of life on the planet. Like the guys at the XXX Church who go to porn conventions and film sets to reconcile that area of life by loving and challenging actors, directors, and retailers. Or my Christian friend who helped rewrite the constitution of the Faeroe Islands from a godly world-view. All areas of life, and every detail, so that, as Tom Marshall used to tell me, "we're saving souls and structures" (from office life to constitutional law).

What I've found helpful in getting my head around the biblical mandate for these areas is to find seminal works that show the systemic principles of God in the domain I want to understand. For instance, Jim Wallace has written along these lines in the area of politics in *God's Politics.* John Templeton has created a forum for godly application in the sciences through the Templeton Foundation (www.templeton.org). Dennis Peacocke wrote a great foundational piece on business in *Doing Business God's Way.* Francis Schaeffer and Hans Rookmaaker have revealed some freeing perspectives on the arts, especially in Rookmaaker's *The Creative Gift.* These books and resources unfold what the Bible calls the "ancient paths", the eternally proven ways of God. They're not prescriptive in the sense that they tell you how to do business. Instead, they cover the foundations of business (like the rule of law, ownership, the place of profit...) so you can build your own application on top of them. Find resources that help you see the deeper wisdom of God at the root level, and customize it from there. If we do our job right, the generations after us should be able to stand on our shoulders to see even further.

Second: Finding or creating your place
There are a lot of boxes out there waiting for you to fit into. The industrial revolution may have given us a cheaper (and crappier) pair of shoes, but it set our personal development back in a huge way by creating systems of conformity such as the standardization of education, work and, by extension, the family and community. We are still reeling from this effect, as is clear in the domination of standardized testing in schools (the biggest mistake since microwave burritos) and hard-wired work hours that control and degrade family life. But again, not on our watch, dammit! Right? We are going to judge angels one day and until then we're meant to rule the earth, so it's time to break out of the boxes waiting for you at the end of college and start creating your own dang job descriptions. And along the way, you might as well create your own curriculum to get you there. It all starts with knowing your:

Identity: Before I get into a list of resources available in this field, I want to say I'm not happy with most of them. It seems to me they all have a bit of that industrial revolution anchor attached. The *Strength Finders* book is really good overall, but still tends towards applications or job descriptions. This is less true with Myers-Briggs testing, but it still gives the impression that if A is true, then your job is B... My sense is that these tools should show different facets to the diamond that is your identity, and from those perspectives you can create a new thing in the world. Like a new way to teach based on dynamic intelligences, or a better computer interface based on eye gestures, or anything that synthesizes all the various elements of your ingenuity or genius. This is why my next book will try to tackle a view of identity that looks beyond outcomes and into possibilities. But again, this is not essential for you to move forward today because I think that the hard work and perspectives offered by the resources below are a great start to a process that, as long as you are creative with it, will meet the needs of your forward movement.

Rick Warren made a great start with *The Purpose Driven Life.* It deals with the fundamentals of the call of God, namely that we are unique and have a calling to be our unique self. I also like that it's not prescriptive, and that it leaves the detailed application to you. I would suggest reading the original *Strength Finders,* and take a Myers-Briggs test or even the FaceBook application called *MyType.* My wife and some friends have found the Enneagram a helpful way to articulate the core motivations and fears that form and drive personality types. Check it out and see if it's helpful for you (www.enneagraminstitute.com/intro.asp). There's another approach which Heather and I have found really helpful called *SIMA* or System for Identifying Motivational Abilities (www.sima.co.uk/Approach/ourapproach.html). What I like about this analysis is that they ask you to tell 16 different stories of your life's successes, or fulfilling things you've done. Things that you felt were achievements and why. From those stories they identify what motivates you and what circumstances, people or resources were involved in that success. Just going through the stories helps you see the threads of your own life, or the memories that mean something to you and why. This is the language that starts to reveal your soul, or at least what's important to it. Which is why I say, the more the merrier. I would look at all of these approaches and develop your own journal or identity map, so you can get in touch with your diversity instead of being pegged to a few strengths, identity types or job descriptions.

As I mentioned earlier, one of the things you're trying to establish in your unfolding identity is the difference between what Robinson distinguishes as "ability" and "interest". You may be interested in music, but are you a musician, producer, roady or avid fan? As you look at the details of your identity, you can start to experiment with these aspects to put the question to a practical test. If you can't play, maybe you can write lyrics. Or if you can play, are you a composer, a studio musician or a producer? The more you know about your identity, the deeper you can go down that path to find your niche. This will unfold over time as you try different angles, an approach that may prevent you from getting stuck on someone else's view of what a musician is or comparing yourself with how someone else does music. Mentors can also help you figure out the difference, so when you have a field or domain you want to pursue, get some feedback from someone who's been there, done that.

Intellect: As you look at the more nuanced levels of your identity, you need to unpack and validate your dynamic intellect. You have intellectual strengths and weaknesses. Knowing your strengths helps deal with the stigma of your "weaknesses". For instance, knowing that my intelligence strengths are interpersonal, spacial, and lingual helps me to not feel stupid for not being math/logical. You're smart and you just need to know how. Have a look at Harvard Professor Howard Gardner's *Frames of Mind* or do one of his multiple intelligence assessments online (here's one, but look around a bit if it doesn't suit you: literacyworks.org/mi/assessment/findyourstrengths.html). Take some time to understand your learning styles as well, because as life-long learners, we need to absorb knowledge and practice that knowledge in a way that plays to our auditory, visual or kinesthetic strengths. This will help you love the things you're learning instead of cringing every time the word "education" crosses your path.

Passion and imagination: Many of us have lost or forgotten our passions. Our imaginations go dormant over time with the loss of this capacity. The result is that we're left to feed off the passion of others, which in the end creates formulaic film and music and the dull amusements of dead people (as in the case of Q. Tarantino. Mind you, his last film was pretty stinking good. I hate it when people I don't like do amazing things; it becomes so hard to judge them in the future...). One way to kick-start that power station of passion is to get inspired again. You may have only a slight clue or memory about what you loved as a child or what moves you to dream. There may be a few people around who inspire you and thus breathe a little onto the embers of your soul. So start there. Take those few clues and follow the trail by going out and getting inspired through whatever means you have available. It may be re-establishing creative foundations through galleries, theaters or science museums. It may be reading the histories or biographies of entrepreneurs like The Body Shop's Anita Roddick or Virgin's Richard Branson. At 16 my son Jordan got on a bus each day and went to Borders to read about the passion, work, and methods of Kubrick and Scorsese in order to understand more about directing film. Anything that reminds you about your passions will give those passions a chance to reconnect with your identity. Passion is like a match; it doesn't take much to re-ignite. You just have to validate that thing you may have discounted because there wasn't any money in it or because you listened to early rejections. If you give your heart the authority to be itself, you will get that passion back in action. And you'll need it in order to discover your tribe and get through all the blockades you'll face in being yourself.

Passion is the precursor to developing talent. Passion weeds out mere interests and forces us to develop what our souls know we're capable of. It connects our dreams and imaginations to the "I am" statements of our identity, creating a sort of fusion of all the facets of the soul, which is where I think true creativity comes from. I can't stress enough how important recovering your passions are, because without them, you can't develop the unique calling you have, especially in a fallen world of people who don't really care enough to help you. In fact, most of the stories of incredible achievements I've mentioned so far are of people who had an uphill battle to achieve those things. Passion was the thing that often kept them going. When Bono was starting out in U2, some of his Christian friends told him to let it go, because "that kind of music" wasn't of God. Good thing he went with his passions instead, eh? Your talent will emerge and be refined as you let your passion push you to try, fail, and learn. Your tribe can help you with the development of your talent(s), but the fastest way for that to happen is to follow the lead of your passions, because they already know where you're going.

Intuition: Related to this is the development of your intuition. I haven't got much to say here because I'm really quite the novice in this area. I'm only beginning to listen closer to my own intuition and I'm learning a lot from people who do it consistently. There's a great TED talk by Elizabeth Gilbert (www.ted.com/talks/elizabeth_gilbert_on_genius.html), where she speaks about inspiration and intuition. Writers like her (she authored *Eat, Pray, Love*) are often challenged to come up with a string of successes, which is impossible to do. In her presentation she talks about being available for the genius to visit you, and maintains that your part is to simply clock in and do what you can. I've learned that a similar thing applies in any creative practice; you have to start the process, even when uninspired and empty, but once you get going, you start to get closer to the place where your intuition kicks in and you can hear it clearly because you're sitting there concentrating. Maybe it's just harder for me as a guy, but in any case, I think identifying and listening to intuition is an essential part of developing our real strength and voice.

Story-telling: One of the tools I've found really helpful in projecting my identity (or calling) into the future is story-telling. Story-telling allows us to get perspective on what we can create in the long term instead of always being limited to just seeing three to six months ahead. A more scientific term would be "scenario planning". A lot of companies like Shell and BP have done this for years (check out www.netmba.com/strategy/scenario/). Basically, you tell a story of a possible or plausible future based on your identity, goals, and dreams. It can be an outline or a short story, but the point is to use your imagination and what you know about your identity to create the lifestyle you want to see happen in 10 or 15 years. It's not just the job you want to have either, but the life you want to live, which includes your work, education, environment, relationships, and creativity. The story describes a month or year in the the future, where you let time tease out all the various aspects you want to develop. You're not predicting the future, you're creating it from what you can possibly do. I carry a story like this in my wallet, and it helps me in a number of ways. First, it gives me a sense of direction and priority so I can say "yes" to some things and "no" to others. Secondly, it gives me something to commit to God so He can establish my ways (Psalm 37:5). Thirdly, I'm always amazed at how much I actually accomplish simply because I've planned to or projected myself into situations that I can actually achieve.

The story can be quite simple or detailed, but speaking out what you want to happen has an amazing creative power, which God modeled by speaking us into existence. And I guess this is the point; we are called to be like our Father in heaven who's always speaking out what He hopes will happen and then puts effort into making it so. I think that, in a micro kind of way, we get to do the same thing. And just so you don't freak out thinking I'm getting all New Age on you, I want to point out that the simple power of speaking out a goal and pursuing it is activated by making choices that will put your energy to work on what you just said. It's really that simple, and godly.

Third: Finding your tribe

I think one of the casualties of our laziness has been our ability to ask, seek, and knock. We've become very mystical (in a bad way) in our approach to getting into the right situations or finding the right people in our lives. We have this vague sense that God will just bring along the right people at the right time, like a puppet-master. Knowing now that that's not gonna happen, you have to switch gear in your thinking so that you start co-operating with God on the matter of relationships and collaboration. Especially when it comes to the difficult task of finding people who will inspire and help you move forward.

Research: It's hard to move out of a status-quo group into a network of people with similar passions, but it's not impossible. The key is to learn how to research. Once you stop praying for which college to go to, you can use that time to get online and on the phone to find out what you're looking for. Start by identifying what your tribe looks like or what your hopes are in connecting with the right school or group of people. If you know what it looks like, you'll know when you see it. It's part of living from the inside out – you define what the domain is and who's working in their fields, and then you pursue them. This will help you refine your queries as you check out education programs, or know what you're listening for in a conversation. You may already know that you want to work with people on a film set or in a medical environment, so researching internships for those domains and meeting with people working in the field might be your next step.

Learn to go deeper in your questions as you pursue opportunities. For instance, don't take a college home page at face value. Ask for a syllabus that goes into detail about what you'd be learning. Get on discussion boards to hear from people who have worked in a job you're interested in. People waste a lot of time by jumping into something they hope the degree might offer, only to find they've wasted two years learning that it's not really for them. The same goes for work. A lot of people spend three or four years training to be a teacher, only to get into a classroom and find they don't work well in structured, overly controlled environments. Go onto job sites like Monster.com and look at job descriptions for the kinds of work you'd like to do. A good job description always lists "I am" statements in the form of "we're looking for people who **are**...". See if you identify with the kinds of character or personality traits the job requires. For instance, some roles require a competitive spirit, while others require a quiet researcher.

Also, move past the general idea of the domain you want to work in and define how *you* want it to look in your best-case scenario. For instance, you may want to teach but don't like how it's done today. Fine. Make it better by committing to a 25-year process in which you're helping to define educational standards and practices. Somebody's got to do it, right? Talk to people who are closest to the way of learning or working that you want to pursue, and ask for the inside story. For instance, if you want to act, join a local acting or theater group, read biographies, watch *Inside the Actors Studio* or ask a friend of a friend to get you a lunch date with someone in the profession so you can find out first-hand what it's really like. The idea is to dig deep both in defining what you really are looking for in a tribe and finding out where they are at, what they're really doing, and what it's like for them. From this base and with God alongside, you'll be in a position to start redeeming or improving that domain.

Experimentation: Following the line of research, you may find that you haven't really been able to define your tribe outside of generic terms like "dancers" or "entrepreneurs". For instance, you may have mapped out 20 or 30 things about yourself, but you're struggling to see how you could fuse some of these elements together and therefore don't know who you really want to work with. In this case, the next step would be to experiment by trying a number of tribes in conjunction with your identity-mapping process.

William Fitzsimmons, the Dean of Admissions at Harvard, has some advice for you. He's noticed that a number of people have been programed from an early age to enter into universities such as Harvard without an opportunity to develop a context for their studies. Context like who they are, why they should be there, what the big questions are that they're asking; context that would make the education worthwhile. Most students are on a treadmill of achievement, racing into and struggling through the program with little real vision as to their distinct place or goals. The results are managers, lawyers or doctors who often "ended up in their profession because of someone else's expectations, or [...] they simply drifted into it without pausing to think whether they really loved their work".[88] Fitzsimmons and other colleagues suggest taking some "time off" or postponing admission for a year to gain a context for education, which would also help you to refine your choice of location or decide if you needed a university at all:

> Perhaps the best way of all to get the full benefit of a "time-off" is to postpone entrance to college for a year. For over thirty years, Harvard has recommended this option, indeed proposing it in the letter of admission. Normally a total of about fifty to seventy students defer college until the next year. The results have been uniformly positive. Harvard's daily student newspaper, The Crimson, reported (5/19/2000) that students who had taken a year off found the experience "...so valuable that they would advise all Harvard students to consider it." Harvard's overall graduation rate of 98% is among the highest in the nation, perhaps in part because so many students take time off. One student, noting that the majority of her friends will simply spend eight consecutive terms at Harvard, "wondered if they ever get the chance to catch their breath."
>
> During her year off, the student quoted above toured South America with an ice-skating company and later took a trip to Russia. Another interviewed in the article worked with a growing e-commerce company (in which the staff grew from ten to a hundred during the year) and backpacked around Europe for six months.
>
> Some Options for the Interim Year Members of one recent class participated in the following activities: drama, figure skating, health-care, archeological exploration, kibbutz life, language study, mineralogical research, missionary work, music, non-profit groups, child welfare programs, political campaigns, rebuilding schools, special needs volunteering, sports, steel drumming, storytelling, swing dance, university courses, and writing – to name some chosen at random.

88 *Time Out or Burn Out for the Next Generation*, posted on the admissions website for Harvard University.

> Many students divide their year into several segments of work, travel, or study. Not all can afford to travel or to take part in exotic activities. A number have served in the military or other national service programs. Some remain at home, working, taking part-time courses, interning, and still finding the time to read books they have never had time to fit into their schedules or begin to write the "great American novel." Others have been able to forge closer ties with parents or grandparents from whom they may have drifted away during the hectic pace of the high-school years.[89]

The main benefit of this time off is that it's intentional. Experimental is not flippant or random; you're meant to be looking for something, and when you have a general idea of the tribe you're seeking, this time off becomes the first step in finding them.

Creating opportunities: Ken Robinson adds to this idea by clarifying another aspect of finding our tribe. On top of the *aptitude* and *passion* we described earlier in the identity section, he points out that moving towards your tribe has the intentional elements of *attitude* ("I want it") and *opportunity* ("where is it"):

> Without the right opportunities, you may never know what your aptitudes are or how far they might take you [...]. Aptitudes don't necessarily become obvious unless there are opportunities to use them [...], opportunities we create [...]. Being in your Element often means being connected with other people who share the same passions and have a common sense of commitment. In practice, this means **actively seeking opportunities** to explore your aptitude in different fields.[90]

Tribes don't generally move towards you, you have to find them, like in running away to join the circus. I mean, don't run away or anything, but if you are not presented with opportunities to test your skills or identity, then create something. I mentioned before that, as a generation, you have more expendable time and money than any generation in history. So, put it to work. And drag your friends along with you by starting a small theater production com-

89 Ibid., page 4.

90 *The Element: How Finding Your Passion Changes Everything*, Viking Adult, 2009, page 25 (my emphasis).

pany or an organic cereal company or whatever suits your aptitude. Because while tribes don't naturally move towards you, people who want to be part of *your tribe* will seek you out once you have something for them to connect with.

Mentors – dead or alive: A key part of our tribe is mentors. They're not present most of the time, and they don't need to be. They're not the chiefs; you are. They're the consultants (eewww, there's a naughty word) or advisors, shamans and wizards who help us see into the realms that exist outside of our own experience. My suggestion is to find the best (meaning, what you think the best is) people in your field and hound them to be part of your life. If you want to carve new skateboard designs, find the guy who invented them or the person doing the most cutting-edge stuff with petrified timbers... If you want to develop a new vaccine for malaria, find the people at the forefront of that craft. Some people you need to learn from are dead, so become a good researcher and avid fan of their history and learn everything you can from them. Then find the ones who are alive and be like the prophet Elisha to them, remembering that really good mentors don't want you bothering them, so you gotta prove you're worth their time.

Move around or stay home: There are advantages to taking some time off and getting out of your comfort zone. For some of you, this will be a must and you already know it. Just be careful not to run away from issues and use your tribal search as an excuse to argue with your dad. I hate it when my kids do that. Some of you need to stay home and make something serious out of the opportunities you already have in Berlin or Nashville, because leaving would just be moving your baggage elsewhere. The tip here is that this question – "should I try elsewhere?" – is an issue of the heart. Only you really know if it's the right thing to do and, if so, when. It may be that you need to deal with some relational issues and then go to Jamaica to practice that cool steel drum you invented – or are about to. In any case, if you do need to move out to find the tribe, make sure you eventually put down some roots, as in getting married or buying a home. Only a few people I know are truly internationals, always on the move from place to place. Most of us are locals and work best when we're connected to a group of people in a place we can all make into a home. If you perpetually move around looking for something, you may never establish anything.

Fourth: Decide already!

One way or another we have to break the inertia of inactivity or the wrong activity. It will hurt, it will be hard, people may not understand and make it even harder, but it has to happen. You will not make perfect choices, but any choice or forward movement in your life will create a context to figure out the next part.

Start with what you know: You already know a lot about yourself and what you'd like to do. In fact, I'm pretty sure you've known for a long time but have been either too lazy or afraid (or, like me, too poor) to act. None of these are good excuses and now we both know it. Even if you only know a little about the bass guitar or your desire to be a chef, you have to make choices to start the process. Even if all you can do today is read, then start reading. If all you can do is earn a bit of money to buy the gear you need, then start working at something you at least won't hate. My daughter, Jasmine, picked potatoes to pay for her first electric guitar. Any choice you make based on the best you know gives God and your friends and family something to work on.

Choice analysis: If you're already moving in a direction but need to make some bigger decisions, you can commit your ways to God but add to that some serious consideration. One tool to help is called "argument mapping". Start with the wikipedia article to get your head around it (en.wikipedia.org/wiki/Argument_map), then look around at other sites to get more resources if needed. Basically, it's best to start by grabbing a sheet of paper or some mind-mapping software (I use NoveMind) and draw out the basic argument (or the choice you think you need to make and why). Under that, draw what supports that idea, and then branch out various assumptions, objections or contentions around the idea. For visual examples, have a look at http://timvangelder.com/2009/02/17/what-is-argument-mapping/ Here's an example of mapping out the decision to pursue writing books or not:

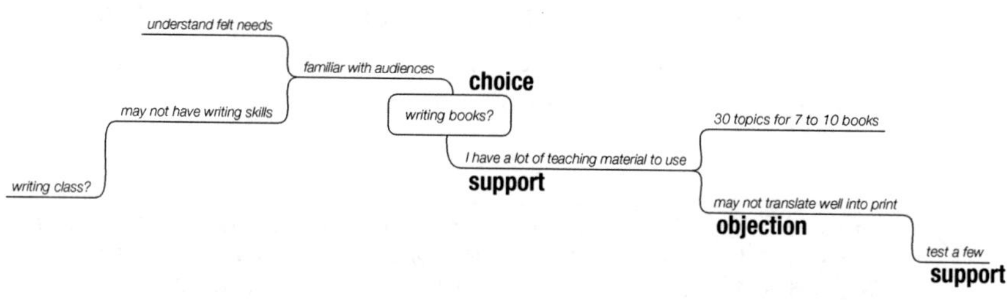

Another way to develop your ability to choose is to refine your critical thinking skills. We've given our kids curricula along these lines to build up their analytical skills, and now it's killing me (they argue with me all the time). Critical thinking teaches you to look at root structures of the issue, gives you a broader context to move past choice biases, and generally gets you out of your own box. You could start by reading *Critical Thinking* by Alec Fisher, or shop around for other titles that may be closer to your interests.[91]

Risk and hard work: When the master walked away from the three guys with the talents, he expected two things from them. He knew they needed to take big risks to double their money and that they would have to hustle. There's no way around risk, and we shouldn't always be avoiding it. There's a reason exploits, adventures, and great things in general all have risk involved; life is not pre-designed. You create it and you have to take risks to create. And, as I've said before, failure is not wrong, it's just failure. Think of risk more as a way of testing out your ideas and abilities. Be a fast learner and build on what you get from the failure or success of your decisions. If you add hard work to risk, you'll probably minimize potential disasters.

One of the best things I ever learned about hard work came while lounging in a friend's living room (ironic, no?). On their bookshelf was *The War of Art* by Steven Pressfield. In this pithy, concise little handbook Pressfield talks about the war to create. How there's a battle going on inside of us with an insidious foe who's trying to stop us from making stuff. One of his key solutions? Hard work. Clocking in whether you feel like it or not. Sitting down and writing (he writes screenplays and novels) whether you're inspired or not. Because in that act of obedience to your gift, you make yourself available to the Muse when she's ready to visit. Sorry, too Greek? Then how about… plugging in and working hard gives the Holy Spirit something to work with should He want to inspire you. Wherever that fleeting whisper comes from, you can only learn to grab and use it when you're concentrating and working hard. You already know this, so just do it already.

---

91 Google Books has an online version of a helpful title called *Critical Thinking: Tools for Taking Charge of Your Professional and Personal Life,* written by Richard W. Paul and Linda Elder. Check out books.google.co.nz/

Commitment: God not only allows for cause and effect, he built a world around it. I think one reason for this is that we could learn and grow up through risk, failure, and success. It's not just a big training ground for heaven; I do think the design of God was to create a wonderfully dynamic environment for us to manage and admire. Same with a new heaven and a *new earth.* But in order to embrace this process, we must learn to commit to things. I mentioned earlier that "we're all eggs and no baskets" because of our unwillingness to make commitments to a certain path we feel will limit us. In fact, we're such free spirits that we don't want to commit to anything, just in case there's a better deal around the corner. And there's the rub. We're not staying flexible in the face of uncertainty, we're really just spoiled shoppers, waiting for Santa to deliver the next round of goodies. Commitment connects us to real risk, vulnerability, and relationships that count. It forces us to identify our eggs and the best baskets to put them into. It makes our "yes" mean "yes" and our "no", "no".

The really cool thing about commitment is that instead of having all flexibility and no definition, you start to define yourself by your commitments. I became an amazing father (and I mean amazing!) when I committed to Heather and to having kids. I became a really good public speaker by embarrassing myself countless times until I figured it out. And while I'm an average writer and story-teller today, in 10 more years, I'm going to be pretty darn good. The point is, by committing to decisions, situations, and people, you define yourself, and your identity goes from the raw stuff it is today to well-formed, solid abilities. People who float don't make anything, and they don't leave anything behind. Over time, flexibility actually becomes a liability. I'm sorry I can't offer any tools for commitment; it's really something you just need to do. Sure, go through some experimental time to see what you want to focus on, but put a limit on it (max two years) and then make some choices and focus for a while.

Fifth: The seasons of your next 20 years

The Christian obsession with Jesus coming back in the last century (like, 10 years ago) is still hurting us. We've become the shortest-term people on the planet. In fact, way too many of us are banking on Jesus' return to help us out of the sticky mess we've helped create. The ironic thing is, people who fully think that their existence ceases when they die are generally the ones making the longest-term plans. They're setting up family trusts for future generations and building long-term solutions for energy needs into the next millennia.[92] So either we know something they don't, or the other way around. I think as Christians we're missing it. Proverbs says that a wise man builds an inheritance for his children's children (13:22). So what does that make the ones who aren't even planning for next year? It makes us stupid butt pies, that's what. We may have bought an escapist line for decades, but now we need to acknowledge that the return of Jesus is His business, while ours is clearly stated in Luke 19:13: "Put this money to work [...] until I come back." And kids, if He's taken over 2000 years to get us all this far, what do you think He's up to? I mean, look at how He talks about the 99 and the 1. Or the woman who searches her house for one coin... Do you think He's actually as preoccupied with returning as we've made Him out to be? Not on your life.

So we have to deal with our "internet-time" mentality. And the best way I know to do that is to look at the natural seasons of our lives, make some plans, and project as far ahead as we can see. I think most of us can do this for a 20-year period. And if you can look ahead 20 years or so and project what you'd like that identity of yours to develop into in terms of a life, you can tell a story about that life which could become a target or goal for yourself and the family you may want to have. From that overall story, you can break down five reasonable seasons that would get you to that place. Here's an example from my friend Esther, a result of some identity mapping we've been doing together (the headers are mine):

> *In 20 years I would like to found a school of midwifery and a birth center in the Badakshan province in Afghanistan. I think when I am in my early 50's if I work at it now I will be able to do this effectively.*
>
> *First Season:* ***Experimentation***
> *Starting this spring I am hoping to spend a 6 months period with a midwife in Winnipeg. She will be mentoring me and preparing me to go to the Philippines to work in a birth center for experience and further mentorship. I am currently working on my Doula certification and will continue this while at*

92 Check out Bill Gates' work on re-using existing nuclear waste for long-term energy creation at www.ted.com/talks/bill_gates.html

home. I have my first birth to attend the beginning of April. I will spend 6 months to a year in the Philippines. The details on this are still in the works.

Second Season: ***Education***
After this I would like to attend University in New Zealand or the Philippines to earn my Bachelor of Midwifery. I've looked into my options for earning my certification in Midwifery and there are many different routes. At this point I believe University is my best option, because I would like to also get my Masters and be able to teach and do research. I am a very hands on learner, so I've looked more into the Universities offering this program and they're all around 50% practical. With hands on experience going into school, I think this will work.

Third Season: ***Apprenticeship***
I would like to get married towards the end of my next 5 years. So I am also working towards that. :-) I've also been experimenting with my creative side more freely and intentionally over the past year. I enjoy many areas of art and creating in general, but I have decided to focus in on photography and film. This is going to be secondary to midwifery in certain seasons, but I want to develop quality skill. I would like to use film and photography as a medium of bringing light to key issues, as well as giving people options and ideas as to how they can actively make a difference. Ex: Today I had the idea to make a short documentary style film on the abortion of mentally handicapped fetus'. As I have been learning more about this topic in my Doula/midwifery studies I feel a strong need to communicate what I am learning to my community.

Fourth Season: ***Production***
I want to offer very holistic care and resources in attending expectant mothers, using my strengths. I want to specialize in birth photography, which I am currently pursuing. I want to get my yoga instructors certification and teach pre-natal and post-natal focused yoga classes. Along with this I plan on gaining as much knowledge on nutrition as possible mostly informal, but possible some formal as well. In my studies I am learning about the emotional baggage women bring into their birth process and how much of it is stirred up at this time of great change and vulnerability. I am a natural counselor, and I would like to develop my knowledge and understanding of this side of the birth process and equip myself with tools for

this area of need. I don't really know where all of this will fit or if it will, but I will sort that out as I go.

Further on: I want to be a mother as well as a wife. I would like a minimum of 3 kids and up to 7. I would also be interested in adopting or fostering. As the main nurturer I want to be able to focus on my children's development, especially in the first 12 years. Yet as you have pointed out in Powerful Equals, I still want to be walking in my identity and involving my children in that. With midwifery at this point, I will be focused on family and community. I see this as a time where the art side will have more of a forefront.

Fifth Season: ***Mentoring and multiplying***
As my children get to puberty and their Dad takes on the role as their main care giver, midwifery will become more of a focus again and a more direct pursuit of the Badakshan vision will begin. This is where I want to hit my stride, and transition into mentoring in due time.

How wonderful is this woman? What I love about her story is that in thinking ahead and basing it all on her identity and passion, she's able to extrapolate the steps or seasons it will take to get where she wants to go. Once you have the story, or a key part of it, it's not difficult to break it down into a reasonable set of seasons. After working with thousands of people over the last 30 years, here's a description of what I've found those seasons to be:

- **First Season, Experimentation**: This is a year or two trying a number of things in tangent with your identity mapping. As you unfold the details of your soul (personality, intellect, "I am" statements), you start making intentional choices that practice these parts of you in real time. Could be a short course in music or an international trip to look at dance culture around the world... The goal is to see where your tribe is and what ignites your passion or, of the many interests you have, which is actually *the* passion, or at least the strongest one to start on. You're also listening for what God thinks about it and what you could do if you focused. You also need to capture this time by journaling or doing whatever helps you process and assess, so you can make a commitment to the next season.

- **Second Season, Education**: Once you have a clue, you need to educate the raw stuff inside you. This four-to-seven-year season is a commitment to formal or non-formal curricula that will add knowledge and understanding to your talents and goals. I would suggest you customize this education to suit your goals instead of getting stuck in a four-year program that's only 50% of what you're looking for. In many cases degrees aren't essential, so don't get hung up on them if they're not part of your future requirements. If they are, find the one that best suits creating long-term possibilities for yourself. Once you have the knowledge, you're ready to put it to work.

- **Third Season, Apprenticeship**: This next four-to-seven-year season is about taking that head knowledge and putting it to work in the real world. It's where you find amazing mentors who will show you what they've learned on the field. It's where you practice and fail and grow in a way that's covered by people who care about you (hopefully) and are passionate about what they're doing. Once you've earned your stripes, cut your teeth, and otherwise paid your dues...

- **Fourth Season, Production**: Now you're ready to make babies, creatively I mean, no, I mean you're ready to make things. Um. Yeah, so now you're hitting your pace and you're actually doing the things you set out to do years ago. You have the actual skills and 10,000 hours of practice behind you, so the party begins. This is where you may start your own business or school or join others with the mature skills and relationships you've fostered. And after seven to ten years of that, you're ready to multiply yourself.

- **Fifth Season, Mentoring and multiplication**: This is where you get to rewrite the rules of your next season and take things even further. You can start another 20-year cycle where, based on the authority of your experience and accomplishments, you can branch out into the other areas of those 20 interests you have. You have a broader foundation to try new things and add your existing depth to whole new fields. And according to the Abrahamic covenant ("I will bless you so that you can be a blessing" Genesis 12:2), you can now share this by mentoring others into the same process you've just mastered. Not that you can't do that anywhere along the way (we're always a step or two ahead of someone), but now you can be more focused and give your time to people who can do some real damage. Here's an example of developing one aspect of your story:

Life Planning 101

1st season: Experiment	2nd season: Education	3rd season: Apprentice	4th season: Production	5th season: Mentor	
	Intelligence	Character	Application	Multiplication	
you are here	theology of you craft	hook up with a pro	start your own business	hire other people	you wanna be here
interested in photography	personal curriculum	take freelance projects	focus in on your strengths	teach in the local schools and colleges	worlds best photographer
Talent	formal education	travel and experiment	develop a reputation	take pro-bono work	
	non formal education	be excellent at what is good	grow steadily	find people who want mentoring	
	4 to 7 years	4 to 7 years	4 to 7 years	4 to 7 years	

Understanding the natural seasons that help us progress through life gives a sense of grace and proportion to our days. For the eager, it gives a sense of pace, while for the laggard, it's a challenge to rise to. I'm both, depending on my mood. But one of the best things about understanding seasons is that it gives a long-term idea of where you're heading. Big projects are beasts to begin because they are so, well, big. But being able to see the whole trajectory means you can then break that down into the one step that needs to happen *today* to start the process. Simple. It's the advantage of having a goal, a vision, or at least a clue. Now, you may not yet have a workable story or long-term goal that you're shooting for, but you can still use your understanding of these seasons to take one step at a time. At least in this way you'll have a sense of where things are going and how to get there.

So now it's your turn. Make a move of some kind and, like the proverbial lamp in the forest, you'll see more of the path as you take steps. Risky and fulfilling steps. The God part is the process. You're walking in His ways when you use your free will and do good. You're being a son or daughter as you commit *your ways* to the Lord so He can establish *your paths.* Give Him something to work with and, like it says in Matthew 25, party on, my son.

Chapter 19 • Your gift

When you have your first child, you see something different in how God feels and thinks about you. The sheer wonder and joy over that child's creation connect you with the purest intentions you'll ever have as a parent. You think about how perfect and beautiful and amazing they are, even though they're covered in blood and amniotic fluids. Before they can say a word or play their first concerto, you're just looking at them, stunned. Most people cry. You DO NOT think about what they can do for you, or how they'll strategically reach Azerbaijan. You don't start scheming about how you'll *use* them to *serve* you. And the last thing you're considering is what you want them to be when they grow up. If a parent in a fallen state can appreciate the complete wonder of a unique, eternal person being brought into the world, how much more does your heavenly Father appreciate who you are, simply because you are.

From God's perspective, watching you learn, mature, and generally be yourself is one of the greatest pleasures. He could pretty much make Himself any gift or wonder He likes (like those giant dust clouds in space, or an exploding supernova turning into a black hole). But instead, His gaze is drawn to this awesome new bundle of pudgy flesh and potential. He loves that you're not controlled, and that you will learn and invent and create on the foundation of the life He's given you. To define or command that process would not only kill the relationship, and the wonder, it would defeat the whole purpose of creation.

Knowing this then, how do we respond? It seems we have this unique ability to give God something He cherishes. I'm not saying He's needy or can't live without us, because He is complete in Himself. But still, He's gone to great lengths to keep the relationship in such a way as to not touch this ability of ours to give back. I guess that's unconditional love, that He gives us the most unique design of all creation (as far as we know anyway) in terms of neurology, physiology, and psychology, and then He lets it go free. And our chubby little selves grow into our adult selves and we look down at our hands and into our hearts and we step back in a similar wonder at this amazing gift. What do we do with all that?

My goal in writing this book was to bring freedom to people trapped by personal fears and institutional weirdnesses. I know that with that freedom could come the tendency to swing away from God altogether and just go hedonist as a reaction to the crap we've done or believed. It's a risk. But to me, the risk is worth it if, in coming to a place of freedom and awe in our fearfully and wonderfully made state, we find a unique way to give back to God. Not the freedom – He doesn't want that. And not the gift of our abilities on the altar of a dead religion. Again, He's not interested. Our gift to God is the act of our creation. Like the making of a better grain of wheat or the cleaning of dirty water to nourish more people. It's the tapping out of a melody on some out-of-tune piano or the creation of relationships that one day may even heal nations. Our gift is being our selves, our emotional, physical, and spiritual selves, and to our fullest potential. This is the thing God cannot get from anything else and He absolutely loves it that way. Which also means He saddens when we lose sight of this potential, or gets angry when we're led astray by the controlling spirits of people who don't properly represent Him.

I wrote this book so we could get back in touch with our ability to give. So that we'd know what we had to work or create with. So that we would take all that goodness and respond to the moral and known will of God (to deal with poverty, justice, loneliness...) that's already mapped into us by the placing of "eternity in our hearts" (Ecclesiastes 3:11). I wrote this so that we would start now in preparation for the great things we're capable of over time, and so that we would be ready for the massive challenges we are currently facing and will face in the coming years. It's going to get really hot in more ways than one (the economy, climate, terror, the list goes on), and we need to be ready. If you could tap into the joy of God over you, and be motivated to make something good with what you've been given, you would change the world, starting with your own. Break out that small but important lunch of yours and start sharing.

Final reflections? Ideas?

appendices

Appendix A

On The Choice Of A Profession

By Robert Louis Stevenson

You write to me, my dear sir, requesting advice at one of the most momentous epochs in a young man's life. You are about to choose a profession; and with a diffidence highly pleasing at your age, you would be glad, you say, of some guidance in the choice. There is nothing more becoming than for youth to seek counsel; nothing more becoming to age than to be able to give it; and in a civilization old and complicated like ours, where practical persons boast of a kind of practical philosophy superior to all others, you would very naturally expect to find all such questions systematically answered. For the dicta of the Practical Philosophy, you come to me. What, you ask, are the principles usually followed by the wise in the like critical junctures? There, I confess, you pose me on the threshold. I have examined my own recollections; I have interrogated others; and with all the will in the world to serve you better, I fear I can only tell you that the wise, in these circumstances, act upon no principles whatever. This is disappointing to you; it was painful to myself; but if I am to declare the truth as I see it, I must repeat that wisdom has nothing to do with the choice of a profession.

We all know what people say, and very foolish it usually is. The question is to get inside of these flourishes, and discover what it is they think and ought to say: to perform, in short, the Socratic Operation. – The more ready-made answers there are to any question, the more abtruse it becomes; for those of whom we make the enquiry have the less need of consideration before they reply. The world being more or less beset with Anxious Enquirers of the Socratic persuasion, it is the object of a Liberal Education to equip people with a proper number of these answers by way of passport; so they can pass swimmingly to and fro on their affairs without the trouble of thinking. How should a banker know his own mind? It takes him all his time to manage his bank. If you saw a company of pilgrims, walking as if for a wager, each with his teeth set; and if you happened to ask them one after another: Whither they were going? and from each you were to receive the same answer: that positively they were all in such a hurry, they had never found leisure to enquire into the nature of their errand: – confess, my dear sir, you would be startled at the indifference they exhibited. Am I going too far, if I say, that this is the condition of the large majority of our fellow-men and almost all our fellow-women?

I stop a banker.
"My good fellow," I say, "give me a moment."
"I have not a moment to spare," says he.
"Why?" I enquire.
"I must be banking," he replies. "I am so busily engaged in banking all day long that I have hardly leisure for my meals."
"And what," I continue my interrogatory, "is banking?"
"Sir," says he, "it is my business."
"Your business?" I repeat. "And what is a man's business?"
"Why," cries the banker, "a man's business is his duty." And with that he breaks away from me, and I see him skimming to his avocations.

But this is a sort of answer that provokes reflection. Is a man's business his duty? Or perhaps should not his duty be his business? If it is not my duty to conduct a bank (and I contend that it is not) is it the duty of my friend the banker? Who told him it was? Is it in the Bible? Is he sure that banks are a good thing? Might it not have been his duty to stand aside, and let some one else conduct the bank? Or perhaps ought he not to have been a ship-captain instead? All of these perplexing queries may be summed up under one head: the grave problem which my friend offers to the world: Why is he a Banker?

Well, why is it? There is one principal reason, I conceive: that the man was trapped. Educations, as practised, is a form of harnessing with the friendliest intentions. The fellow was hardly in trousers before they whipped him into school; hardly done with school before they smuggled him into an office; it is ten to one they have had him married into the bargain; and all this before he has had time so much as to imagine that there may be any other practicable course. Drum, drum, drum; you must be in time for school; you must do your Cornelius Nepos; you must keep your hands clean; you must go to parties – a young man should make friends; and, finally – you must take this opening in a bank. He has been used to caper to this sort of piping from the first; and he joins the regiment of bank clerks for precisely the same reason as he used to go to the nursery at the stroke of eight. Then at last, rubbing his hands with a complacent smile, the parent lays his conjuring pipe aside. The trick is performed, ladies and gentlemen; the wild ass's colt is broken in; and now sits diligently scribing. Thus it is, that, out of men, we make bankers.

You have doubtless been present at the washing of sheep, which is a brisk, high-handed piece of manoeuvring, in its way; but what is it, as a subject of contemplation, to the case of the poor young animal, Man, turned loose into this roaring world, herded by robustious guardians, taken with the panic before he has wit enough to apprehend its cause, and soon flying with all his heels in the van of the general stampede? It may be that in after years, he shall fall upon a train of reflection, and begin narrowly to scrutinize the reasons that decided his path and his continued mad activity in that direction. And perhaps he may be very well pleased at the retrospect, and see fifty things that might have been worse, for one that would have been better; and even supposing him to take the other cue, bitterly to deplore the circumstances in which he is placed and bitterly to reprobate the jockeying that got him into them, the fact is, it is too late to indulge such whims. It is too late, after the train has started, to debate the needfulness of this particular journey: the door is locked, the express goes tearing overland at sixty miles an hour; he had better betake himself to sleep or the daily paper, and discourage unavailing thought. He sees many pleasant places out of the window: cottages in a garden, angles by the riverside, balloons voyaging the sky; but as for him, he is booked for all his natural days, and must remain a banker to the end.

If the juggling only began with school-time, if even the domineering friends and counsellors had made a choice of their own, there might still be some pretension to philosophy in the affair. But no. They too were trapped; they are but tame elephants unwittingly ensnaring others, and were themselves ensnared by tame elephants of an older domestication. We have all learned our tricks in captivity, to the spiriting of Mrs. Grundy and a system of rewards and punishments. The crack of the whip and the trough of fodder: the cut direct and an invitation to dinner: the gallows and the Shorter Catechism: a pat upon the head and a stinging lash on the reverse: these are the elements of education and the principles of the Practical Philosophy. Sir Thomas Browne, in the earlier part of the Seventeenth Century, had already apprehended the staggering fact that geography is a considerable part of orthodoxy; and that a man who, when born in London, makes a conscientious Protestant, would have made an equally conscientious Hindu if he had first seen daylight in Benares.

This is but a small part, however important, of the things that are settled for us by our place of birth. An Englishman drinks beer and tastes his liquor in the throat; a Frenchman drinks wine and tastes it in the front of the mouth. Hence, a single beverage lasts the Frenchman all afternoon; and the Englishman cannot spend above a very short time in a café, but he must swallow half a bucket. The Englishman takes a cold tub every morning in his bedroom; the Frenchman has an occasional hot bath. The Englishman has an unlimited family and will die in harness; the Frenchman retires upon a competency with three children at the outside. So this imperative national tendency follows us through all the privacies of life, dictates our thoughts, and attends us to the grave. We do nothing, we say nothing, we wear nothing, but it is stamped with the Queen's Arms. We are English down to our boots and into our digestions. There is not a dogma of all those by which we lead young men, but we get it ourselves, between sleep and waking, between death and life, in a complete abeyance of the reasoning part.

"But how, sir," (you will ask) "is there then no wisdom in the world? And when my admirable father was this day urging me, with the most affecting expressions, to decide on an industrious, honest and lucrative employment--?" Enough, sir; I follow your thoughts, and will answer them to the utmost of my ability. Your father, for whom I entertain a singular esteem is, I am proud to believe, a professing Christian: the Gospel, therefore, is or ought to be his rule of conduct. Now, I am of course ignorant to the terms employed by your father; but I quite here from a very urgent letter, written by another parent, who was a man of sense, integrity, great energy, and a Christian persuasion, and who has perhaps set forth the common view with a certain innocent openness of his own: "You are now come to that time of life," he writes to his son, "and have reason within yourself to consider the absolute necessity of making provision for the time when it will be asked, Who is this man? Is he doing any good in the world? Has he the means of being 'One of us'? I beseech you," he goes on, rising in emotion, and appealing to his son by name, "I beseech you do not trifle with this till it actually comes upon you. Bethink yourself and bestir yourself as a man. This is the time--" and so forth.

This gentleman has candour; he is perspicacious, and has to deal apparently with a perspicacious pick-logic of a son; and hence the startling perspicacity of the document. But, my dear sir, what a principle of life! To "do good in the world" is to be received into a society apart from personal affection. I could name many forms of evil vastly more exhilarating whether in prospect or enjoyment. If I scraped money, believe me, it should be for some more cordial purpose. And then, scraping money? It seems to me as if he had forgotten the Gospel. This is a view of life not quite the same as the Christian, which the old gentleman professed and sincerely studied to practise. But upon this point, I dare dilate no further. Suffice it to say, that looking round me on the manifestations of this Christian society of ours, I have been often tempted to exclaim: What, then, is Antichrist?

A wisdom, at least, which professes one set of propositions and yet acts upon another, can be no very entire or rational ground of conduct. Doubtless, there is much in this question of money; and for my part, I believe no young man ought to be at peace till he is self-supporting, and has an open, clear life of it on his own foundation. But here a consideration occurs to me of, as I must consider, startling originality. It is this: That there are two sides to this question as well as to so many others. Make more? – Aye, or spend less? There is no absolute call upon a man to make any specific income, unless, indeed, he has set his immortal soul on being "One of us."

A thoroughly respectable income is as much as a man spends. A luxurious income, or true opulence, is something more than a man spends. Raise the income, lower the expenditure, and, my dear sir, surprising as it seems, we have the same result. But I hear you remind me, with pursed lips, of privations – of hardships. Alas! Sir, there are privations upon either side; the banker has to sit all day in his bank, a serious privation; can you not conceive that the landscape painter, whom I take to be the meanest and most lost among contemporary men, truly and deliberately prefers the privations upon his side – to wear no gloves, to drink beer, to live on chops or even on potatoes, and lastly, not to be "One of us" – truly and deliberately prefers his privations to those of the banker? I can. Yes, sir, I repeat those words; I can. Believe me, there are Rivers in Bohemia! – but there is nothing so hard to get people to understand as this: That they pay for their money; and nothing so difficult to make them remember as this: That money, when they have it, is for most of them, at least, only a cheque to purchase pleasure with. How then if a man gets pleasure in following an art? He might gain more cheques by following another; but then, although there is a difference in cheques, the amount of pleasure is the same. He gets some of his directly; unlike the bank clerk, he is having his fortnight's holiday, and doing what delights him, all the year.

All these patent truisms have a very strange air, when written down. But that, my dear sir, is no fault of mine or of the truisms. There they are. I beseech you, do not trifle with them. Bethink yourself like a man. This is the time.

But, you say, all this is very well; it does not help me to a choice. Once more, sir, you have me; it does not. What shall I say? A choice, let us remember, is almost more of a negative than a positive. You embrace one thing; but you refuse a thousand. The most liberal profession imprisons many energies and starves many affections. If you are in a bank, you cannot be much upon the sea. You cannot be both a first-rate violinist and a first-rate painter: you must lose in the one art if you persist in following both. If you are sure of your preference, follow it. If not – nay, my dear sir, it is not for me or any man to go beyond this point. God made you; not I. I cannot even make you over again. I have heard of a schoolmaster, whose speciality it was to elicit the bent of each pupil: poor schoolmaster, poor pupils! As for me, if you have nothing indigenous in your own heart, no living preference, no fine, human scorn, I leave you to the tide; it will sweep you somewhere. Have you but a grain of inclination, I will help you. If you wish to be a costermonger, be it, shame the devil; and I will stand the donkey. If you wish to be nothing, once more I leave you to the tide.

I regret profoundly, my dear young sir, not only for you in whom I see such a lively promise of the future, but for the sake of your admirable and truly worthy father and your no less excellent mamma, that my remarks should seem no more conclusive. I can give myself this praise, that I have kept back nothing; but this, alas! is a subject on which there is little to put forward. It will probably not much matter what you decide upon doing; for most men seem to sink at length to the degree of stupor necessary for contentment in their different estates. Yes, sir, this is what I have observed. Most men are happy, and most men dishonest. Their mind sinks to the proper level; their honour easily accepts the custom of the trade. I wish you may find degeneration no more painful than your neighbours, soon sink into apathy, and be long spared in a state of respectable somnambulism, from the grave to which we haste.

R.L.S.
Saranac, New York – in the winter of 1887-88

Chatto & Windus, London, 1916

Appendix B

A list of scriptures to tape onto your refrigerator :-)

I've listed most of these scriptures throughout the book but wanted to offer them here under the main headings of the general, extraordinary and call to be your self. I found these as I've processed the questions of guidance and calling with God. I suggest you add to this with your own process and move past a passive acceptance or interpretation by digging for yourself.

Please note that I have used a variety of translations throughout this book including the NIV, NAS and KJV. I also have used Young's Literal Translation in trying to get a little closer to the original words as you'll see in the list below.

1. General call of God

"Come, follow me," – Matthew 4:19

The Ten Commandments – Exodus 20
1 And God spoke all these words:
2 "I am the LORD your God, who brought you out of Egypt, out of the land of slavery.
3 "You shall have no other gods before [1] me.
4 "You shall not make for yourself an idol in the form of anything in heaven above or on the earth beneath or in the waters below.
5 You shall not bow down to them or worship them; for I, the LORD your God, am a jealous God, punishing the children for the sin of the fathers to the third and fourth generation of those who
hate me, 6 but showing love to a thousand {generations} of those who love me and keep my commandments.
7 "You shall not misuse the name of the LORD your God, for the LORD will not hold anyone guiltless who misuses his name.
8 "Remember the Sabbath day by keeping it holy. 9 Six days you
shall labor and do all your work, 10 but the seventh day is a Sabbath to the LORD your God. On it you shall not do any work, neither you, nor your son or daughter, nor your manservant or maidservant, nor your animals, nor the alien within your gates. 11
For in six days the LORD made the heavens and the earth, the sea,

and all that is in them, but he rested on the seventh day. Therefore
the LORD blessed the Sabbath day and made it holy.
12 "Honor your father and your mother, so that you may live long
in the land the LORD your God is giving you.
13 "You shall not murder.
14 "You shall not commit adultery.
15 "You shall not steal.
16 "You shall not give false testimony against your neighbor.
17 "You shall not covet your neighbor's house. You shall not covet
your neighbor's wife, or his manservant or maidservant, his ox or
donkey, or anything that belongs to your neighbor."

The Widow, the Poor and the Alien
Zechariah 7
9 "This is what the LORD Almighty says: 'Administer true justice;
show mercy and compassion to one another. 10 Do not oppress the
widow or the fatherless, the alien or the poor. In your hearts do not
think evil of each other.'

Worship and service:
Deuteronomy 30:19
This day I call heaven and earth as witnesses against you that I have set before you life and death, blessings and curses. Now choose life, so that you and your children may live

Joshua 24:15
But if serving the LORD seems undesirable to you, then choose for yourselves this day whom you will serve, whether the gods your forefathers served beyond the River, or the gods of the Amorites, in whose land you are living. But as for me and my household, we will serve the LORD ."

Health
Numbers 19
10 The man who gathers up the ashes of the heifer must also wash
his clothes, and he too will be unclean till evening. This will be a
lasting ordinance both for the Israelites and for the aliens living
among them.
11 "Whoever touches the dead body of anyone will be unclean for
seven days. 12 He must purify himself with the water on the third
day and on the seventh day; then he will be clean. But if he does

not purify himself on the third and seventh days, he will not be clean.

Numbers 19:18
Then a man who is ceremonially clean is to take some hyssop, dip it in the water and sprinkle the tent and all the furnishings and the people who were there. He must also sprinkle anyone who has touched a human bone or a grave or someone who has been killed or someone who has died a natural death.

Evangelism
Matthew 28
18 Then Jesus came to them and said, "All authority in heaven and on earth has been given to me. 19 Therefore go and make disciples of all nations, baptizing them in the name of the Father and of the Son and of the Holy Spirit, 20 and teaching them to obey everything I have commanded you. And surely I am with you always, to the very end of the age."

Loving God and your neighbor
Deut 6:4 Hear, O Israel: The LORD our God, the LORD is one. [1] 5 Love the LORD your God with all your heart and with all your soul and with all your strength. 6 These commandments that I give you today are to be upon your hearts. 7 Impress them on your children. Talk about them when you sit at home and when you walk along the road, when you lie down and when you get up. 8 Tie them as symbols on your hands and bind them on your foreheads. 9 Write them on the door frames of your houses and on your gates.

Mark 12
30 Love the Lord your God with all your heart and with all your soul and with all your mind and with all your strength.'[1] 31 The second is this: 'Love your neighbor as yourself.'[2] There is no commandment greater than these."

Leviticus 18:20
"'Do not have sexual relations with your neighbor's wife and defile yourself with her.

Leviticus 19:18
"'Do not seek revenge or bear a grudge against one of your people, but love your neighbor as yourself. I am the LORD .

Proverbs 6:3
then do this, my son, to free yourself, since you have fallen into your neighbor's hands: Go and humble yourself; press your plea with your neighbor!

Exodus 22:7
"If a man gives his neighbor silver or goods for safekeeping and they are stolen from the neighbor's house, the thief, if he is caught, must pay back double.

Exodus 22:14
"If a man borrows an animal from his neighbor and it is injured or dies while the owner is not present, he must make restitution.

Deuteronomy 4:42
to which anyone who had killed a person could flee if he had unintentionally killed his neighbor without malice aforethought. He could flee into one of these cities and save his life.

Deuteronomy 19:14
Do not move your neighbor's boundary stone set up by your predecessors in the inheritance you receive in the land the LORD your God is giving you to possess.

Deuteronomy 23
23 Whatever your lips utter you must be sure to do, because you made your vow freely to the LORD your God with your own mouth.
24 If you enter your neighbor's vineyard, you may eat all the grapes
you want, but do not put any in your basket. 25 If you enter your
neighbor's grain field, you may pick kernels with your hands, but you must not put a sickle to his standing grain.

Deuteronomy 24
9 Remember what the LORD your God did to Miriam along the way after you came out of Egypt.
10 When you make a loan of any kind to your neighbor, do not go

into his house to get what he is offering as a pledge. 11 Stay outside and let the man to whom you are making the loan bring the pledge out to you.

Psalm 12:2
Everyone lies to his neighbor; their flattering lips speak with deception.

Psalm 101:5
Whoever slanders his neighbor in secret, him will I put to silence; whoever has haughty eyes and a proud heart, him will I not endure.

Proverbs 3:28
Do not say to your neighbor, "Come back later; I'll give it tomorrow"- when you now have it with you.

Proverbs 14:21
He who despises his neighbor sins, but blessed is he who is kind to the needy.

Proverbs 24:28
Do not testify against your neighbor without cause, or use your lips to deceive.

Proverbs 25
9 If you argue your case with a neighbor, do not betray another man's confidence,
10 or he who hears it may shame you and you will never lose your bad reputation.

Proverbs 27:10
Do not forsake your friend and the friend of your father, and do not go to your brother's house when disaster strikes you- better a neighbor nearby than a brother far away.

Proverbs 27:14
If a man loudly blesses his neighbor early in the morning, it will be taken as a curse.

Luke 14
11 For everyone who exalts himself will be humbled, and he who

humbles himself will be exalted." 12 Then Jesus said to his host,
"When you give a luncheon or dinner, do not invite your friends,
your brothers or relatives, or your rich neighbors; if you do, they
may invite you back and so you will be repaid. 13 But when you
give a banquet, invite the poor, the crippled, the lame, the blind,

Romans 13:10
Love does no harm to its neighbor. Therefore love is the fulfillment of the law.

Romans 15:2
Each of us should please his neighbor for his good, to build him up.

Ephesians 4:25
Therefore each of you must put off falsehood and speak truthfully to his neighbor, for we are all members of one body.

James 4:12
There is only one Lawgiver and Judge, the one who is able to save and destroy. But you, who are you to judge your neighbor?

Note: All of the general call of God scriptures do not give specific application in terms of things like, where you live, what Job you take, who you marry...

Love
Romans 13

Communication
Most of Proverbs

General Behavior
All the Epistles... You get the point

2. The Extraordinary Call of God

Abraham

Genesis 12

1 The LORD had said to Abram, “Leave your country, your people
and your father’s household and go to the land I will show you.
2 “I will make you into a great nation and I will bless you; I will
make your name great, and you will be a blessing.
3 I will bless those who bless you, and whoever curses you I will
curse; and all peoples on earth will be blessed through you.”
4 So Abram left, as the LORD had told him; and Lot went with
him. Abram was seventy-five years old when he set out from Haran.
5 He took his wife Sarai, his nephew Lot, all the possessions they
had accumulated and the people they had acquired in Haran, and
they set out for the land of Canaan, and they arrived there.

Moses

Exodus 3

1 Now Moses was tending the flock of Jethro his father-in-law, the
priest of Midian, and he led the flock to the far side of the desert
and came to Horeb, the mountain of God. 2 There the angel of
the LORD appeared to him in flames of fire from within a bush.
Moses saw that though the bush was on fire it did not burn up. 3
So Moses thought, “I will go over and see this strange sight-why the
bush does not burn up.”
4 When the LORD saw that he had gone over to look, God called
to him from within the bush, “Moses! Moses!” And Moses said,
“Here I am.”
5 “Do not come any closer,” God said. “Take off your sandals, for
the place where you are standing is holy ground.” 6 Then he said, “I
am the God of your father, the God of Abraham, the God of Isaac
and the God of Jacob.” At this, Moses hid his face, because he was
afraid to look at God.
7 The LORD said, “I have indeed seen the misery of my people in
Egypt. I have heard them crying out because of their slave drivers,
and I am concerned about their suffering. 8 So I have come down
to rescue them from the hand of the Egyptians and to bring them
up out of that land into a good and spacious land, a land flowing
with milk and honey-the home of the Canaanites, Hittites, Amori-
tes, Perizzites, Hivites and Jebusites.

9 And now the cry of the Israelites has reached me, and I have seen the way the Egyptians are oppressing them. 10 So now, go. I am sending you to Pharaoh to bring my people the Israelites out of Egypt."

Jeremiah

Jeremiah 1:4 The word of the LORD came to me, saying,
5 "Before I formed you in the womb I knew [1] you, before you were born I set you apart; I appointed you as a prophet to the nations."
6 "Ah, Sovereign LORD ," I said, "I do not know how to speak; I am only a child."
7 But the LORD said to me, "Do not say, 'I am only a child.' You must go to everyone I send you to and say whatever I command
you. 8 Do not be afraid of them, for I am with you and will rescue you," declares the LORD .
9 Then the LORD reached out his hand and touched my mouth
and said to me, "Now, I have put my words in your mouth. 10 See,
today I appoint you over nations and kingdoms to uproot and tear down, to destroy and overthrow, to build and to plant."

Hosea

Hosea 1
1 The word of the LORD that came to Hosea son of Beeri during the reigns of Uzziah, Jotham, Ahaz and Hezekiah, kings of Judah, and during the reign of Jeroboam son of Jehoash king of Israel:
2 When the LORD began to speak through Hosea, the LORD said to him, "Go, take to yourself an adulterous wife and children of unfaithfulness, because the land is guilty of the vilest adultery in
departing from the LORD ." 3 So he married Gomer daughter of
Diblaim, and she conceived and bore him a son.

Jesus

John 18
37"You are a king, then!" said Pilate. Jesus answered, "You are right in saying I am a king. In fact, for this reason I was born, and for this I came into the world, to testify to the truth. Everyone on the side of truth listens to me."

Paul
Romans 1:1 Paul, a servant of Christ Jesus, called to be an apostle and set apart for the gospel of God-- 2the gospel he promised beforehand through his prophets in the Holy Scriptures

Acts 16:9 During the night Paul had a vision of a man of Macedonia standing and begging him, "Come over to Macedonia and help us." 10 After Paul had seen the vision, we got ready at once to leave for Macedonia, concluding that God had called us to preach the gospel to them.

3. The call to be yourself

– where God does not micromanage us.

The Parable of the Talents - and investing yours...
Matt 25:14 "Again, it will be like a man going on a journey, who called his servants and entrusted his property to them. 15 To one he gave five talents of money, to another two talents, and to another one talent, each according to his ability. Then he went on his journey. 16 The man who had received the five talents went at once and put his money to work and gained five more. 17 So also, the one with the two talents gained two more. 18 But the man who had received the one talent went off, dug a hole in the ground and hid his master's money.
19"After a long time the master of those servants returned and settled accounts with them. 20 The man who had received the five talents brought the other five. 'Master,' he said, 'you entrusted me with five talents. See, I have gained five more.'
21"His master replied, 'Well done, good and faithful servant! You have been faithful with a few things; I will put you in charge of many things. Come and share your master's happiness!'
22"The man with the two talents also came. 'Master,' he said, 'you entrusted me with two talents; see, I have gained two more.'
23"His master replied, 'Well done, good and faithful servant! You have been faithful with a few things; I will put you in charge of many things. Come and share your master's happiness!'
24"Then the man who had received the one talent came. 'Master,' he said, 'I knew that you are a hard man, harvesting where you have not sown and gathering where you have not scattered seed.

25 So I was afraid and went out and hid your talent in the ground.
See, here is what belongs to you.'
26"His master replied, 'You wicked, lazy servant! So you knew
that I harvest where I have not sown and gather where I have not
scattered seed? 27 Well then, you should have put my money on
deposit with the bankers, so that when I returned I would have
received it back with interest.
28" 'Take the talent from him and give it to the one who has the
ten talents. 29 For everyone who has will be given more, and he
will have an abundance. Whoever does not have, even what he has
will be taken from him. 30 And throw that worthless servant out-
side, into the darkness, where there will be weeping and gnashing of
teeth.'

The Sheep and the goats story follows. Is there a correlation between not applying ourselves and ending up as a goat?

God delegating the earth to us
Genesis 1 and 2
1:27 So God created man in his own image, in the image of God he
created him; male and female he created them.
28 God blessed them and said to them, "Be fruitful and increase in
number; fill the earth and subdue it. Rule over the fish of the sea
and the birds of the air and over every living creature that moves on
the ground."
31 God saw all that he had made, and it was very good. And there
was evening, and there was morning-the sixth day.

2:19 Now the LORD God had formed out of the ground all the beasts of the field and all the birds of the air. He brought them to the man to see what he would name them; and whatever the man called each living creature, that was its name.

What God gave us to work with
Psalm 139
13 For you created my inmost being; you knit me together in my
mother's womb. 14 I praise you because I am fearfully and wonder-
fully made; your works are wonderful, I know that full well.
15 My frame was not hidden from you when I was made in the
secret place. When I was woven together in the depths of the earth,

Trusting in God, being yourself
Psalm 37
3 Trust in the LORD and do good; dwell in the land and enjoy safe
pasture. 4 Delight yourself in the LORD and he will give you the
desires of your heart. 5 Commit your way to the LORD ; trust in
him and he will do this: 6 He will make your righteousness shine
like the dawn, the justice of your cause like the noonday sun.

23 If the LORD delights in a man's way, he makes his steps firm;
24 though he stumble, he will not fall, for the LORD upholds him
with his hand.

God want's to empower your ideas
II Thess:1:11
With this in mind, we constantly pray for you, that our God may
count you worthy of his calling, and that by his power he may
fulfill every good purpose of yours and every act prompted by your
faith. 12 We pray this so that the name of our Lord Jesus may be
glorified in you, and you in him, according to the grace of our God
and the Lord Jesus Christ

General stuff

Does God have a 'PLAN' for our lives?
Ps 33:11 – **New American Standard**
The counsel of the LORD stands forever, The plans of His heart from generation to generation

33:11 – **Young's Literal Translation**
The counsel of Jehovah to the age standeth, The thoughts of His heart to all generations.

Pr 16:1 – **NAS**
The plans of the heart belong to man, But the answer of the tongue is from the LORD

Pr 16:1 – **YLT**
Of man [are] arrangements of the heart, And from Jehovah an answer of the tongue.

Pr 16:3 – **NAS**
Commit your works to the LORD And your plans will be established

Pr 16:3 – **YLT**
Roll unto Jehovah thy works, And established are thy purposes,

Pr 16:9 – **NAS**
The mind of man plans his way, But the LORD directs his steps

Pr 16:9 – **YLT**
The heart of man deviseth his way, And Jehovah establisheth his step.

Pr 19:21 – **NAS**
Many plans are in a man's heart, But the counsel of the LORD will stand

19:21 – **YLT**
Many [are] the purposes in a man's heart, And the counsel of Jehovah it stand

Pr 21:5 – **NAS**
The plans of the diligent {lead} surely to advantage, But everyone who is hasty {comes} surely to poverty

Pr 21:5 – **YLT**
The purposes of the diligent [are] only to advantage, And of every hasty one, only to want.

Jer 29:11 – **NAS**
'For I know the plans that I have for you,' declares the LORD, 'plans for welfare and not for calamity to give you a future and a hop

Jer 29:11 – **YLT**
For I have known the thoughts that I am thinking towards you -- an affirmation of Jehovah; thoughts of peace, and not of evil, to give to you posterity and hope.

Ps 31:3 – **NAS**
For You are my rock and my fortress; For Your name's sake You will lead me and guide me.

Ps 31:1 – **YLT**
To the Overseer. -- A Psalm of David. In Thee, O Jehovah, I have
trusted, Let me not be ashamed to the age, In Thy righteousness
deliver me. 2 Incline unto me Thine ear hastily, deliver me, Be to
me for a strong rock, For a house of bulwarks to save me. 3 For my
rock and my bulwark [art] Thou, For Thy name's sake lead me and
tend me. 4 Bring me out from the net that they hid for me, For
Thou [art] my strength. 5 Into Thy hand I commit my spirit, Thou
hast redeemed me, Jehovah God of truth

Ps 48:14 – **NAS**
For such is God, Our God forever and ever; He will guide us until death

Ps 48:14 – **YLT**
That this God [is] our God -- To the age and for ever, He -- he doth lead us over death!

Can we plan for the future?
James 4:13
Now listen, you who say, "Today or tomorrow we will go to this or
that city, spend a year there, carry on business and make money."
14 Why, you do not even know what will happen tomorrow. What
is your life? You are a mist that appears for a little while and then
vanishes. 15 Instead, you ought to say, "If it is the Lord's will, we
will live and do this or that." 16 As it is, you boast and brag. All
such boasting is evil. 17 Anyone, then, who knows the good he
ought to do and doesn't do it, sins.

Young's Literal Translation:
13 Go, now, ye who are saying, `To-day and to-morrow we will go
on to such a city, and will pass there one year, and traffic, and make
gain;' 14 who do not know the thing of the morrow; for what is
your life? For it is a vapor that is appearing for a little, and then is
vanishing; 15 instead of your saying, `If the Lord may will, we shall
live, and do this or that;' 16 and now ye glory in your pride; all
such glorying is evil;

17 to him, then, knowing to do good, and not doing, sin it is to him.

Waiting on God or for God?

General:

Psalm 38:15 I wait for you, O LORD ; you will answer, O Lord my God.
16 For I said, "Do not let them gloat or exalt themselves over me when my foot slips."

Isaiah 30:18
Yet the LORD longs to be gracious to you; he rises to show you compassion. For the LORD is a God of justice. Blessed are all who wait for him!

Isaiah 64
3 For when you did awesome things that we did not expect, you came down, and the mountains trembled before you.
4 Since ancient times no one has heard, no ear has perceived, no eye has seen any God besides you, who acts on behalf of those who wait for him.
5 You come to the help of those who gladly do right, who remember your ways.

Why?

Special Wisdom:

Numbers 9:7 and said to Moses, "We have become unclean because of a dead body, but why should we be kept from presenting the LORD's offering with the other Israelites at the appointed time?"
8 Moses answered them, "Wait until I find out what the LORD commands concerning you."

Desperate need:

Psalm 5
2 Listen to my cry for help, my King and my God, for to you
I pray. 3 In the morning, O LORD , you hear my voice; in the
morning I lay my requests before you and wait in expectation.
Protection and ultimate justice:

Psalm 27:12 Do not turn me over to the desire of my foes, for false witnesses rise up against me, breathing out violence. 13 I am still confident of this: I will see the goodness of the LORD in the land of the living. 14 Wait for the LORD ; be strong and take heart and wait for the LORD .

Psalm 33:20
We wait in hope for the LORD ; he is our help and our shield.

Psalm 37:7
Be still before the LORD and wait patiently for him; do not fret when men succeed in their ways, when they carry out their wicked schemes.

Psalm 37:34
Wait for the LORD and keep his way. He will exalt you to inherit the land; when the wicked are cut off, you will see it.

Psalm 38:14 I have become like a man who does not hear, whose mouth can offer no reply. 15 I wait for you, O LORD ; you will answer, O Lord my God. 16 For I said, "Do not let them gloat or exalt themselves over me when my foot slips."

Psalm 59:3
See how they lie in wait for me! Fierce men conspire against me for no offense or sin of mine, O LORD .

Proverbs 20:21 An inheritance quickly gained at the beginning will not be blessed at the end. 22 Do not say, "I'll pay you back for this wrong!" Wait for the LORD , and he will deliver you.

Isaiah 30:18 Yet the LORD longs to be gracious to you; he rises to show you compassion. For the LORD is a God of justice. Blessed are all who wait for him! 19 O people of Zion, who live in Jerusalem, you will weep no more. How gracious he will be when you cry for help! As soon as he hears, he will answer you.

Waiting for the things we cannot have or see here:
1 Corinthians 4:5
Therefore judge nothing before the appointed time; wait till the Lord comes. He will bring to light what is hidden in darkness

and will expose the motives of men's hearts. At that time each will receive his praise from God.

Philippians 3:20
But our citizenship is in heaven. And we eagerly await a Savior from there, the Lord Jesus Christ,

James 5:7
Be patient, then, brothers, until the Lord's coming. See how the farmer waits for the land to yield its valuable crop and how patient he is for the autumn and spring rains.

Jude 1:21
Keep yourselves in God's love as you wait for the mercy of our Lord Jesus Christ to bring you to eternal life.

Summary: Waiting is for what only God can do, not what we must do.

Sloth, the enemy of calling. Calling, the cure for Sloth.

From the Pocket Catholic Catechism:
Sloth is the desire for ease, even at the expense of doing the known will of God. Whatever we do in life requires effort. Everything we do is to be a means of salvation. The slothful person is unwilling to do what God wants because of the effort it takes to do it. Sloth becomes a sin when it slows down and even brings to a halt the energy we must expend in using the means to salvation.

Medieval theologian Thomas Aquinas said Sloth is "sluggishness of the mind which neglects to begin good... [it] is evil in its effect, if it so oppresses man as to draw him away entirely from good deeds." (2,35, ad 1)

Why are the Seven Deadly Sins considered "deadly"?
They are called "deadly" because they wound love, and therefore do great harm to our relationship with God and others. Eventually, they can kill the soul, in a sense. And they aren't much fun to live with, either.

Lightning Source UK Ltd.
Milton Keynes UK
UKOW04f2059150813

215462UK00013B/757/P

9 780986 462610